G000229301

British Rail Standard Diesels of the 1960s

David N. Clough

Ian Allan
PUBLISHING

First published 2009

ISBN 978 0 7110 3373 3

Published by Ian Allan Publishing

an imprint of Ian Allan Publishing Ltd, Hersham, Surrey, KT12 4RG

Printed by Ian Allan Printing, Hersham, Surrey, KT12 4RG

Code: 0908/B1

Visit the Ian Allan website at www.ianallanpublishing.com

Contents

Introduction

In 2003 I met with Peter Waller, Ian Allan Ltd's commissioning editor, in our usual London rendezvous and out of this evolved the *Diesel Pioneers* book, published in 2005. This covered both the various prototype and engine test bed locomotives, together with the Pilot Scheme classes ordered as part of the 1955 Modernisation Plan. Back at the same venue in July 2007 we discussed taking the story of the BR diesel to its next phase. This would look at how BR settled on a number of designs for main-line applications, some 'standard' (for general use across the network) and others specific for a particular requirement. In this context, 'main-line' excludes trip locomotives that were conceived purely for local work. Arguably, this was the golden age for enthusiasts, when diversity was at its greatest, up to the point when the National Traction Plan resolved a thinning-out of classes on the grounds of unreliability or excess capacity.

This book cannot be a definitive study of the locomotives covered; quite simply, there is just not the space. For this reason, designs that were covered in detail in *Diesel Pioneers* are not dwelt on here. It aims to be a general survey of the core main-line diesel fleet of British Railways during a fascinating transitional phase – the 1960s. In this context, 'core' means 'standard', because the non-standard was already on borrowed time and, in fairness, the panoply of designs that emerged within the Pilot Scheme were dealt with in *Diesel Pioneers*. Researching the text, it quickly became apparent that, while some classes had been well covered in print, others had had virtually nothing written about them at all. Although this might be unsurprising for the short-lived Class 17 'Claytons', it was revealing that the 'Peaks' have been almost ignored. For simplicity, the TOPS classification for locomotive types has been adopted throughout to avoid confusion and aid ease of reference, even though this form of notation only just appeared within the period covered by this book.

Several 'standard' works on the diesel fleet were published during the 1980s, but these came too early for their authors to have been able to access files provided by BR to the National Archive. Such files remain closed for 30 years, but are now available and I am most indebted to my wife, Jo, for unstinting efforts over many days in trawling the dusty documents. Regrettably, there is a far from complete record of key events of the period, but the correspondence has brought a new insight into some of the decision-making processes and views of those involved. While a full set of minutes for the BTC and BR is available, these often refer to briefing papers, provided for meetings by railway committees, such as Works & Supply, with the minutes merely recording endorsement of unspecified committee proposals. Nevertheless some fascinating comments are recorded, notably those of the BTC chairman, Sir Brian Robertson. Information elicited from these records has also helped to tie down precisely dates when locomotives were ordered and to which Region they were to be allocated. This has brought fresh material into the public domain for the first time.

Locomotive liveries have proved to be something of a minefield, with BR's official schemes often not being adhered to, even when locomotives emerged from the manufacturers' workshops. There were also quite a number of alterations as the decade progressed. Regrettably, photographs cannot be relied upon because of the risk that what is reproduced does not truly reproduce the colours. Again, National Archives' material has helped, not least in highlighting the conflicting views of those who made the decisions. Descriptions in this book are based on the most reliable sources. The same difficulty applied when producing the tables of particulars because of inconsistency between reference sources. The simplest solution was therefore to use a single source – the BR Diagram Book.

Sourcing quality, unpublished, relevant and comprehensive illustrations from the period is extremely difficult because, these days, such material is in high demand and low supply. Browsing magazines from the era has proved a double-edged sword. Some lovely photographs were published at the time but, regrettably, many of the photographers are no longer with us and their collections have been dispersed or lost. As with *Diesel Pioneers*, I am indebted to Peter Waller for his unstinting work in combing the publisher's photographic library for suitable material. The photographic selection is a key part of this book and should therefore not disappoint.

I would like to thank Michael Hunt for many helpful suggestions. Input from Hugh Dady, Clive Burrows and Peter Meredith has also been of assistance. Finally, the support of my wife with research and proofing the text is greatly appreciated.

Abbreviations

AEI	Associated Electrical Industries
BP	Beyer Peacock
BR	British Rail
BRCW	Birmingham Railway Carriage & Wagon Co Ltd
BTC	British Transport Commission
BTH	British Thomson Houston
CME	Chief Mechanical Engineer
CMEE	Chief Mechanical & Electrical Engineer
CP	Crompton Parkinson
cwt	hundredweight
ECML	East Coast Main Line
ECS	Empty coaching stock
EE	English Electric
ER	Eastern Region
ETH	Electric train heating
GC	Great Central line
GE	Great Eastern line
GEC	General Electric Company
GN	Great Northern line
hp	horsepower
KM	Krauss-Maffei
LMR	London Midland Region
LTS	London, Tilbury & Southend line
mgr	'Merry-go-round' (coal trains)
MML	Midland Main Line
NBL	North British Locomotive Co Ltd
NER	North Eastern Region
Paxman	Davey, Paxman & Co Ltd
pws	permanent way slack
rhp	rail horsepower
RSH	Robert Stephenson & Hawthorn
ScR	Scottish Region
SR	Southern Region
VF	Vulcan Foundry
WCML	West Coast Main Line
WR	Western Region

Class 14

Whereas all the Regions bar the WR (and the SR, which didn't want the type) received diesels in the Type 1 range under the Pilot Scheme, it was to be some time before that Region plugged this gap, and in a different fashion from the others.

On 21 December 1961 the BTC approved the transfer of construction of the last ten of Swindon's share of the order for the Type 4 'Westerns' to Crewe. This was to free up capacity at the Works in order to bring forward to 1963 the construction of 26 Type 1s that had been scheduled for 1964. It was, however, not until 8 February 1962 that approval for the new design was affirmed. The estimated cost was £34,520, considerably lower than other Type 1s. Once drawings had been produced, the Board authorised that tenders be invited for the remaining 30 locomotives being sought, and the minutes record that multiplication beyond 56 was planned. In the event, on 14 March 1963 the Board agreed to Swindon building the second and final batch of 30.

Four sources are inconsistent in the Swindon lot numbers for the class, a quite remarkable example of the unreliability of published material! This also serves to highlight the difficulty faced in producing accurate information when official records no longer survive. One source even splits the lots into 25 and 31 locomotives, which is at variance to the BTC minutes. Swindon Lot 456 was assigned to the first 26 and Lot 460 for the last 30, whilst Lot 500 appears to be the BR number in a new series range.

Swindon undertook the design and Allen Barnes, Bowden Ltd, which had earlier also acted as consultant in the design of the Class 17, was appointed as the external consultant for styling. What emerged differed radically from other Type 1s, reflecting the planned duties which required an axle load that would permit use across the whole Region. The minimum curve radius was no better than other Type 1s, so there was no advantage when it came to negotiating curved track in collieries and docks.

Unsurprisingly, the power train was diesel-hydraulic, not diesel-electric. Significantly, the twin-bogie carrying arrangement found on all other BR diesels was dropped in favour of six coupled driving wheels, mounted on three axles, reminiscent of a shunting locomotive. In truth, the class was not a main-line locomotive as generally accepted and this is reinforced by the low top speed.

The condition of No D9549 suggests that it is probably nearly new. Its profile clearly aligns the design more towards a shunting locomotive than one for traditional main-line use.
Ian Allan Library

Left: Most of the work of the Class 14 was undertaken in the Principality. On 14 April 1967 No D9510 is at Pontypool Road, possibly during shunting operations at this once-busy location.
Ian Allan Library

Frames were from 1¼-inch-thick steel plate sections, riveted to deep heavy-section buffer-beams that also acted as ballast weights to provide even distribution of weight on the coupled wheels. One such buffer beam was 5 inches thick ('A' end) and the other 1½ inches thick. Independent laminated springs bore directly onto inside roller-bearing cast-steel axleboxes, running in manganese steel-faced cast-steel hornblocks. The superstructure and equipment layout was neatly subdivided into three units: the fore or 'A' end comprised the bonnet or hood, which was the longer of the two; the cab was placed above the jackshaft drive assembly; and the shorter 'B' or aft end was the bonnet.

At the very front of 'A' bonnet was the cooler group (with the radiators protected by hand-operated shutters), the cooling fan with its hydrostatic motor, controller, hydrostatic tank and associated pipework all supplied by Serck Radiators Ltd as a complete unit. To the rear of the cooling unit was a fabricated stand carrying a pair of electrically driven vacuum brake exhausters.

Next came the Davey Paxman 'Ventura' 6 YJXL four-stroke diesel engine, with six cylinders in 'vee' formation; this delivered 650bhp at 1,500rpm continuously. A triple-throw crankshaft meant that this engine was inherently unbalanced; this is also the situation with four-cylinder-in-line and V8 engines, which require special dynamic balancing shafts, along the lines of those patented by Frederick Lanchester in 1906. On this Paxman engine, two Lanchester-type balancing shafts were necessary, together with the usual Holset viscous vibration damper. Whereas the other WR diesel-hydraulics were fitted with a dynastarter, the Class 14 had a starter motor and auxiliary generator, the former being coupled to the engine flywheel.

From the engine flywheel, a long Hardy Spicer cardan shaft was angled upwards under the cab to the input flange of the Voith L 217 U turbo-transmission located in and beneath the 'B' bonnet. This incorporated two torque converters, the third stage being through a single fluid coupling. A Hardy Spicer output cardan shaft ran from the transmission below the input shaft to a Hunslet Type 650 triple-reduction reversing and final drive gearbox with jackshaft assembly, having an overall ratio of 6.75:1; this was supplied through Voith, yet manufactured by Hunslet in Leeds. The jackshaft was located beneath the cab between the intermediate and trailing wheel centres.

From the transmission, a Laycock Engineering cardan shaft with two 'Layrub' flexible couplings drove the auxiliary generator, mounted at the far end of 'B' bonnet. This was a Lancashire Dynamo & Crypto type C12W Special unit, rated at 20kW, 110V.

For such a small locomotive, the livery was something of a coat of many colours. Standard Locomotive Green was used for the bonnet side and roof panels, exhaust stack, running plates and tool boxes, with Sherwood Green for the cab sides and ends. Grey was chosen for the cab roof and black for the wheels, underframes and drawgear. A break with the traditional red came with the selection of yellow for the buffer-beams and stocks. Bonnet ends received black and yellow warning chevrons and the handrails and footsteps were white. Lettering was painted in a white 'Grotesque' typeface on the cabsides, surmounted by the BR Coaching Stock cypher. The numbering series commenced with No D9500.

Construction began during late 1963 and No D9500 went to Bristol Bath Road on 24 July 1964. No D9555 completed the build when it entered traffic on 22 October 1965, also at Bristol. Other examples went new to Cardiff Canton and later some moved to other depots in South Wales, where the class found employment on coal traffic over routes where larger locomotives were not permitted. Nos D9521-4 went new to Old Oak Common to cover local trip freight and parcels duties that took them as far afield as Basingstoke, Newbury and Didcot. By October 1965 the quartet had migrated west to join the rest of the fleet.

The class was rapidly overtaken by events because the traffic for which it was conceived began to disappear, even as construction was in progress. The loss of freight traffic to road haulage and the rundown of the Welsh coalfield meant that the work for which the Class 14 had been built went into sharp decline; many examples were put in store, mainly at Worcester, during 1966.

A unique situation then came about, which brought the only instance of main-line diesel-hydraulic traction allocation away from the WR. The Hull Area of the Eastern (NE) Region needed to eliminate steam power, which comprised 15 8F 2-8-0 'WD' and four 5MT 'B1' 4-6-0 engines. The ER requested an initial allocation of 20, later increased to a total of 33, which the WR was prepared to release.

Although allocation to Hull Dairycoates shed is shown as from the end of December 1966, the first four did not reach their new home until 4 January 1967. All 20 were there by the 23rd, and by the end of the month 18 were serviceable, but only two were being used by the beginning of April, with only one failure reported. The problem was that the Hull Division Movements Manager didn't want them, deeming them unsuitable and also uneconomic. Matters came to a head with a meeting at Regional headquarters on 14 April.

The intention was to deploy the interlopers on a variety of duties, not just in Hull Docks but also to Howden, Beverley and Bridlington. Trials established that the brake force imposed a

Nos D9521-24 were sent new to Old Oak Common for local trip work. This undated view of No D9521 suggests that it had not long since arrived from Swindon. Note the yellow buffer-beam, a change from the traditional red, and typically applied to shunters.
Ian Allan Library

limitation on loads on certain downgrades, while consideration was given to the use in tandem on heavier duties; to this end, fitting multiple-unit equipment was considered.

History records that eventually Hull received a total of 33, but the stay did not prove lengthy. Again, this is likely to have been due to a sharp decline in traffic, and the Region's allocation were all withdrawn on 1 April 1968. Nevertheless, surviving correspondence proves that the popular myth of the ER being palmed off with unwanted WR locomotives is not true, and that the Regional senior management (at least) was a willing recipient in order to eliminate steam.

The locomotives that remained on the WR fared little better. Withdrawals had begun on 30 December 1967 with Nos D9522/31 – the latter had probably the shortest career of the fleet, entering service on 2 February 1965 and being put in store on 5 December 1967. Eventually the last handful succumbed on 26 April 1969.

A report produced in October 1967 by the BRB's Chief Engineer (Traction & Rolling Stock) sets out the state of play. At the end of June availability was around 80%, but reliability was a very poor 6,000 miles per casualty. Although two of the 12-cylinder version of the Paxman engine were performing satisfactorily in Class 42 No D830, the rating was set slightly less per cylinder. The ScR also had 14 locomotives of Class 29, with the 12-cylinder version, rated at 1,350hp at 1,500rpm, and these were giving trouble, so possibly the higher rating in the Classes 14 and 29 pushed the design too far. Cylinder head failures had already brought a decision to exchange the original aluminium type for a cast iron variant from October 1966 in the Class 14. As noted above, the Class 14's six-cylinder variant was inherently less well balanced and prone to vibration, which caused failures to turbocharger support brackets and mounting bolts.

The auxiliary generator armature banding failed on some machines due to engine overspeeding. The CAV starter motor suffered defects due to switch failure, ingress of brake block dust and cleaning solvent. The flexible coupling was also prone to fail. A programme of modifications had been mapped out to deal with

An interesting picture of a Class 14 performing banking duties. Regrettably, no other information is available. *Ian Allan Library*

these issues; No D9506 had been experimentally modified to give different characteristics at the generator drive.

Indeed, unlike some of the Type 2 classes discussed at the time, the report did not then envisage an early demise for the Class 14s, though the need for this type of locomotive was to be kept under review. Although surplus to BR, these nearly new machines were seen by British Steel and the National Coal Board as ideal replacements for steam, with the result that 45 found a new life in industry. In fact, several still survive in preservation today.

Length	34ft 7in
Width	8in 7¾ in
Height	13ft
Weight	50 tons
Sanding gear	Fitted
Fuel tank capacity (gallons)	323
	(three tanks combined)
Minimum curve radius (chains)	4½
Maximum speed (mph)	40
Engine	
Paxman 'Ventura' 6 YJXL	650 at
Engine output (bhp)	1,500rpm
Tractive effort (lb)	
Maximum	30,910
Continuous	26,690 at 5.6mph
Gear ratio	
N/a	

Class 15

The Pilot Scheme for the dieselisation of BR, which was part of the 1955 Modernisation Plan of the railways, ordered several types of locomotive in each of three power classifications. Initially, these classifications were designated 'A', 'B' and 'C', but this was later changed to Types 1, 2 and 4, there being no order for any designs within the Type 3 power range within the Pilot Scheme. With one exception, all the Pilot Scheme orders were made on 16 November 1955, and British Thomson Houston (BTH) was awarded a contract for ten Type A locomotives (Nos D8200-09), which were specified to be of up to 1,000hp and to have a single cab.

Planned use was on branch and local trip workings and as station and yard pilots, with a multiple-unit capability to enable two examples to be driven from one cab. No provision was made for train heating, though a through heating pipe meant that a piloting locomotive could supply steam to a train. Original allocation was planned to be to the LMR but this was changed later to the Great Eastern and London, Tilbury & Southend lines. As part of the move towards the rapid dieselisation of BR, and thus abandonment of the Pilot Scheme concept of service evaluation of competing designs, a further 33 examples were ordered in three batches as follows:

Nos	Ordered
D8210-09	17.12.1958
D8220-36	5.9.1959
D8237-43	18.12.1959

The last seven were ostensibly for the King's Cross (six) and Sheffield (one) areas and were part of the 1960 building programme. By the date of this last order, BTH had merged with

Ex-works No D8241 poses for an official photograph.
Ian Allan Library

Above: This interesting view shows the layout of Class 15 equipment within the body. From left to right are the cooler group, engine, generator, cab and control cubicle.
Ian Allan Library

Left: Initial duties for the Class 15 comprised trip workings in East London and transfer freights around the capital. On 11 September 1959 an example takes a Willesden Junction to Ripple Lane freight across North London Junction, Bromley-by-Bow, on the LT&S route.
BR

Metropolitan Vickers to form Associated Electrical Industries (AEI).

A full description of the design was included in *Diesel Pioneers*, though with a few minor technical changes the production series are covered in this volume. The salient features were a 'bonnet', which housed the cooler group, engine and generator set. Next to this was the cab, and this was followed by the control cubicle superstructure; this was mounted on the frames, which were carried on two, twin-axle bogies.

A 16-cylinder Paxman YHXL diesel, rated at 800bhp at 1,250rpm, was used, the rating being 200bhp lower than the manufacturer's continuous figure. Coupled to the engine was a 6-pole BTH RTB 10858 main generator, rated at 500kW, 720/1320A, 690/377V at 1,250rpm. Overhung from the end of the main generator was an RTB 7420 40kW auxiliary alternator. Unusually, there was a separate differential exciter (model DY2816) for the main generator, which was belt-driven from the latter and mounted on top of the auxiliary generator. Four BTH 137BZ traction motors, continuously rated at 144hp, 330A, 380V at 375rpm, were mounted one per axle in the usual nose-suspended arrangement. Strictly speaking, from

D8237 onwards this should be quoted as the AEI (BTH) 137BZ.

Establishing the identity of the constructors of the Pilot Scheme and production series batches throws up inconsistencies between sources. BTH (later AEI) subcontracted construction for No D8210 onwards to the Clayton Equipment Company. This company's works at Derby were not capable of handling the building of main-line locomotives and sublet the task to International Combustion, a member of the same group as Clayton, which was also located in Derby. This arrangement was later adopted for the Class 17. The Yorkshire Engine Co Ltd, which had led the construction of Nos D8200-09, is believed to have contributed some of the mechanical parts, though precise details cannot be verified.

The superstructure was painted Standard Locomotive Green, with light grey applied to the front and rear-facing cab panels. The undergear and bogies were black.

No D8200 was handed over on 18 November 1957 at a ceremony at Euston, but three months were to elapse before No D8201 was accepted into stock. Although intended for the ER, initial allocation was to the LMR's

No D8201 passes Kensal Green Junction. Note that the cab front is in a lighter livery in order to aid visibility for those working on the track. *BR*

Devons Road depot in East London, though there had been a reassignment to the ER by 1960. The type was tried out by the LMR outside London and also by the ScR shortly after delivery, but these Regions eventually took allocations of the competing Type 1 design from English Electric instead.

A two-month gap separated the commissioning of No D8209 and the order for the second batch, the first of which was not in traffic until late 1959. No D8243 completed the class when delivered to Finsbury Park in February 1961; in fact, all the last batch ordered went to this depot. Most of the Class 15s spent all their lives in East Anglia, generally on Stratford depot's books, though Norwich, Ipswich and March were among other locations that had responsibility for the type, which reflects the pattern of use.

The Class 15 shared the same engine model with the North British Locomotive Company's Class 16, which was also ordered under the Pilot Scheme. While the latter was not re-ordered, the BTH design was multiplied. Nevertheless, the Paxman engine appears to have been its Achilles heel, with several design faults emerging over the years. Availability figures over 80% point to a satisfactory performance, certainly far from the disaster tag with which other commentators have labelled the class. In fact, these were the standard Type 1 in East Anglia.

As late as October 1967 the BRB Chief Mechanical Engineer put forward further proposals for reliability modifications to the Paxman engine because the locomotives were seen as having a future, subject to the BR's revenue forecast forward to 1974, which envisaged a substantial downturn in traffic. Some engine modifications had already been done and availability and reliability were 76% and 10,000 miles per casualty respectively, superior to the Class 16. Even so, the CME was unable to plan for an availability of 90%, as laid down in the prevailing National Traction Plan.

Events overtook this because road competition brought a drastic decline in local trip working, together with an associated fall in the need for yard pilots. Withdrawals therefore began in 1968, and it is reported that the final 23 survivors all succumbed on 28 March 1971. Four examples, Nos D8203/33/37/43, were taken into Departmental use as carriage heating units. No D8233 is now the sole survivor and was last reported at the East Lancashire Railway, restored to its original number undergoing restoration.

Nos D8210-43

Length	42ft 3⅜ in
Width	9ft 2in
Height	12ft 6in
Weight	68 tons
Fuel tank capacity (gallons)	400
Wheel diameter	3ft 3½ in
Minimum curve radius (chains)	3½
Max speed (mph)	60

Engine
Paxman 16YHXL

Engine output (bhp)	800

Tractive effort (lb)

Maximum	39,500
Continuous	20,000 at 11.5 mph

Gear ratio
65:16

Nos	BTH Works Numbers	Clayton Works Numbers
D8210-17	1108-15 of 1959	CE 3579/1-27
D8218-36	1116-34 of 1960	
D8237-43	*CE 4095/1-7	

By this date BTH had merged with Metropolitan Vickers to form Associated Electrical Industries, and no AEI works numbers were assigned to the locomotives.

Class 17

R. C. Bond, the BTC's Chief Officer (Traction & Rolling Stock), informed the Board on 11 February 1960 that he wished to invite tenders for 88 of a new design of Type 1. While the English Electric (EE) Type 1 had proved successful mechanically, operationally the siting of the single cab at one end had caused some difficulty with the observation of signals. Thus was born the ill-starred new Standard Type 1 project that resulted in the contract being let to the Clayton Equipment Company Ltd, Record Works, Hatton, Derbyshire (hereafter Clayton) for what was to become Class 17 under the TOPS classification. (It is worth noting that the Clayton company referred to here has absolutely no connection to the Clayton Manufacturing Company, Steam Generator Division, El Monte, California, USA, which manufactured steam heating generators to permit locomotives to provide train heating. Vulcan Foundry (VF) of Newton le Willows, which, by the date covered by this book had been absorbed within English Electric, was the UK licensee for the American company.)

Award of the order to Clayton brought a strong reaction from the Scottish Trade Union Congress. By virtue of the planned allocation of the class to Scotland, the TUC argued that the work should have gone to the North British Locomotive Company Ltd (NBL), whose Glasgow Hyde Park Works was under threat of closure. BR argued that NBL was inferior on both price and delivery to Clayton's bid, while previous experience with NBL's diesels had shown them to be of poor design and build quality. Needless to say, the TUC felt these issues could be overcome, but NBL took no part in the Class 17s.

On 24 April 1961 the BR CME wrote to the BR Design Panel as follows:

'An order has been placed with Clayton for the supply of 88 of the above. Although many components are identical with the BTH Type 1 [TOPS Class 15] already in being, these new locomotives will be of the centre-cab type and will represent a new styling job. The sponsoring region is LMR and the first meeting with the firm has just been held. Will you nominate a design consultant since styling of BTH's Type 1 was one of the more successful achievements, so far as single-cab locos are concerned. You may consider it desirable to use the same stylist.'

Thus John Barnes of Allen Barnes, Bowden Ltd was duly appointed.

When new, class doyen No D8500 was sent to Marylebone for inspection by the hierarchy in BR's offices there. The locomotive sits resplendent in the goods yard. Interestingly, BR's caption gives the upper cab and cab front livery as grey/green, though it was very close to Sherwood Green, which was also being applied to Class 47 at the time. *BR*

Described by BR as its Standard Type 1 design, the No D8500 series was controversial from its inception. Intended for the ScR, the Scottish Trade Union Congress was extremely annoyed that the order did not go to the struggling NBL company in Glasgow, rather than to Claytons in England. On 25 October 1962 No D8505 was just eight days in traffic when captured at Tarbolton on the Ayr to Mauchline line on trial with a Falkland Junction-Saltney (Chester) fitted freight. *The late Derek Cross*

A precise date for the order of these 88 locomotives is unavailable, but it was made during April 1961 at a price per locomotive of around £57,000. A later order for 29 examples was awarded to Beyer Peacock (Gorton) Ltd (BP), and sanctioned by the BTC on 12 July 1962; these locomotives cost £53,520 each. Numbering was D8500-87 for the Clayton batch and D8588-616 for those from BP.

By October 1961 good progress on styling had been made, but Mr Barnes's suggestion for a different livery at solebar level was rejected in favour of all-over Locomotive Green but with either a black or charcoal grey roof. Reviewing the official livery description compared with that in which the class actually left the builders shows some variation. It should have been:

Body and cab sides, bonnet ends, skirt	– *BR Locomotive Green*
Roof, door panel and step, radiator louvers	– *Mid Grey*
Bogies and all equipment below skirt	– *Black*
Buffer-beams and stocks	– *Red*
Bonnet panel	– *Yellow*

It appears, though, that the bonnet tops were Mid Grey, while the radiator louvres were Light Grey, and the upper cab was a light shade of green, possibly the Sherwood Green in which the Class 47s were appearing. Ultimately there was universal approbation for the looks of the locomotive when it made its debut at Marylebone, BR's headquarters, on 27 July 1962.

Opting for a centre cab meant using two engines. Davey, Paxman & Co Ltd ("Paxman") of Standard Works, Colchester, Essex, apparently felt that it had not won a sufficient share of the UK locomotive market and offered its six-cylinder ZHXL engine, rated at 450hp at 1,500rpm. This was a horizontal version of the YHX unit, which had been fitted in 16-cylinder form in the Class 15. Under Paxman's coding, the number at the start of the engine code gives the number of cylinders; the first two letters in the engine code refer to cylinder configuration (in line) and size; the X that the engine is turbo-supercharged without air intercooler; and the L is for rail traction application. The 6ZHXL had already seen service powering Derby-built railcars of 1957 vintage, where performance had been satisfactory.

For reasons that will be discussed later, the last two of the order placed with Clayton, Nos D8586/7, had two Rolls-Royce engines instead of the Paxman variant. This was the

DV8TCMW and was supplied by that company's diesel engine division at Shrewsbury (the former Sentinel works). These 'D' series engines were of 'Vee' configuration, eight-cylindered and turbocharged. The 'C' and 'W' implied water-cooled charge-air cooling. Engine output was set to a continuous site rating of 450bhp at 1,500rpm to comply with the requirements of the electric transmission, because the electrical machines of the duo were identical to those in the Paxman-engined locomotives, Nos D8500-85.

In fact, the Rolls-Royce engine was designed to deliver its output at 1,800rpm in general application. A comparison of the engine height with that of the Paxman engine will explain the necessity for the elevated section of the engine hood that so readily identified these two variants of locomotive. Electrical equipment for all the Clayton-built examples came from the General Electric Company (Engineering) Ltd of Witton, Birmingham (GEC).

BP's order comprised 29 locomotives, Nos D8588-616. Although these had the Paxman engine, a switch was made in the supplier of the electrical machines. These came from Crompton Parkinson Ltd, of Chelmsford, Essex (CP), while control gear was from Allen West & Co Ltd of Brighton. Details of the different sets of main and auxiliary generators are tabulated above.

The traction characteristic was very much 'freight', with a maximum speed of 60mph and full engine output available between 3 and 60mph. Nevertheless, as already noted, the plan was to equip at least 20 with train heating generators. These were to come from Spanner Boilers Ltd, Bracknell, Berks, of model J3479/98. In the event this fitment never came to pass, possibly due to trade union pressure about siting such equipment inside the cab. Nevertheless passenger duties were undertaken during the summer, while a through steam pipe was fitted so that a leading locomotive could supply heat via a Class 17 to the train. Although capable of working in multiple, the Red Diamond coupling code was unique to the design. Cabside recesses were provided for fitting automatic tablet exchange equipment, though none received this facility.

For such small locomotives, there was considerable complexity with the control gear in respect of the number of options for generator/traction motor combinations available to drivers. This applied to all the class. Both engines ran independently, and they could run as single units or as a pair. When running as a pair both engines were controlled simultaneously in step to deliver power through their generators. Each engine drove a generator, which delivered power to a pair of traction motors. Thus, under normal conditions, the two engine/generator sets combined to supply the total power of the locomotive. Either set could be shut down and isolated, leaving the locomotive to be run on half power. In addition, provision was made for switching all four motors on to either generator; in this case the resulting series-parallel grouping of the four motors

Nos D8500-87/Nos D8588-616

Main generator (*two per locomotive*)	GEC WT 800 6-pole, self-ventilated	CP CG1086A1 4-pole, self-ventilated
Ratings	274kW, 700/420A, 397/650V at 1,500rpm	274kW, 900A, 305V at 1,500rpm; 276kW, 512A, 540V at 1,500rpm
Auxiliary generator (*two per locomotive*)	GEC WT 763	CAG1087A1
Ratings	35kW, 318A, 110V at 625/1,500rpm	34kW, 310A, 110V at 595rpm
Traction motors (*four per locomotive*)	GEC WT 421 4-pole force-ventilated	CP C1066A1 4-pole, force-ventilated
Continuous ratings	158hp, 350A, 397V at 470rpm at 12.8mph*	160hp, 450A, 305V at 670rpm

* *Source: Class 17 Electrical Machines Maintenance Manual*

permitted the maximum possible starting tractive effort to be applied to all wheels. The choice of these power combinations was made through the power selector switch in the main control cubicle, which had six positions:

1. Both engine/generator sets shut down and all four traction motors isolated.
2. No 2 engine/generator set shut down and Nos 3 and 4 traction motors isolated; Nos 1 and 2 traction motors connected in parallel across No 1 generator, with the locomotive thus reduced to half power.
3. No 1 engine/generator set shut down and Nos 1 and 2 traction motors isolated; Nos 3 and 4 traction motors connected in parallel across No 2 generator with the locomotive thus reduced to half power.
4. Nos 1 and 2 traction motors connected in parallel across No 1 generator and Nos 3 and 4 traction motors connected in parallel across No 2 generator (the normal position with both engine/generator sets running).
5. No 2 engine/generator set shut down and the four traction motors connected in series-parallel across No 1 generator, with the locomotive thus reduced to half power but with a high starting tractive effort available.
6. No 1 engine/generator set shut down and the four traction motors connected in series-parallel across No 2 generator, with the locomotive thus reduced to half power but with a high starting tractive effort available.

Service experience

Construction of the 88 units for the ScR was divided between Clayton's Hatton works and those of its parent, International Combustion (Holdings) Ltd, also at Derby. The plan was to divide Scotland's fleet between Glasgow south of the River Clyde and Fife; the Class 20s would be based north of the Clyde. No D8500 was taken to Marylebone for exhibition on 25 July 1962. Although accepted into stock at Glasgow Polmadie on 10 September, it was observed at Leeds Holbeck on 7 October. By then, other class members had penetrated as far south as Carlisle while in service. Initial reaction among footplate staff was a preference for the Class 20.

Deliveries continued up to No D8513 on 7 December, when the problems to be described below brought a curtailment. By January 1963 these problems caused all those in service to be stopped and stored at the closed Glasgow Parkhead steam shed. The official date for their withdrawal from service was 10 February, and the delivery of engines from Paxman also ceased. When a resolution was found, locomotives in Scotland went to Perth shed for modification.

Meanwhile, Clayton continued to assemble locomotives, and those up to No D8536 spent at least some time in store in the Derby area before making their way to the ScR from May to July. By early May 1963 the Class 17s were beginning to return to traffic, and on the 15th D8531 was seen at Bonnybridge on the 'Hielan Piper' freight. Prior to electrification of routes south of the Clyde, during the summer of 1963 the 'Claytons' (as the class is generally known) were used extensively on the Glasgow to Gourock and Wemyss Bay passenger services. No D8518 was noted on an Isle of Man boat train from Ardrossan Pier.

Polmadie's Nos D8545-9 were based at Thornton Junction for training. No D8554 was the first to be allocated permanently to Edinburgh Haymarket, which was the destination for all the remaining Clayton batch. The depot used its fleet on empty stock movements and local freight, and also sent them further afield, such as to Grangemouth on cement traffic. On 5 September Nos D8501/36 were loaned to the NER for trials on the Consett

Early in 1963, when only a few months old, technical troubles were such that all deliveries to date were taken out of service. Rectification work was subsequently carried out at Perth, where Nos D8503/4/11 were found on 13 April. *David C. Smith*

iron-ore workings; No D8500 was also reportedly loaned to the Region for training purposes. A year on from the initial crisis, failures from several causes remained common. A gap of several months separated the last of the Paxman variants to be built by Clayton and the two with Rolls-Royce engines, with No D8587 not entering traffic until 5 February 1965.

No D8588, the first of the BP order, went new to Thornaby on 20 March 1964, with the NER allocating deliveries from No D8593 to Gateshead. Use was primarily on local trips around north and south Tyneside, Wearside and Teesside; initial sightings were at Middlesbrough and Haverton Hill. During August 1964 trials were carried out on the Blyth & Tyne and it was established that the diesel was superior to the steam 'J27' 0-6-0s. An added advantage was the Class 17's potential to haul vacuum-brake-fitted pigeon specials when required, instead of Blyth shed's 'K1' 2-6-0s. The survivors from these CP-equipped locomotives migrated to Haymarket in mid-1971, where they lingered until October before final withdrawal. This suggests a preference for the BP examples, as they displaced those from Clayton.

The ER received from No D8604, allocated initially to Sheffield Tinsley until the new depot at Barrow Hill opened in April 1965. December 1964 saw the ER's No D8608 trialled on Warsop coal trains as a prelude to the short-lived

deployment on Nottinghamshire and Derbyshire coal trips. No D8616 entered traffic on the 23rd of that month. It is alleged that the ER disliked the new arrivals, which might explain why all moved to Haymarket in July 1966; most lasted there until October 1971, again a preference for the BP build.

Commencing in September 1967, the LMR eventually received Nos D8500-34 at Carlisle Kingmoor depot, from where they took over some of the tasks performed previously by Class 28s on both passenger and freight around Cumbria. One report refers to Class 17s displacing steam at Tebay for banking duties up Shap. The stay proved short-lived, in some cases only a few months, because the LMR rid itself of the type by October 1968, either by withdrawal from stock or passing some back to Polmadie. In fact, some withdrawn examples were reinstated in Scotland to meet an upturn in traffic in 1969.

Almost from the start, the 'Claytons' were in trouble. Several issues emerged with the Paxman engines. One source reports that marrying the engine to the GEC main generator caused unforeseen torsion vibration in the engine crankshafts, to which the generators were attached. The vibration affected not only the crankshafts but also other parts of the engine. These engine problems were almost totally related to shortcomings in the design and its durability. By the end of

Above: Beyer Peacock built 29 examples, which had Crompton Parkinson electrical equipment, and these were regarded as of superior quality to the GEC-equipped Clayton builds. On 31 August 1964 No D8595 passes Penshaw North with an up freight. *I. S. Carr*

Left: The ER also received a small allocation at Barrow Hill for transfer and trip duties, principally on coal traffic. The driver of No D8610 is probably glad of the excellent visibility offered by the commodious cab as he assembles his train at Ireland Colliery, Staveley, on 15 May 1965. *J. S. Hancock*

In 1967 the LMR was coerced into taking a large allocation of Class 17s, which were surplus in Scotland. With all based at Carlisle Kingmoor, they were used on Cumbrian line passenger services in the summer, train banking on Grayrigg and Shap banks and a range of freight turns. Bullgill Junction looks derelict as an unidentified pair of locomotives wheel a steel train along the former Maryport & Carlisle main line.
P. Robinson

1962, with only 13 delivered, three engines had suffered crankshaft failures.

The crankcases and frames were aluminium alloy castings, incorporating seven housings for the main bearing shells integrally cast, which began to fracture almost from day one, and with monotonous regularity. The engine camshafts were steel stampings, the cams and journals of which were hardened, ground and phosphated. As if the crankcase fractures were not enough, there came an epidemic of camshaft failures at the same time. Oil leakage from the fractures caused the engine compartments to run awash, and the most worrying aspect was that oil was finding its way into the main generators.

So serious were these failures and such were the implications that, from 10 February 1963, BR refused to allow new locomotives to enter the commissioning/acceptance procedure. Paxman hastily designed replacement cast iron crankcases/frames, and the affected engines were rebuilt by them so as to dispense with the aluminium alloy members, at considerable cost to the company. Even then, the engine was always prone to oil leaks, and the exhaust manifolds were single-skin stainless steel and dripped oil from the bellows.

There was a strong reluctance on the part of the LMR when it was asked to take an allocation of surplus locomotives from Scotland. Eventually agreement was reached, provided that the first one was ex-works. A visit to Carlisle to examine the chosen machine found that local maintenance staff had rigged up paint pots, suspended under leaking joints, to collect dripping oil. The LMR insisted on double-skin exhaust manifolds being fitted to curb leakage and fracturing.

With oil deposited everywhere in the engine compartment, maintenance was an unpleasant job, made worse because much of the work involved lying on top of the engine, which could only be done when it had cooled down. It was therefore unsurprising that there are allegations that depot staff were not as thorough in their work as they should have been and minor problems became major failures in consequence.

No doubt all these issues prompted the trial fitting of Rolls-Royce diesels in the last of the Clayton order, Nos D8586/7. Chosen possibly by virtue of being the only diesel that would fit within the available space (even then, the bonnet housing had to be raised slightly), these did not prove entirely trouble-free and two of the four suffered crankcase failures; these failures were reported to have been replaced by Paxman engines.

When BR was considering placing an order for further Type 1s in 1964, it decided to order from EE instead of opting for more Class 17s. This sealed the fate of the design. Many of the class saw long periods of storage at various locations, notably St Rollox Works and Ardrossan. Those that survived into the 1970s were mainly withdrawn in October 1971, though a few made it to December. Nos D8512/21/98 were retained for Departmental use, but none survived the 1970s. No D8568 was bought for industrial use by Hemelite Ltd at its Harpenden site during 1972, with a further sale in 1977 to Ribblesdale Cement Ltd for use at Clitheroe. In 1982 the locomotive passed into preservation with the Diesel Traction Group.

Settling on the locomotives that worked for the shortest time is made difficult because of the periods of storage, but Nos D8595/6 can probably claim the mantle. These entered service on 21 and 28 July 1964 respectively and were withdrawn on 22 December 1968, though quite a number of locomotives managed five years or less.

A potentially good design was marred by a serious weakness in a major component. The usefulness of Type 1 locomotives operating singly diminished rapidly during the second half of the 1960s as local freight work disappeared. This meant that both Class 17 and Class 20 spent much of their time operating in multiple, and the latter's signal-sighting problems were thus removed. It would be difficult to conclude otherwise than that the 'Claytons' were a very expensive mistake.

Length	50ft 7½ in
Width	8ft 9½ in
Height	12ft 8in
Weight	68 tons
Sanding gear	Fitted
Fuel tank capacity (gallons)	500
Minimum curve radius (chains)	3½
Maximum speed (mph)	60

Engines (two per locomotive)

Nos D8500-85/88-616	Paxman 6ZHXL
Nos D8586/7	Rolls-Royce DV8TCMW
Engine output (bhp)	450hp at 1,500rpm

Tractive effort (lb)

Nos D8500-87	
Maximum	40,000
Continuous	18,000 at 12.8mph
Nos D8588-616	
Maximum	43,000
Continuous	18,400 at 12.6mph

Gear ratio

GEC-equipped	66:15
CP-equipped	81:13

Clayton-built locomotives

D8500-85	Order No 4365
D8586/7	Order No 4924

Construction numbers:	D8500-10	4365 U 1-4365 U 11

Thereafter consecutive numbering was not kept, resulting in the following:

No D8511 - 14	No D8521 - 17
No D8512 - 16	No D8522-34 - 24-36
No D8513 - 13	No D8535 - 21
No D8514 - 12	No D8536 - 37
No D8515 - 20	No D8537 - 40
No D8516 - 19	No D8538 - 41
No D8517 - 18	No D8539 - 38
No D8518 - 15	No D8540 - 39
No D8519 - 22	No D8541-87 – 42-88
No D8520 - 23	

BP-built locomotives

Nos	Order Number	Works Numbers	Date
D8588-92	1739		1964
D8593-97	17311	8010-14	1964
D8598-8602	17312	8015-19	1964
D8603-07	17313	8020-24	1964
D8608-11	17314	8025-28	1964
D8612-16	17314	8029-33	1965

Class 20

Although No D8000 was the first of the Pilot Scheme orders delivered to BR in June 1957, and despite the success of the design, it quickly fell out of favour with its owners. This was because its bonnet or hood layout required double-manning on the footplate for reliable signal sighting when the bonnet end was leading, whereas BR wanted single-manning in the driving cab. It therefore appeared that the EE Type 1 would not become a standard design, confirmed when an order was given to Clayton for the Class 17, which was referred to as the standard Type 1. History rarely ploughs a straight furrow and ultimately fate proved kind to the D8000s.

Like the other Type 1s ordered under the Pilot Scheme, the EE variant had a single cab and this was mounted at one end of the locomotive. In front of this and under the bonnet housing was, first, the control gear, then the diesel power unit and finally (at the other end of the locomotive) the cooler group. This was a logical layout and, during the period covered by this book at least, facilitated easy access for maintenance because large bonnet side doors gave good access to all the equipment while standing on the footplating. Later in the life of the class, Health & Safety decreed that a locomotive could only be worked on if the depot had staging for staff to step onto from the locomotive footplating. The height restriction imposed by the BR loading gauge meant that the cab could not be raised to give visibility along the bonnet top, an option EE employed in a later order for Portugal.

Class 20 was, in many ways, an archetypal EE offering. It was rugged and unsophisticated – some might argue 'basic'. It was this combination, however, that helped to make it a winner. The engine was the EE SVT Mark 2, which had performed creditably in the Southern prototype No 10203, but here in its eight-cylinder configuration. EE used its 6-pole 819/3C main generator, which was attached to the diesel and was continuously rated at 642kW, 1,070A, 600V at 850rpm. The 8-pole EE911/2B 48kW auxiliary generator was overhung at the former's free end. Four EE 526/5D traction motors (Nos D8000-49 only, the remainder the EE 5268D) were continuously rated at 212hp at 362rpm, 600A

The London area saw the first deployment of Class 20s. While this was primarily on freight, the ER also used its allocation on suburban passenger services out of King's Cross during summer months when train heating was not needed. An unidentified example powers an eight-car working out of Hadley Wood Tunnel. *www.railphotoprints.co.uk*

Order date	Quantity	ER	NER	LMR	ScR
16.11.55	20		D8000-19		
14.1.59	30	D8020-7/45-9	D8035-44*		D8028-34
5.2.60	78	D8050-69		D8070-127	

* Originally allocated for delivery to the ER but exchanged for the same number of BTH Type 1s.

at a nominal 300V, and connected in series-parallel and nose-suspended, one per bogie axle; the motor gearing was for a 75mph top speed. Standard Locomotive Green for the body was complemented by a mid grey bonnet roof, red buffer-beam and black for the undergear. Nevertheless some new locomotives appeared with green cab roofs.

Construction of the Pilot Scheme batch was at Vulcan Foundry, and new builds were given trial runs, generally from Liverpool Edge Hill Carriage Sidings over either Shap or Ais Gill. No D8000 arrived at Willesden on 18 June 1957 before moving to Devons Road, its home depot, a few days later. The remainder of this first order followed until No D8019 arrived on 4 March 1958. A repeat order did not come until January 1959, with the work being split between the Robert Stephenson & Hawthorns (RSH) works at Darlington, which was part of the EE group, and Vulcan Foundry; the former built Nos D8020-34 and the latter the remainder. The table above sets out the

regional allocations, as well as those for a subsequent order for 78 units. Capacity issues at Vulcan Foundry meant that all of the third order was constructed by RSH, the last, No D8127, emerging during May 1962.

Some minor detail differences marked later builds from the first 20; the first batch had oval buffers, whereas the remainder had circular ones. Early examples, up to around No D8056, had a ladder on the body. Yellow warning panels also began to be applied at both ends, initially small, then full height, though one source says that Nos D8000-127 did not have warning panels from new. Scottish Region locomotives (Nos D80028-34/70-127) had some detail differences. There was a slightly different arrangement of the pipework on the buffer-beam and snowplough brackets were fitted. Also the cabside windows were more deeply recessed due to the inclusion of a recess in the side sheet below to accommodate single-line tablet exchange equipment, though only Nos D8028-34 actually had the gear fitted.

During the 1950s and 1960s the LMR allocated most of its fleet to the Midlands. This 1966 view depicts No D8143 at Galton, near Birmingham, with an engineer's train. *Michael Mensing*

For so long associated with coal traffic, the class was used extensively in the Nottinghamshire and Derbyshire coalfield, as well as in Scotland. Nos D8149 and 8184 bring empty hoppers from Blackwell past Westhouses station, bound for Silverhill on 17 August 1968. *J. S. Hancock*

Utilisation

Although there was no immediate rush to conduct road trials with the new arrivals, No D8000 was taken for this purpose between July and September 1958, when it had run 18,650 miles. The trials largely confirmed EE's predicted performance. Of the 1,000hp engine rating, auxiliary equipment absorbed 82hp, generator and motor losses were 43hp and 101hp respectively, and the locomotive's own resistance was 12hp. Temperature tests of the main generator determined that the manufacturer's rating was conservative.

While allocated to Devons Road, a former North London Railway shed in Bow, East London, the Pilot Scheme batch was deployed mainly on trip and short-distance freight work around the docks and yards in the Greater London area. As deliveries of the second and third orders arrived, their respective regions assigned a range of work, including ECS moves at Euston or in pairs on longer-distance freights. During the summer months passenger work could be undertaken at weekends, not possible in the winter due to the lack of a steam heat generator. By 1960 the class was taking a hand with freights in the Crewe and Chester areas. No D8036 had an unusual duty on 19 February 1961 when it hauled a massive transformer up the Conway Valley line to the site of the new power station at Trawsfynydd.

By February 1960 Hornsey's Nos D8045-9 were at work on cross-London freights and passenger services out as far as Huntingdon. Outbased at Hatfield, they also appeared on both passenger and freight movements on the Dunstable branch. In Scotland staff training took place in the Edinburgh area (the former Leith Central steam shed being the first base for diesels in the city), at Aberdeen Kittybrewster, and at Glasgow area sheds north of the Clyde. While at Parkhead shed for this purpose, Nos D8070/2 filled in for Class 303 'Blue Train' EMUs, which had been temporarily removed from service. On 8 February 1960 No D8032 was noted on the 9.20am Perth to Inverness train, paired with No D5346.

With the output against the third order coming into traffic during 1961, the ER sent its share to Sheffield Darnall. Later, as part of steam displacement in the Hull area, the class took over passenger workings along the coast to Scarborough. The ScR opted to base its allocation at Eastfield, from where forays took place along the West Highland Line and outings were made on passenger services in the summer. When Class 17s began to arrive in

Left: No D8198 has custody of a short goods near Langwith Junction in Nottinghamshire on the ex-Great Northern line on 4 May 1968.
J. S. Hancock

Below: Despite the visibility issue for the driver, No D8308 is running bonnet-leading at the head of a down goods passing Milford South Junction heading for Dringhouses, York, on 5 August 1969.
J. S. Hancock

1963, the plan was to keep the Class 20s on work north of the Clyde, though Polmadie crews preferred them to the new Standard Type 1s. The policy was not enforced rigidly, because by 1963 pairs of Scottish Class 20s were in charge of the car trains between Hillman's plants at Johnstone and Coventry. No D8041 arrived at Aston on 19 August 1963 for training purposes, then moved to Bescot.

The standard Type 1

On 19 December 1963 the BRB authorised the purchase of a further 100 Type 1s, but problems with the Class 17s led to a deferment of the placing of an order for that design. The matter was reconsidered at the Board's meeting on 23 April 1964, in the light of a recommendation by both the Chief Operating Officer and CME to procure 50 locomotives for delivery commencing in 1965. The recommendation was to place the order with EE at a cost of £2,975,000. A decision regarding the balance of 50 Type 1s was deferred again to assess progress with the 'Claytons', which were still preferred in principle. During the remainder of 1964 no decision was taken, but on 28 January 1965 the Board gave the go-ahead for the ordering of the last 50 Type 1s to be given to EE. Consideration had been given to allocating the

work to BR's own workshops, but this was not possible on capacity grounds.

Thus, after a gap of six years, Vulcan Foundry recommenced construction of Class 20s. Nos D8128-33/8 went to Darnall and Nos D8300-15 were split between York and Thornaby. The LMR sent almost all of Nos D8134-99 to Toton and Nos D8316-27 made their way to either Haymarket or Polmadie in Scotland. Production at Vulcan Foundry slowed to a crawl at the end, due to labour relations issues arising from the lack of future orders. A gap of eight weeks separated Nos D8326/7 from their sisters, with delivery on 7 February 1968; the new arrivals thus eliminated steam in several areas.

Some changes were introduced in these final two orders. EE referred to examples up to No D8127 as the 'old' locomotives and from No D8128 as 'new' locomotives. Route indicator boxes were added – those on the cab front protruding in a rather incongruous manner – and red tail warning lights were fitted below the route indicator boxes. Nos D8317-27, destined for Scotland, almost warrant designation as a separate sub-class. They had train air brake gear, as well as grab handles on the nose-end buffer-beam, but other, less obvious, changes were made, as will be described below.

The main generator rating on all of the 'new' locomotives changed to a more generous

Above: The adoption of a universal multiple operation system for most of BR's diesel-electric Types 1-3 enabled different classes to be controlled by one driver. With cab leading, No D8121 is paired with Class 27 No D5404, pictured at Waterside on a coal trip to Ayr on 4 April 1969. *The late Derek Cross*

Left: A rural setting on the Deeside branch from Aberdeen finds No D8034, recently ex-works, with the branch freight in 1964. *Michael Mensing*

645kW, 1,200A, 537V at 850rpm; they had an anti-wheelslip brake valve, and a newer model of Reavell exhauster in place of the Reavell exhausters on the 'old' locomotives, with a larger capacity.

Of more significance was the adoption of an electronic control system in the last 50 ordered, from No D8178. This used a closed-loop scheme based around a KV10-B1 torque regulator or field supply unit, identical to that used later in the Class 50. This featured an NPE7-A2 input board, except for No D8179 and Nos D8317-27, which incorporated Slow Speed Control (SSC), and here an NPE7-A1 input board was employed. All of these 'new' locomotives were delivered with:

1. A Driver's Controller Potentiometer, as it was then called (what in the Class 50 was termed the Current Setting Potentiometer)
2. A Current Limit Potentiometer
3. An Air-Operated Potentiometer, which supplied the current setting signal to the central control unit when one of the 'new' locomotives was required to work in multiple with any other Blue Star multiple-working system locomotive
4. A Speed Setting Potentiometer, additional to Nos D8179, D8317-27.

D8317 and 8179 underwent trials during mid-1967 in the Derby area to prove the new system, and this explains a six-month gap between the commissioning of No D8316 and the remainder. The ScR deployed the batch in pairs or triples on coal movements to power stations in Fife and to installations in Strathclyde.

The LMR found the slow-speed prototype, No D8179, to be troublesome and tried to transfer it to Scotland to join Nos D8317-27. The ScR rejected the locomotive but agreed to investigate the persistent KV10 'lock-ons'. No D8176 and from No D8178 onwards were delivered in the new Rail Blue livery, which was all-over blue except for full yellow ends and black undergear and buffer-beams.

With a fleet size of 228, the unexpected further multiplication of the class firmly made it the Standard Type 1. Its only drawback was the signal sighting issue, but otherwise the design proved to be the most reliable BR-ordered diesel. Gradually it became the norm for locomotives to be paired up, with cabs facing out, and this combination provided a formidable traction unit for the installed power.

ength	46ft 9⅜in
Width	8ft 9in
Height	12ft 7⅝in
Weight	72 tons
Wheel diameter	3ft 7in
Fuel tank capacity (gallons)	400
Minimum curve radius (chains)	3½
Maximum speed (mph)	75
Engine	
EE 8SVT Mk II	
Engine output (bhp)	1,000
Tractive effort (lb)	
Maximum	42,000
Continuous	19,500 at 14.8mph
Gear ratio	
63:17	

Works Numbers

Loco Nos	VF	RSH	EE Rotation No	EE Contract No
D8000-19	D375-94		2347-66	CCF 0873
D8020-34		8052-66	2742-56	CCL 1029
D8035-49	D482-96		2757-71	CCL 1029
D8050-127		8208-85	2956-3033	CCM 1113
D8128-177	D998-1047		3599-3648	CCS 1372
D8178-325	D1054-1101		3659-3705	CCS 1399
D8326/7	D1078/80		3683/5	CCS 1399

It appears that Nos D8302/4 were not assigned Works Numbers.

Class 21 & 29

Like nearly half the classes described in this book, the Class 21 design first saw service as a result of a Pilot Scheme order, which was covered in *Diesel Pioneers*. A North British Locomotive Company product to meet the criteria laid down by the BTC in the 1,000 to 1,250hp category, the Pilot Scheme order had been for ten examples, numbered Nos D6100-09. Allocation was for suburban workings out of King's Cross.

Expansion of the ordering of diesel traction in advance of the delivery of any of the Pilot Scheme building programme saw NBL awarded an order for a further 28 units on 1 May 1957 for delivery in February 1959. Allocation was to be to the King's Cross and London, Tilbury & Southend dieselisation schemes. This was followed on 4 July 1958 with an order for a further 20 for the ScR with delivery from July 1959, bringing the fleet size to 58.

The two production series batches were constructed at the Queen's Park (Order No QP 94) and Hyde Park Works (Order No HP 94) respectively. The MAN L12V18/21BS diesel engine was rated at 1,100hp at 1,500rpm (more precisely 1,445rpm), an increase of 100hp over the Pilot Scheme batch. This drove a GEC WT 880A 6-pole main generator, rated continuously at 712kW, 1,940A, 367V at 1,500rpm. On generators of this output and speed, special attention has to be paid to satisfactory commutation, and in this case a duplex lap winding was used in order to produce the reactance voltage while maintaining a moderate voltage between segments. The result was a complex and rather expensive machine.

A GEC WT 761 auxiliary generator supplied 35kW, 318A, 11V at 600/1,500rpm. Four GEC WT 440 traction motors were rated in the production series at 207hp, 48A, 367V at 350rpm, and had a gear ratio of 64:15. All four traction motors were connected in parallel across the main generator in order to obtain good adhesion characteristics. A change in the control scheme meant that the standard Blue Star multiple operation coupling code was adopted. Some sources claim that all the production series were Blue Star, while other sources say that the

The cabside recess on No D6148 is clearly visible here, but no tablet exchange apparatus has been installed. On 4 August 1962 the locomotive calls at Portknockie on the circuitous 10.20am Aberdeen to Elgin and Forres service via the coastal route. *Anthony Vickers*

29

change only commenced from the second batch of the production series.

NBL had four orders under the Pilot Scheme, a Type 1 diesel-electric, two Type 2s (Classes 21 and 22) and a Type 4 diesel-hydraulic. The latter was prioritised by the BTC, with drawings for the others being sent to the BTC in January 1956. Styling for the Type 2s broadly followed that agreed for the Type 4, except that there was no need for a nose end. This created some difficulty for the styling consultant because the same window frames fitted to the Type 4 had to be used for the cut-off nose. Nevertheless, by 25 June 1956 the stylist reported to the BTC that he had resolved the matter. There was then some debate over livery, but eventually the BTC laid down that the body would be Standard Locomotive Green, with a mid-grey roof section between the cabs. Whereas the Class 22 appears to have received a light grey horizontal band at solebar height, new deliveries of the Class 21 do not feature this.

The production series deliveries followed the initial build and No D6110 entered traffic at Stratford on 20 May 1959, followed by the next nine deliveries. Norwich was allocated Nos D6120-37, which were in traffic by the end of 1959. The ScR based its stud of 20 at Kittybrewster, No D6157 being accepted on 7 December 1960. It appears likely that all the latter had cabside recesses to permit automatic tablet exchange apparatus to be fitted.

Problems began from the first deliveries of the Pilot Scheme order. Those relating to the MAN engines are dealt with in the sections covering Classes 22 and 43. Sources give conflicting information about the actual engine ratings at delivery, but what seems reasonably certain is that NBL experimented with ratings of 1,000 and 1,100hp during the attempts to resolve the problems, which manifested themselves during the early stages of construction of the production series. One commentator from within the railway industry considered that setting the engine to the higher rating was, in itself, a source of trouble, and NBL may well have used 1,000hp during the evaluation of modifications.

Regrettably, the electrical machines also proved troublesome and the availability by the end of 1959 was dire. A programme of modifications was drawn up, to be carried out by NBL at its Glasgow works. To facilitate this, and no doubt after lobbying by the ER, the whole class were reallocated to Scottish depots during 1960.

Operationally, the ScR deployed the class as part of the planned elimination of steam on the West Highland Line, as well as between Glasgow, Dundee and Aberdeen. On the latter the locomotives were at times used in multiple, probably to cut schedules. Kittybrewster also put the class to use on routes north of Aberdeen. The class also performed on freight movements, with reported sightings in the Ayrshire coalfield and even at Carlisle.

A lovely night study at Buchanan Street on 1 November 1963 of a Glasgow to Dundee service, with Nos D6134+49 at the head. Over the years the ScR diagrammed either a single or pair of Class 21s to these duties. *Norman Pollock*

Twenty-six days later the pioneer Class 29 has sole charge of the 10.15am Buchanan Street to Aberdeen train, captured passing St Rollox. By now the locomotive is in two-tone green, but has not received the route indicator panel that was to be fitted to later converts. *Norman Pollock*

The final external livery for the Class 29 was all-over blue, as seen here on No D6129 in this November 1968 illustration. The train, the 12.25 from Oban to Glasgow Queen Street, is approaching Crianlarich. *C. W. R. Bowman*

For whatever reason, the ScR seemed to experience more difficulty in keeping its fleet in traffic than did the WR with the Class 22, and some examples were laid up for long periods. One commentator cites a shortage of spares for the engines as an issue, though this was not referred to in relation to the WR fleet of MAN-engined locomotives.

With a view to addressing the unreliability of the MAN engine and the inadequacy of the cooling system, No D6123 was selected for a trial re-engining. The unit chosen was the same already in use in Class 42 No D830, a Paxman 'Ventura' 12YJXL, but now continuously rated at 1,350bhp at 1,500rpm, which was also the highest rating that could be accommodated by the existing electrical equipment. The work was carried out by Paxman at its Colchester works and completed in June 1963, with trials in Scotland commencing in July.

A decision was taken to convert a further 19 locomotives, the work being shared between Glasgow and Inverurie Works. The programme was scheduled between September 1965 and August 1966 but was delayed initially by late delivery of engines from Paxman, then by AEI, which was carrying out modifications to the main generators, and was not concluded until December 1967.

A report prepared in October 1967 for the BRB refers to poor availability and a decision to send the main generators for the re-winding of the armatures, so this work appears to have been additional to the original re-engining programme. The report also identifies several issues with the 'Ventura' engines: main and big-end bearing failures, piston scuffing and seizures, defective turbo-charger exhaust intake bellows and cylinder liner wear.

Locomotives converted to what became Class 29 were Nos D6100/01/02/03/06/07/08/12/13/14/16/19/21/23/24/29/30/32/33/37. Although photographic evidence confirms that No D6123 re-entered traffic in all-over green, the remainder received a two-tone green livery and had their front-end doors sealed and fitted with a four-character route indicator box. Some later received Rail Blue livery.

By October 1967 30 of the 38 surviving Class 21s were stored unserviceable and deemed surplus to prevailing requirements. Unsurprisingly, many were withdrawn at the end of the year, with more in 1969. Despite the expenditure on the Class 29 conversions, and planned retention into the 1970s, the release of the Class 27 by the LMR meant that all the NBL diesel-electric Type 2s had gone by the end of 1971.

Length	51ft 6in
Width	8ft 8in
Height	12ft 8in
Weight	72 tons 10 cwt
Sanding gear	Fitted
Fuel tank capacity (gallons)	
Class 21	360
Class 29	375
Minimum curve radius (chains)	4½
Max speed (mph)	
Class 21	75
Class 29	80
Engine	
Class 21	MAN L12V18/21BS
Class 29	Paxman 'Ventura' 12YJXL
Engine output (bhp)	
Class 21	1,100 at 1,500rpm
Class 29	1,350 at 1,500 rpm
Tractive effort (lb)	
Maximum	
Class 21	45,000
Class 29	47,000
Continuous	
Class 21	30,000 at 10.2mph
Class 29	24,400 at 16 mph
Gear ratio	
64:15	

Nos	NBL Progressive Numbers
D6110-37	27840-67 of 1959
D6138-57	27942-61 of 1960

One of the Pilot Scheme orders awarded to NBL on 16 November 1955 was for a diesel-hydraulic version of the Type 2 diesel-electric for which the company had already been contracted. BR intended these two classes to provide as close a comparison as possible between the different forms of transmission. In the event, for several reasons, this comparative study never came about, mainly because both types were beset by design and manufacturing problems. The six examples of Class 22 were also designed to be compatible with the Type 4 diesel-hydraulics also ordered from NBL to facilitate operation in multiple.

On 5 November 1957 a further 52 units were ordered against NBL's tender of the previous April (Swindon Lot No 440, NBL Order No L97), although the Pilot Scheme six had yet to emerge from the manufacturer. This order was allocated by the BTC between the WR Area 1 modernisation scheme (West of England, 44 units) and Area 2 (Bristol, 8 units), and had (eventually) around 70 modifications, a number of which arose from initial experience with the first few No D6300s. The total of 58 units comprised the envisaged Type 2 requirement under Stage 1 of the WR's diesel programme, which embraced the area west of Exeter. All freight and secondary (non-DMU) passenger and banking duties were to be assigned to the class. Based on German Federal Railways' practice, the engines and transmissions were to be interchangeable with the Maybach engines and Mekydro transmissions being fitted to the Swindon-built Type 4s (TOPS Class 42). In the event, this facility was never used. Running numbers D6306-57 were assigned and NBL allocated Progressive Numbers from 27879 to 27930.

The engine was the MAN L12V18/21 in its 'B' form, whereas the Pilot Scheme batch had the 'A' version. Power output was now 1,100hp at 1,530rpm, a 100hp uplift. Transmission was a Voith LT306r, whereas Nos D6300-5 had the Voith L306r. The newer units had a higher transmission power input capacity of 1,036hp and were lighter and more compact. Germany supplied 22 transmissions, NBL the rest. Gear reduction in the drive differed, with 3.43:1 for the first

This study of No D6321 at Newton Abbot in June 1960 shows the locomotive in as-built condition, being just two months old. Note the distinctive NBL diamond-shaped works plate under the cab number. It is awaiting its next banking duty up to Dainton and onward to Plymouth. *David Adams*

batch and 4.45:1 for the production series. Other detail differences existed between the two series in the transmission and drive arrangement.

A hydrostatic motor and pump was used to drive the radiator fan, a change from the electric motor drive used in Nos D6300-5. All the class had a separate radiator compartment, which drew air in from both sides of the body to cool the Serck radiator blocks. Externally, the fitment of horizontal louvres in the bodyside of Nos D6300-5 was changed to a single square grille for the remainder, providing a clear visual difference between the types. Other differences saw the substitution of GEC for BTH electrical equipment and Davies & Metcalfe for Westinghouse train brake gear.

Four-character headcode panels were provided from new on Nos D6334-57, and were fitted retrospectively by Swindon Works on the remainder. Further amendments to the design were made during delivery of the production batch, largely to fulfil BTC requirements. Included in these were snowplough brackets, though it is not certain whether all class members received these. All appeared in BR standard Locomotive Green, with a light grey line along the underframe between the cabs. Some of the class received BR Monastral Blue, the so-called Rail Blue livery, in 1967/8. Yellow

was added to cab fronts, initially as a painted panel, then to the entire front, in later years.

Delivery and operation

Numbered Nos D6300-57, delivery of the first example was in December 1958, 18 months late, with the first of the production batch entering service in October 1959. Production was slowed after No D6333 in August 1960 to enable NBL to concentrate on its order for Type 4s. No D6337 did not arrive until March 1962, with No D6357 completing the order in the following November.

Initially allocated to 83D (Plymouth Laira), as part of the WR's plans to eliminate steam in the West Country, the Class 22 became the Region's standard Type 2. As steam was gradually phased out, and branch lines in Devon and Cornwall closed, so the class was split between Laira, Newton Abbot, Bristol Bath Road and Old Oak Common. Although there were several reallocations between these depots, the lower-numbered examples generally stayed in the West Country, while Bristol received around ten of the middle order in September 1967 for almost a year, though that depot had received smaller allocations at other times. Old Oak Common tended to have locomotives in the higher number range from around 1965 in any quantity.

Schoolboys in uniform look on as friends depart for Central station from Exeter St David's behind No D6301. Class 22s were used on secondary passenger duties around Exeter right to the end of their days, the last diagram being on a Plymouth train in December 1971.
David N. Clough

In Cornwall the class was generally deployed in multiple and on all manner of work. Even titled trains were taken over at Plymouth for the continuation to Penzance, as with No D6307 and a classmate in June 1963, proudly displaying the 'Cornishman' headboard. The location is Truro. *David Adams*

Being non-standard with the production series, Nos D6300-5 were kept at Plymouth. The incompatibility arose because the Pilot Scheme examples had electro-pneumatic driving control in order to multiple with the NBL Pilot Scheme Type 4s, Nos D600-4. The remainder had electric control, which was used on the production series NBL Type 4s (TOPS Class 43).

By virtue of being the only WR Type 2 meant that the Class 22s were assigned a range of work. Prior to the arrival of Type 4 locomotives in any quantity, they were deployed in Cornwall in pairs on top-line passenger turns. In fact, one contemporary report claims that almost all Laira's diagrams were for pairs. This included a passenger service between Par and Newquay, although a single machine was sufficient for the two coaches that comprised the train set for the Chasewater to Newquay service, shortly before closure. Most of the mileage was run on the (at the time) extensive china clay traffic. In fact, around a dozen locomotives were based at St Blazey depot for this traffic and the class was popular with drivers because of the strong pulling power at low speed; such traffic was worked as far afield as Meeth in North Devon. Class 22s replaced Class 45xx 'Prairie' steam engines on the Padstow to Bodmin Road service, and from April 1960 one powered the daily Plymouth to Exeter freight via the former Southern route; a revised diagram later in the year meant that it returned with a portion off a passenger service, which had originated at Waterloo at 3pm. Milk traffic as far afield as Chard was also covered. With control of former SR routes in Devon and Cornwall placed with the WR from late 1963, during the summer of 1964 Class 22s displaced much of the steam power on those lines, including Ilfracombe and Barnstaple to Torrington.

Banking duties were performed over the South Devon hills, at Evershot on the Weymouth line, up Ashley Down bank out of Bristol, and on Sapperton bank between Gloucester and Swindon. Despite extensive use of DMUs on second-tier long-distance Class 1 and 2 passenger duties, Class 22s fulfilled a role here too. For example, from January 1960 a pair of No D6300s were rostered for the 7.55am Taunton to Paddington.

There were diagrams off Old Oak Common on empty coaching stock in and out of Paddington, and local freight movements as far north as Banbury and west along both the Thames Valley and Berks & Hants routes were assigned to the class. Milk traffic was another No D6300 duty, while Bath Road-based examples found their way into South Wales and to Gloucester on freight. It is said that, while working in the Gloucester area, No D6320 carried the unofficial name *Lister* for a time.

Technical issues and rundown

The technical issues were dealt with in some detail in *Diesel Pioneers*, but, essentially, there were serious problems with the MAN engines and exhaust system, the electrical systems (including control gear) and the steam heating generators, of which three types were installed across the fleet. It has often been said that a key issue was the quality of manufacture by NBL, when compared to German-built equipment. Explaining this, it has also been pointed out that the BTC negotiated a very hard deal with NBL, the latter cutting corners in consequence. All these served to pull down availability, especially when spare parts became scarce after NBL's closure. As early as 23 July 1959 the BTC minutes record problems of overheating and with fuel injection nozzles to the extent that it was resolved not to place any further orders with NBL, whose fate was therefore sealed.

The 1968 National Traction Plan envisaged phasing out the Class 22, made possible by spare Type 2 capacity on other regions due to the shrinking of the rail network. In 1966 the WR identified a need for 45 Type 2s, which might explain why some of its fleet of 58 were put into store. It must, though, be noted that, during the mid-1960s, the D6300s returned the highest availability of any WR diesel class, generally above 80%. Withdrawal of the Pilot Scheme series came first during 1967/8, although a number of the production series also succumbed in 1968. Among these was No D6357, which saw just six years and one week on BR's books, while several others ran for barely any longer

before being put into store, followed by withdrawal. The storage of a large proportion of the No D6300s from 1968 was probably due to shortage of spares. The survivors then enjoyed a period of grace until 1971, with the last few going on 1 January 1972. No D6338 might have been the last to work a train because it is reported as catching fire on 20 December 1971 while hauling the 16.11 Drinnick Mill to St Blazey china clay service.

Nos D6306-57

Length	46ft 8½ in
Width	8ft 8in
Height	12ft 10in
Weight	65 tons
Fuel tank capacity (gallons)	450
Wheel diameter	3ft 7in
Minimum curve radius (chains)	4½
Maximum speed (mph)	75

Engine
MAN L12V18/21BS

Engine output (hp)	1,100 at 1,530rpm

Tractive effort (lb)

Maximum	43,500
Continuous	30,000 at 8mph

Gear ratio
N/a

At the end of the line, Penzance, No D6308 and another example reverse their train out and head for Long Rock carriage sidings. *David Adams*

Eventually the WR's standard Type 2 spread to Bristol and London depots. Complete with route indicator boxes and half yellow end, No D6356 draws out of Temple Meads with empty stock from a local working in 1964. *David Adams*

Old Oak Common found quite a variety of tasks for its stud. No D6327 had acquired BR Blue by 28 April 1967 when captured on a weedkilling train at Newbury. Note the position of the BR emblem, set high in the middle of the body. *D. E. Canning*

As late as 1970 the Wallingford branch from Cholsey & Moulsford retained a daily freight. No D6326 heads back to the main-line junction amid a rural scene. This time the BR emblem has been sited below the secondman's side window. *John H. Bird*

Class 24

British Railways had very extensive workshop facilities at the time, a carry-over from pre-Grouping days, when each railway had its own mechanical engineering establishments. The intention was to allocate as much work as possible to the shops at Crewe, Derby and Swindon, while Darlington also played a small part. However, capacity constraints meant that orders had also to be placed with private-sector locomotive builders in order to facilitate deliveries in the required timescale.

The first 20 of this design were part of the Pilot Scheme, and comprised an order awarded to BR's Derby Works to its own design. Official records show that the drawing office took no notice of recommendations made by Mr E. G. M. Wilkes, who had been appointed as design consultant by the BTC Design Panel, and the result was something of an ugly duckling. In fact, in 1962, when Mr Wilkes was asked to advise on a change of livery, he replied that 'it was not possible to make a silk purse out of a pig' – harsh words. A particular black mark could be awarded to the plethora of bodyside

grilles, which gave the impression of a patchwork quilt and allowed brake block dust inside the engine room. The exterior styling of the equivalent BRCW design (Class 26) was judged much superior, with air intake grilles at cantrail level.

Leaving external styling aside, the choice of a Sulzer 6LDA28A engine and British Thomson Houston (BTH) electrical machines proved successful; *Diesel Pioneers* set out full details of the design components. The engine rating was 1,160hp at 750rpm. The main generator was the 12-pole model RTB15656, continuously rated at 735kW, 1,400A, 525V at 750rpm. In the first 50 locomotives a separate exciter for the main generator was fitted, but this was dropped on later builds in favour of the main generator having separate shunt and differential windings. Control was then direct from the auxiliary generator via the load regulator.

The 8-pole 32/50kW auxiliary generator was the RTB 7440. The four traction motors were type 137BY, continuously rated at 213shp, 350A, 525V at 549rpm, and were mounted conventionally (that is, nose-suspended on each axle), and connected in parallel across the main generator. Gearing was fairly low to reflect the envisaged duties, and this gave a predicted continuous rating speed of 13.5mph, later revised to 14.8mph. Nevertheless, full engine output was available between 7.7 and 69mph and the rail horsepower at the continuous rating speed was 843.

Against a specified maximum overall weight of 75 tons, No D5000 tipped the scales at 4cwt short of 80 tons when it finally emerged from Derby on 24 July 1958 to be displayed at Marylebone; it had been due the previous February. The excess weight caused a headache when used on the SR, whose Chief Civil Engineer was much less willing to accept the situation than his counterparts on other Regions. Consequently, some examples had their steam generators removed to reduce weight. As built, Nos D5000-113 had a hinged valance at solebar level, but this corroded and was later removed.

The class was eventually multiplied to a total of 151, and the table below has been extracted from a 1961 report produced by the CME Department.

The 1957 order was initially assigned to the ER, but an exchange was arranged that saw an order of the same size for BTH Class 15s moved from the LMR. Construction was split between Crewe and Darlington as well as Derby; the latter was responsible for Nos D5000-29/66-75/5114-50, while Darlington was allocated Nos D5094-113 and Crewe dealt with the remainder. For a time during late 1959 and the first half of 1960 two workshops were producing locomotives concurrently, which explains why

delivery dates are not numerically consecutive.

According to *Trains Illustrated*, it was not until No D5094 emerged from Darlington in February 1960 that the weight issue was resolved, the contemporary reports quoting 72 tons 17 cwt. In contrast, A. H. Tayler's book *Sulzer Types 2 and 3* states that No D5050 was the first to appear at the lower weight when it emerged from Crewe the previous November. What is indisputable is that Darlington's No D5096 was the first Type 2 allocated to the NER. No D5150 completed the orders when it went to Gateshead on 27 February 1962.

In common with virtually all the new designs in this period, full dynamometer car trials were conducted with No D5008 during November 1959. By virtue of the main generator characteristic, the maximum starting tractive effort was established to be 40,000lb, as predicted, but the continuous rating figure was higher than predicted at 22,700lb. Full engine output was available between 9.3 and 58.3mph, the latter figure lower than predicted, and peak transmission efficiency was 79.2%, representing about 910rhp. The control system and engine governor combined to give a good level of fuel efficiency and the overall results were regarded as satisfactory.

The ER used its class members in East Anglia on passenger work. No D5044 departs from Haddiscoe beside the River Waveney in June 1963 with a Lowestoft to Newcastle express. *David N. Clough*

Order date	Quantity	ER	NER	LMR	ScR
16.11.55	20			D5000-19	
28.2.57	10	D5020-9			
13.2.58	84	D5047-83/94/5	D5096-113	D5030-46 D5084-93	
8.1.59	37		D5147-50	D5133-46	D5114-32

Utilisation

Although intended for steam displacement on the LMR, the first 15 were loaned to the SR from February 1959 until June 1962 as a stopgap on Kent Coast passenger services until that Region's own diesel locomotives had been procured. A Class 24 did, however, reach Southampton on a boat train. On their return to the LMR some worked in the London area, while others went to Crewe, from where examples began to be cast aside from early 1969. Although No D5000 was withdrawn on 4 January, it was reinstated later in the year and saw further service in Scotland with its classmates.

Ipswich and March were the principal recipients of the ER's batch and used the type extensively in Norfolk and Suffolk on secondary passenger as well as freight movements – in the 1960s, of course, the rail network in East Anglia was far more extensive than today. The surviving remains of the (then) recently closed Midland & Great Northern Joint line from Norwich witnessed Class 24s on the remaining passenger and freight turns. Longer-distance deployments included the 7.53am Norwich to Birmingham New Street and 3.55pm return, with stabling at the now long-defunct Monument Lane shed during the layover time.

Hornsey received a batch of 25 in exchange for Class 26s because the latter were too heavy for cross-London freights to the SR. Deployment was additionally on empty stock and peak-hour suburban services. Part of a typical five-day diagram is listed in the table below. Later in the week the locomotive visited Feltham, Hither Green and New Southgate on freight, while it went to Dalston and Bounds Green on ECS, in addition to further trips to locations already covered previously.

The ER quickly decided it preferred the Brush No D5500s as its standard Type 2 and, as deliveries of these increased, the Region displaced many of its Class 24s to other regions, particularly the LMR and Scotland. From late 1960 March gave up some locomotives to Longsight, Manchester. Nevertheless, Finsbury Park retained an allocation as late as 1966.

Meanwhile, the LMR put its fleet to use on empty stock and suburban services out of Euston. By February 1961 double-heading of outer suburban services to Northampton had begun, which helps to explain the appearance of Willesden depot machines finding deployment between Rugby, Peterborough and Northampton. Further north, Crewe's examples took a share of freight and even appeared on semi-fast passenger trains between Liverpool and Birmingham New Street forward from Crewe. There was also extensive diagramming on freights – the Class 24s were the Region's standard Type 2 until this mantle was assumed by the nearly identical Class 25s.

The North Eastern Region began receiving its allocation at Gateshead with No D5096 on 9 April 1960. Early use included freight traffic between the Newcastle area and Carlisle, while the new timetable in May saw a unit substitute for a DMU between Newcastle and Leeds. By October Gateshead was turning out pairs of the class on parcels and even express passenger workings along the East Coast Main Line. For example, during November Nos D5107/8 powered the 'Heart of Midlothian' from Edinburgh to Newcastle. Elimination of steam on the Tyne Dock to Consett iron-ore traffic resulted

Day	Terminal	Arr	Dep	Class
1	Finsbury Park Carriage Sdgs		05.50	
	Potters Bar	06.25	08.10	B
	Moorgate	08.45	08.59	ECS
	Finsbury Park Western Sdgs	09.23		ECS
	Ferme Park		10.35	Freight
	Hither Green	12.00	13.45	Freight
	Ferme Park	15.10	20.08	Freight
	Norwood	21.23	22.12	Freight
2	Ferme Park	23.31	02.28	Freight
	Bricklayers Arms	03.35	04.35	Freight
	Ferme Park	05.53		
	Hornsey – daily exam			
	Ferme Park		09.20	Freight
	Bricklayers Arms	11.10	12.35	Freight
	Ferme Park	13.55		
	Finsbury Park Carriage Sdgs		17.30	ECS
	Moorgate	17.56		
	King's Cross		18.44	ECS
	Hornsey Sdgs	19.50		
	Ferme Park		22.58	Freight
3	New Cross Gate		23.52	Freight

in Nos D5102-11 being fitted with an extra air compressor and also control gear to operate the wagon doors (though the class had reached Consett beforehand on other freights). A pair of locomotives avoided the need for banking assistance on the 1 in 35 climb.

No D5114 was the first to be allocated to the Scottish Region, at Inverness, on 23 April 1960, and it was also the first to have a four-character route indicator box. An early reported working for the class later that month was the 7.07pm Perth to Edinburgh train. Nos D5114-32 of Inverness had the tablet exchange apparatus fitted in a cabside recess below the driver's windows at Glasgow St Rollox Works in October 1960, so that loops on the Highland Line could be passed at 40mph.

Crews preferred the BRCW Class 26s and regarded the Class 24s as inferior traction units with an inferior cab environment. On the Highland Line, when two Type 2s were operated in multiple, the most common arrangement in the 1960s was a pairing of a Class 24 and a Class 26. Class 24s suffered markedly more cylinder liner wear than their BRCW counterparts, and Inverness depot was selected to investigate this because it had both

types, operating on identical duties. Attention quickly turned to the engine room air intake grilles, because the BR design had these scattered across the bodyside, while BRCW had placed them at cantrail height. Close monitoring of filter dirt quickly established that those at low level had to cope with a large amount of particles and became overloaded; this meant that the filters were not capable of working effectively and more dirt entered the engine room than on the Class 26.

During the first few years, main generator flashovers were too common, but a modification reduced their incidence; a facility

The route between Blackburn and Bolton has not seen regular loco-hauled services for several decades. No D5027 passes Hoddlesden Junction, near Darwen, with an empty coaching stock on 26 July 1968. *J. S. Hancock*

In pre-electrification days the LMR also deployed some of its fleet on passenger turns into and out of Birmingham New Street. The platform inspector prepares to signal No D5136's departure from Manchester Piccadilly on an express for Birmingham. *AEI*

A different route to Birmingham, this time from Rugby, as No D5026 heads a down parcels train at Canley, near Coventry, on 16 April 1961. *Michael Mensing*

for rotating the generator brushgear during maintenance tended to stick due to dirt, and checking the brushes at the bottom position is said to have involved the electrician lying on his back in the oil drip tray, a strong deterrent to doing the job. The equipment layout generally was not as well planned as on the BRCW design.

By June 1962 the class, in conjunction with Class 26, had virtually eliminated steam north of Perth, including the Far North and Kyle lines. Even the Aberfeldy branch service was dieselised. On 17 January 1963 No D5083 inaugurated a Glasgow Gushetfaulds to Birmingham 'Condor' container flow, the locomotive having been transferred to Crewe from Willesden for the purpose. In September 1967 Scottish-based Nos D5127/31 had a headlight fitted to improve visibility on ungated level crossings.

Casualties up to the end of the 1960s were Nos D5005/43/51/93/122/138/139, of which Nos 5043/93/138/139 all succumbed on 9 July 1969 as a result of being hit by a runaway freight, which was diverted into Chester depot.

A snapshot of depot allocations in September 1967 was as follows:

Crewe	81	York	1
Longsight	8	Eastfield	6
Gateshead	18	Haymarket	15
Holbeck	3	Inverness	19

Overall the class proved successful, though build quality was not to the same standard as that of BRCW. Political considerations aimed at keeping BR shops fully occupied led to the large number built, while in truth the Class 26 was a better traction unit in just about every respect.

Length	50ft 6in
Width	9ft 1in
Height	12ft 8in
Weight	
D5000-49	79 tons 16 cwt
D5050-5101/12-50	73 tons
D5102-11	71 tons
Fuel tank capacity (gallons)	500
Minimum curve radius (chains)	4½
Wheel diameter	3ft 9in
Maximum speed (mph)	75

Engine
Sulzer 6LDA28A

Engine output (hp)	1,160 at 750rpm

Tractive effort (lb)

Maximum	40,000
Continuous	21,300 at 14.8mph

Gear ratio
81:16

Nos D5102-11 were not fitted with a steam heat generator.

In the early days of dieselisation, the lighter weight of locomotives when compared to the previous steam power meant that there was insufficient brake force to handle unfitted freights. To address this, redundant locomotive tenders were converted to provide a braked vehicle, attached in front of the locomotive. In the industrial setting of the ICI plant, No D5112 leaves Billingham for Middlesbrough with a 350-ton train of iso-octanol for export to Australia. *ICI*

Brake tenders were often needed on a rake of mineral wagons, as seen here at Manors, Newcastle-upon-Tyne. No D5106 comes from the Heaton direction on 28 May 1962. *Michael Mensing*

The last batch of Class 24s had route indicator boxes, though these were little used in Scotland. No D5130 calls at Helmsdale with the up 'Orcadian' from Wick to Inverness. *AEI*

Class 25

Between January and December 1959, the dates of the last order for Class 24 and the first for Class 25, Sulzer had got development work on its LDA28 engine through UIC testing and was able to offer it in 'B' form. By revising the cylinder heads and fuel pumps, increasing the turbocharger capacity and adding charge-air cooling, the engine in six-cylinder form could now develop 1,250hp at 750rpm, a modest increase of 90hp. It was the adoption of this 'B' engine that marked the new class designation of the subsequent orders, combined with a requirement for a top speed of 90mph.

Over successive orders there were several changes to the electrical equipment, and the easiest way to present these is in tabular format (*see below*). Under TOPS, sub-class designations were applied to the successive changes and these designations are used here.

Just to confuse the picture, the AEI/Sulzer Operating Manual gave the maximum tractive effort as 46,500lb and the continuous rating 20,500lb at 18mph.

The main generator was, essentially, the same machine as fitted in the later builds of Class 24, the AEI 12-pole RTB15656, rated at 817.5kW, 1,500A, 545V at 750rpm. An RTB 7440 auxiliary generator was fitted, rated at 50kW up to No D7597 and 54kW in the remainder. The Class 25/0 used the traction motor that was virtually identical to that fitted to the Class 24, but with a higher gear ratio of

79:18 to permit a 90mph top speed. It had a rating of 245hp at 375A, 545V, and its revised characteristic also improved its efficiency. Whereas for Class 24 the rail horsepower at the continuous rating speed was 843, it rose by 106hp to 949 in the Class 25/0, an improvement beyond the engine's extra 90hp uplift.

Meanwhile, British Thomson Houston had now merged with Metropolitan Vickers to form Associated Electrical Industries Ltd (AEI), and the company had developed a new traction motor for a wide range of applications from metre-gauge railways upwards. When the next batch of Class 25s was ordered, the AEI 253AY motor was substituted, rated at 234hp, 650A, 315V, with a gear ratio of 67:18. It was lighter than its predecessor but offered a superior traction characteristic, even though pairs of motors were connected in series-parallel, rather than all four motors being connected in an all-parallel configuration, as on earlier builds. It is, though, generally considered that having motors in an all-parallel arrangement reduces the risk of slipping. Employing six stages of field weakening enabled full engine output to be available over a slightly wider range than Nos D5151-75. Locomotives of this type comprised Classes 25/1 and 25/2 and, were numbered D5176-5299 and D7500-97. A minor change from AEI Series 1 to Series 2 electrical equipment distinguishes these two sub-classes, Nos D5176-232 forming Class 25/1 and the remainder Class 25/2.

Finally, from No D7598 to No D7677, there was a further slight change to the main generator, which now had 10 poles and a slightly amended characteristic. This pushed up the speed at which the main generator could utilise full engine output to 80mph, but came at the expense of a slightly lower maximum tractive

	Class 25/0	Class 25/1	Class 25/2	Class 25/3
Main generator rating at 750rpm	817kW, 1,500A, 545V	819kW, 1,300A, 630V	819kW, 1,300A, 630V	819kW, 900A, 910V
Max tractive effort (lb)	39,000	45,000	45,000	41,500
Continuous rating (lb)	20,800 at 17.1mph	20,800 at 17.1mph	20,800 at 17.1mph	20,800 at 17.1mph
Full output range (mph)	9.3 to 77.6	7 to 77.5	7 to 77.5	7 to 80

The first batch of Class 25s continued the Class 24 body styling, with cab-front doors and a plethora of bodyside grilles, which allowed brake dust to enter the engine room. No D5155 is in original guise in this view at Dringhouses Yard, York. *AEI*

effort. Electronic control of traction motor field weakening was also employed on this batch, with an electronic speedometer providing a signal input into the system. Train air braking equipment was added from new, while earlier builds had this fitted retrospectively.

Bodyside styling underwent some evolution. From No D5176 the warning horns were moved to a slightly revised train indicator box. The later Class 24 design, with train indicator box, prevailed up to No D5232, and on Nos D7568-97. Subsequently, the bodyside was cleaned up by emulating BRCW styling, with air intake grilles at cantrail level. This followed the research carried out at Inverness, which established that the extra cylinder liner wear on the Class 24, when compared to Class 26, was due to the location of grilles low down on the body side, where dust from the brake blocks was sucked into the engine room and thus the engine.

Front-end styling also changed. Correspondence dated 21 November 1962 from the BR CME to the BR Design Officer sought views on restyling the cab front, in the light of dispensing with nose-end doors, though building work was already under way. The CME preferred to use three windscreens so

that the outer two could be of the existing pattern, and although the Design Officer favoured the use of just two windscreens, he accepted that the economics of stocking an additional size of windscreen outweighed the aesthetic benefits. No D5233 was the first to be built to the new arrangement and was the start of a new batch at Derby.

Initially, the Class 24 paint scheme was adopted: a green bodyside with a light grey horizontal band at solebar level along the full length, mid grey roof and front cab windows, small yellow cab-front warning panel, and black undergear. During 1963 there was much debate about revising this scheme. On 12 November the design consultant E. G. M. (Ted) Wilkes commented that 'nothing could make this locomotive look worse than it is at present'. He went on to note that Derby had been un-cooperative with its design and the standard of workmanship was terrible. Wilkes recognised the type's importance by virtue of being a standard design. What finally emerged was the adoption of the two-tone scheme applied to the Class 47s, but with only one Locomotive Green band for the upper body and Sherwood Green for the lower body below

By way of comparison, No D7548 displays the revised body styling and smart two-tone green livery of the Class 25/3. It is passing Lenton South Junction, Nottingham, on 27 July 1965 with a special coal train. *J. S. Hancock*

cab window height. Again, No D5233 was the first to emerge in two-tone green.

In anticipation of a change of 'house' style, No D7660 emerged from Derby at the end of 1966 in all-over BR blue livery, with yellow ends. Numbers were located not under the driver's cabside windows but behind the cab doors at the other end of the locomotive. When blue began to be applied more generally, the BR 'reversed arrows' emblem was carried under the cab windows at both ends, with the number behind the cab doors.

Some variation existed within the driving cabs. Nos D5151-75 continued the Class 24 practice of having a cab lining of removable aluminium panels, but these proved draughty at the joints. The AEI/Sulzer Operating Manual shows that Nos D5176-232 and 7568-97 had a different driver's desk from the remainder.

Not all the class was equipped with a train heat generator. The AEI/Sulzer Operating Manual gives the locomotives fitted with a Stone Vapor L4610 generator as Nos D5176-8/83-237 and D7568-97. This reflects the duties planned, for many of the class would not be involved in winter passenger trains, but even those with heating equipment sometimes had it isolated or even removed. It is perhaps unsurprising that

there was considerable variation in locomotive weights; the following summarises the position:

D5151-65	70 tons 5 cwt
D5167-75	72 tons 7 cwt
D7176-8/83-232, 7568-97	73 tons 15 cwt
D5179-82	71 tons 9 cwt
D5233-7	73 tons 1 cwt
D5238-99, 7500-67/98-677	70 tons 14 cwt

Source: AEI/Sulzer Operating Manual.

The first order for Class 25s came on 7 December 1959 and comprised 25 locomotives for the North Eastern Region's Area 2. Numbered D5151-75, BR's Darlington shops received the contract. A two-year break in orders followed until the next 57 were authorised in late 1961 under the 1963 building programme, divided between Derby (47) and Darlington (10). Derby had been fully committed building Class 45s, to the extent that some production of this type had been moved to Crewe. Once Type 4 construction was concluded, Derby could turn its attention in earnest to its design of Type 2.

On 12 July 1962 the BTC sanctioned a total of 165 locomotives, 123 for Derby and 53 for Darlington, at a unit price of £66,837. During

The Class 25 driving position, clearly showing why it was described as 'knee hole'. *AEI*

its meeting on 19 December 1963 the BRB (as successor to the BTC) considered the relative merits of ordering additional Type 3s from EE or Type 2s from BR's shops; speed of delivery was thought to be quicker from EE. It sanctioned that an application be made to the Ministry of Transport for both additional Type 2s and 3s and, with Ministry go-ahead, the meeting on 12 March 1964 affirmed the ordering of 26 locomotives from Derby Works at a unit cost of £70,348 and from Beyer Peacock for 54 at £68,150 each. The latter was the only instance of a BR main-line design being built by a private contractor.

Concurrent with the placing of the order with BP was the announcement of BR's rationalisation plan for its own workshops. This involved the closure of Darlington, which lobbied for additional Type 2 work. The BRB minutes record an unwillingness to accede to this on the grounds that the Works' build costs were too high, and this would not stave off the closure plan. It was therefore unsurprising that the rail unions reacted against BP being contracted to construct locomotives using jigs transported from Darlington after completion of No D7597 in August 1964. In the event, the company sought release from the last 18 of the order so that its affairs could be liquidated.

By the end of 1964, with 327 machines delivered or on order, the position was as follows: deliveries comprised 20 in 1961, 5 in 1962, 78 in 1963 and 95 in 1964, while expected in 1965 were a further 82, and 47 in 1966.

The Class 25/0s were built at Darlington for the NER at Thornaby and had no steam generators. Entry to traffic spanned 12 months from April 1961, and thereafter there was an overlap in construction of different batches from the various workshops; the accompanying table sets out the details.

Service experience and utilisation

Once the NER had received the first 28 of the class, the Midland Lines of the LMR took Nos D5183-7597, 214 locomotives. Of the next 52, the ER's Sheffield area got 39, 13 being allocated to Glasgow Eastfield. Finally, the LMR assigned the last batch to Willesden and Toton. With the rundown of steam in North West England, some of the LMR's fleet were transferred to depots in the area. Gradually, the ER gave up its locomotives during the latter part of the 1960s, Nos D7633-7, for example, going to Wigan

Works	Nos	First deliveries	Last deliveries
Darlington	D5151-85	15 April 1961	25 May 1963
	D5223-32	6 July 1963	14 December 1963
	D7578-97	30 November 1963	12 August 1964
Derby	D5186-222	23 March 1963	21 September 1963
	D5233-99*	14 December 1963	28 September 1963
	D7500-67	2 October 1964	20 January 1966
	D7568-77	28 September 1964	16 November 1963
	D7598-7623	5 February 1966	8 September 1966
	D7660-77	31 December 1966	9 April 1967
BP	D7624-59	30 July 1965	21 July 1966

**In completion, No D5299 was fitted with a 6LDA28-R engine, which Sulzer had rated at 1,750hp. Further development work was, however, channelled into Sulzer's 'V' engine, and No D5299 does not appear to have entered revenue service until fitted with a standard engine. In consequence the locomotive entered traffic a year later than its contemporaries on 16 October 1965.*

Springs Branch as steam replacements. The ScR swapped its units with the LMR for Class 27s off the Midland Lines in 1968/9. By October 1969 the class was allocated as follows:

Birmingham Division	37
Liverpool Division	50
London Division	34
Manchester Division	38
Nottingham Division	90
Preston Division	34
Gateshead	3
Holbeck	23
Thornaby	8
Eastfield	2
Haymarket	8

Much of the work of the class during the 1960s was unglamorous, largely because the majority of miles run were not on top-flight passenger services. There were exceptions, such as a nocturnal mail train between York and Manchester, while appearances at Oban were not unknown, and regular diagrams existed on passenger and parcels services between Edinburgh and Carstairs. During the summer holiday season Class 25s would be turned out, either singly or in multiple, on trains to seaside destinations on the East and North West coasts of England and North Wales. A pair from Eastfield's stud might also find their way across the Border, bound for Blackpool. It was only

when deputising for a BR Type 4 on the Midland Main Line that the class would be fully extended for long periods. With up to 100mph being reported, one can only imagine how the AEI 253 motors fared with the high voltage and high speed bouncing over pointwork, which are conditions that tax even robust equipment.

The former Midland Main Line was standardised on the Sulzer LDA28B engine for all its Type 2 and 4 requirements, which reduced spare parts stocks at depots. Freddie Harrison (CME on the LMR at the time of the Pilot Scheme) had therefore achieved his objective. Class 25s appeared singly or in pairs on a variety of freight and parcels duties across the LMR, though trains whose traction was diagrammed off Crewe tended to receive Class 24s. In Cumbria the type displaced the Class 28 Crossley Metrovicks.

In Scotland some examples had tablet exchange equipment fitted under the driver's cab windows. Probably because Inverness drivers lacked knowledge of the type, the class was very rarely seen on the Highland Line, though examples did penetrate beyond Aberdeen on the former Great North of Scotland routes. On the NER, freight and parcels duties represented the main activities.

Generally, the Sulzer 6LDA28B engine gave less trouble than its 12-cylinder counterpart, probably because it was not pushed as hard for as long during operation.

Typical Class 25 activity during the early 1960s involved transfer and trip freights. This official picture depicts No D5212 at Cricklewood Yard.
Ian Allan Library

Left: The Midland Main Line witnessed much activity by the class working in multiple. On 11 May 1963 Nos D5184+5183 pass Hathern, Loughborough, in charge of an up mineral train. *Kenneth L. Seal*

Below: Deep in the South Manchester suburbs at Fallowfield, onlookers observe a busy scene. No D5207 brings a transfer freight from Trafford Park to Dewsnap Yard (Guide Bridge), while Class 40 No D303 waits for the road with coal empties, also bound for Guide Bridge. *Dr R. Elston*

There were some failures of welds due to stress, and coolant leakage from cylinder liners and cylinder head core plugs. The engine exhaust was routed via a roof-mounted chamber on the earlier series. The engine crankcase breather also vented into this compartment, and the combination of hot exhaust gases and oil mist from the breather sometimes proved, literally, an explosive mix.

The February 1967 issue of *Modern Railways* carried a feature celebrating the success of the combination of the Sulzer engine and the AEI 253 traction motor, the success being measured in terms of the quantity in traffic, not only in this country but also overseas. Whether these motors were a success operationally is a moot point; being smaller than the type they superseded certainly aided maintenance, but it

Although the first series of Class 25s went to the NER for freight use, No D5161 was commandeered for an excursion from Ushaw Moor to Seaburn on 4 July 1964. The train is descending the 1 in 78 grade from Fawsett Street Junction to Sunderland. *S. Rickard*

The ScR tended to keep its allocation off the lines to the West Highlands and also north of Perth, and in South West Scotland the type shared duties with the Class 27. Although closed in 1964, Waterside station is being kept tidy as No D7617 pilots 5MT 'Black Five' 4-6-0 No 45167 on a coal train for Ayr on 1 August 1966. *The late Derek Cross*

A good array of semaphore signals at Spondon Junction on the Derby to Nottingham line frame No 5269 and its lengthy rake of empty stock on 3 August 1968.
J. S. Hancock

meant that there were fewer copper windings to handle the same current. One engineer has described the windings as more akin to fuse wire, and was therefore unsurprised at the much higher failure rate than the earlier variant. A member of the Railway Technical Centre was alarmed to find two Class 25s deputising for a Class 45 on an express out of St Pancras, as he considered the traction motors unfit for sustained 90mph running. Matters with the motors were not helped by being connected in series-parallel across the main generator, which made them more prone to slipping, which is also unhelpful to motor reliability. Additionally, incorrect field diversion could cause excessive currents in the motors.

Corrosion was a problem, partly due to indifferent build quality that allowed water through cab roof welds. In dealing with corrosion, Derby Works would remove an entire cab, which might then not be refitted to the same locomotive; this led to instances of cab fronts being mismatched to body style. It is generally considered that Nos D7624-59, which came from BP, had a better build quality. Frame strength forward of the bogie centre line pivot proved to be rather weak, and collision damage often resulted in the frames bending downwards at this point.

Length	50ft 6in
Width	9ft 1in
Height	12ft 8in
Weight	See table above
Fuel tank capacity (gallons)	500
Wheel diameter	3ft 9in
Minimum curve radius (chains)	4½
Maximum speed (mph)	90

Engine
Sulzer 6LDA28B

Engine output (hp)	1,250 at 750rpm

Tractive effort
See table above

Gear ratio

Class 25/0	79:18
Class 25/1/2/3	67:18

BP Works Numbers
D7624-46 8034-56

Class 26

Another of the Pilot Scheme orders went to Birmingham Railway Carriage & Wagon Co Ltd (BRCW), and the specification was identical to that for the BR Type 2, namely a power rating between 1,000 and 1,250hp, a maximum axle load of 18.75 tons and a top speed of 75mph; a steam generator for train heating was also to be provided. The order date for these 20 locomotives was the same as for all the Pilot Scheme classes, 16 November 1955, with the first example to be delivered during January 1958. By virtue of being destined for the ER, Doncaster was appointed as the parent drawing office.

BRCW also collaborated with Sulzer to produce this design of Type B locomotive, with Crompton Parkinson providing the electrical machines and Allen West the control gear. Thus the same 6LDA28A power plant as that fitted to Class 24 was married to a CG391A1 10-pole main generator, continuously rated at 757kW, 1,720A, 440V at 750rpm, with an overhung 8-pole CAG193A1 auxiliary generator, continuously rated at 57kW, 518A, 110V at 450/750rpm.

Four 4-pole C171A1 traction motors, continuously rated at 224hp, 430A, 440V at 340rpm, were fitted to the Pilot Scheme locomotives and were connected in parallel across the main generator. Having as many as five stages of field weakening no doubt helped to ensure that full engine output was available between 7 and 75mph. Subsequent orders used a C171D3 motor instead, but retained the same power rating, albeit at a fractionally higher continuous rating speed. Although the difference between the two motors was slight, it led to the Pilot Scheme locomotives eventually being classified as Class 26/1 (later Class 26/0), while the remainder were Class 26/2 (later Class 26/1). The latter were permitted a higher maximum speed of 80mph, though when the increase came into effect is unclear, and some of Class 26/0 (BR design code 26/0BV) were reportedly also permitted 80mph.

This busy scene at Kyle of Lochalsh on 13 July 1967 offers a comparison between the front ends of the two variants of Type 2 that were used around Inverness at the time. The single-line token is exchanged by the crew of Class 26 No D5326 on the 11.00 to Inverness while, in the background, Class 24 No D5050 sits on a rake of vans and freight stock. *Ian Allan Library*

Another comparison of the two Inverness Type 2s on an Inverness to Edinburgh service at Perth on 8 September 1962. Class 26 No D5321 leads Class 24 No D5125, with the former's cantrail-level air intake grilles clearly evident, while the latter has these located in the bodyside.
The late Derek Cross

It is worth setting out the respective performance figures for the BR and BRCW Type 2s, which had identical engines.

	BR	BRCW
Maximum tractive effort (lb)	40,000	42,000
Continuous tractive effort (lb)	21,300	30,000
Continuous rating speed (mph)	14.8	11.25
Continuous rating (rhp)	843	900
Full engine output range (mph)	7.7-69	7-77

It is therefore evident that the Class 26 offered a superior performance to its rival.

The mechanical parts followed conventional practice of the period in using a strength underframe, and nose-end gangway doors were fitted. More effort was made in body styling than with the comparable BR Derby Type 2s, and the engine room air intake grilles were sited at cantrail level. Back in 1956 a mock-up of the design featured carriage maroon livery, but BR standard Locomotive Green was actually used for the body, with grey for the roof and black below solebar level and for the two-axle bogies. Cab windows were off-white, the same colour as a thin line that wrapped round the body circumference just below cab window height; the overall effect was very smart, and much superior to the offering from Derby Works. All the Production Series (Nos D5319-46) had cabside recesses to permit the fitment of single-line tablet exchange apparatus. All had a Stone Vapor steam generator for train heating.

No D5300 was delivered to Doncaster Works for acceptance and there was some consternation when overall weight was found to be 77 tons 17 cwt, against the specified 75-ton upper limit. It was eventually accepted for allocation to Hornsey on 30 July 1958. Completion of the order came when No D5319 arrived at Hornsey on 13 March 1959. By now two further batches had been ordered by the BTC, 18 on 5 May 1957 and nine on 2 January 1959. Bearing in mind that BRCW was under pressure to deliver a brand-new design of Type 3 for the SR, the

On 21 September 1963 No D5330 is rostered on its own to work a Glasgow to Inverness service, captured coasting past Hilton Junction on the run down to Perth. *The late Derek Cross*

company did well to fulfil its promised delivery date of August for the last tranche, the order for which had only been received eight months before. The manufacturer also managed to slim down the weight on the production series, achieved partly by a small change in the design of the traction motors.

No comparable road trials to those performed on No D5008 were carried out. Perhaps BR was concerned that the Class 26 might perform better than its own design, thus making it harder to justify repeat orders for the latter. A decompounding winding on the main generator meant that the machine could not exceed its maximum rating, and this was a useful facility when starting a heavy train. This aspect of electrical machine design was not incorporated in the BTH main generator in the Class 24. The traction motors also had a different characteristic from those on the Derby-designed locomotives.

Utilisation

The type was to undertake a mix of duties that encompassed transfer freights between Ferme Park yard and the SR, as well as empty stock movements into and out of King's Cross and Class 2 peak-hour passenger work. By virtue

of the axle load being higher than planned, the SR Civil Engineer rejected the 'D5300s', which caused the BRCW Pilot Scheme pool to be reallocated to (initially) Leith Central and (when the new depot opened) Haymarket in the Edinburgh area during mid-1960, as lighter Class 24s became available from BR's shops. The two production-series orders went new to Edinburgh but migrated to Inverness during 1960.

Following commissioning during October 1958, No D5303 went to Scotland for trials before heading for Hornsey. It spent some time at Inverness and in December 1958 ran a trial on the West Highland Line. The train was the 5.45am Glasgow Queen Street to Fort William (the overnight sleeper from London King's Cross), conveying nine cars for 320 tons. On a schedule laid down for a Class 5 4-6-0 with seven bogies, No D5303 nearly kept time, tending to drop ½ to 1 minute between stops, despite being driven on full power. While some commentators at the time regarded this as disappointing, a 1,160hp diesel was never really expected to be the equal of a Class 5 steam locomotive, so the achievement was quite worthy.

Nevertheless, the trial did highlight that the capacity for diesel to improve on steam required a like-for-like transition. In truth, perplexingly, no Pilot Scheme design embraced the steam Class 5 power category, a most strange omission because the ER 'B1s', LMR 'Black 5s' and WR 'Halls' were the mainstay of all the Regions except the Southern.

Overall, the trials in Scotland clearly proved the type suitable for the replacement of Class 5 4-6-0 steam power because virtually the entire Production Series spent almost all of the 1960s at the Highland depot. Meanwhile, the Pilot Scheme sub-class was retained at Haymarket, largely on freight duties, once Scottish dieselisation had been completed.

On 18 January 1960 Nos D5337/8 worked an 11-car rake of coaches between Edinburgh and Aberdeen, and this presaged the class being used singly on services that terminated at Dundee or in pairs to Aberdeen. Surprisingly, during the week commencing 3 October 1960 D5311 was trialled on mineral wagons between Doncaster and Barnetby, the exercise being repeated the following week using a Brush Type 2.

Edinburgh-based units took over local passenger work on the Waverley route to Carlisle, and while there the LMR borrowed them for local duties. Through services from Inverness to Glasgow Queen Street saw the class used either singly or in pairs. Cecil J. Allen published a run with Nos D5325/33 on the 10am ex-Glasgow loaded to nine vehicles, grossing 325 tons. By using pairs of Type 2s, the Perth to Inverness schedule was cut by 19 minutes.

Cecil J. Allen was full of praise for the high-quality running, and picked out the early acceleration from 30 to 49mph from Stanley to MP 8½ on a 1 in 93 gradient, while on subsequent 1 in 82/5 sections speed was around 42. Climbing from Blair Atholl to Dalnaspidall, the hardest section is more than 7 miles at 1 in 70, and here the rate only fell from 42 to 41mph. The passing time to the summit at MP 53 was 26min 3sec for the 17.8 miles, including four intermediate station calls. Adding the start-to-stop schedules gives an overall Perth to Inverness time of 174 minutes, which included 8 minutes of recovery time. Allowing for a couple of interruptions to the running, Mr Allen estimates a gain on the schedule, net of recovery

Haymarket-allocated Class 26s ventured south of the Border on Waverley Route duties. On 18 August 1962 No D5301 waits to leave Carlisle for Edinburgh while 7P 'Royal Scot' 4-6-0 No 46107 is at the head of a train for Glasgow St Enoch. *The late Derek Cross*

allowance, of 18 minutes, achieved without excessive speed.

Assessing the power produced by the locomotive, on the 1 in 82 and 1 in 85 ascents the rail horsepower comes out at around 1,700, while between MPs 44 and 49 on the 1 in 70 it was 1,970. The predicted rail horsepower at the continuous rating speed was 900hp per loco, 1,800 for two, so the performance reported here points to a better-than-expected effort. Such efforts became common by Inverness-based Class 26s and was appreciated with the down 'Royal Highlander' London to Inverness sleeper, which habitually loaded to 600 tons and more, with no banking required.

During the 1960s the only casualty was No D5328, which was involved in an accident at Inverkeithing during June 1968 and never ran again, being withdrawn in 1972. Undoubtedly the ScR got a winner in the No D5300s, for they proved generally trouble-free and reliable. Their modest top speed was no handicap on a Region where, during the period under review, there was an overall ceiling of 75mph. Although a single locomotive was not a match for the Class 5 steam power it displaced, they could be used in multiple with only one footplate crew in order to accelerate schedules on express services.

Production series, No D5320 onwards

Length	50ft 9in
Width	8ft 10in
Height	12ft 8in
Weight	73 tons 6 cwt
Fuel tank capacity (gallons)	500
Wheel diameter	3ft 7in
Minimum curve radius (chains)	5
Maximum speed (mph)	75 (original)
	80 (later)

Engine
Sulzer 6LDA28A

Engine output (hp)	1,160bhp at 750rpm

Tractive effort (lb)

Maximum	42,000
Continuous	30,000 at $11\frac{1}{2}$ mph

Gear ratio
63:16

Nos D5300-D5319 carried BRCW Works Nos DEL 45-64, while Nos D5320-46 carried DEL65-91.

Based on initial experience with the Class 26, it was hardly surprising that, on 29 February 1960, BRCW received a fourth order for 69 Type 2 locomotives to facilitate elimination of steam in several areas. Twelve examples, Nos D5347-58, were for the ScR's Area 6 (Fife) as part of the 1960 programme, for delivery in January 1961, though this was later revised to March. As part of the 1961 programme, three were assigned to ScR Area 5 (Glasgow-Aberdeen) and eight to Area 6; these were Nos D5359-69 and were expected in May (then July) 1961. Nos D5370-8 were allocated to the NER Area 2, due for delivery in September (later November) 1961. Finally under this order, 37 units were destined for LMR Area 3 (Midland Lines) and would be Nos D5379-5415, due in October 1961 but changed to December. Building these Type 2s was concurrent with the Class 33s.

There were three main differences from the company's Class 26. As noted in the description of the Class 25 above, the 'B' version of the Sulzer 6LDA28 engine was available, rated at 1,250hp. Crompton Parkinson was fully committed to supplying electrical equipment for both the Class 33 and Class 45, so BRCW had to seek an alternative supplier. GEC had provided equipment to NBL for its Type 2

diesel-electric design, but a different set of equipment was supplied for what was to become Class 27.

The main generator was a GEC Whitton 10-pole WT 981, rated at 803kW, 1,940A, 414V continuously at 750rpm. Mounted on the same hub was a 6-pole WT 782 auxiliary generator of 57kW. Four WT 459 traction motors each had a rating of 236hp, 485A, 415V at the continuous rating speed of 14mph and employed three stages of field weakening. Finally, as with the Class 25, a 90mph top speed was required, and the traction motor gearing was 60:17, quite a bit higher than the Class 26, with its 75mph limit. Nevertheless, full engine output was available between 7½ and 80mph.

As with the Class 26, the radiator fan employed an electric motor drive arrangement. Similarly, the train heat equipment was a Stone

Although the Class 27 is traditionally associated with the ScR, the LMR received an allocation from new and these were deployed on the Midland Lines. In this official photograph on 25 June 1962 No D5389 is less than a month old. *BR*

Vapor steam generator, though this was not fitted to the NER's batch, which were intended primarily for freight or summer Saturday passenger work. Revised secondary springing and the addition of shock absorbers marked a difference from the Class 26 bogies, and was in response to vertical riding problems on poor track. A four-character route indicator box was added above the nose-end gangway doors, and some changes were made to the cab interior to facilitate easier maintenance and cleaning. The livery mirrored that applied to the Class 26.

Into traffic

The first two examples are reported as going initially to Thornton Junction shed on 30 June and 17 July 1961 respectively, but they moved to Eastfield within a matter of days. By virtue of the ER serving as the sponsoring design office, all deliveries went first to Doncaster Works for commissioning. No D5369 brought up the end of deliveries to the ScR on 17 January 1962, which was also the date that No D5370 arrived at Thornaby on the NER. Finally, the LMR began to receive its allocation at Cricklewood with No D5379 on 31 March 1962, and No D5415 completed the order on 6 October. In fact, this was also the last locomotive produced by BRCW for BR.

In Scotland the type quickly displaced steam on the two routes from Glasgow to the West Highlands, namely the West Highland Line to Fort William and Mallaig, and the Callendar & Oban route via Dunblane. Although the NBL Type 2s had already penetrated these areas, their indifferent reliability did not endear them for use on these isolated routes, where rescue was not close at hand. Thus the Class 27 was preferred and, after an initial report in the October 1961 issue of *Trains Illustrated* of their use on a Queen Street to Fort William train, later sightings were of a swift takeover. The class also found use south of the Clyde on the former Glasgow & South Western routes, reaching Stranraer. For single-line working, all the Scottish fleet had cab recesses for automatic tablet exchange apparatus.

Thornaby depot required the class for freight work around Teesside, and there were also visits to York and Leeds. On summer Saturdays the class duly appeared at East Coast resorts, such as Scarborough, on passenger services.

Cricklewood assigned a variety of work to its fleet, which appeared as far north as Derby on freights, while other duties included empty stock moves around St Pancras. Finally came forays on passenger services: the long-gone St Pancras to Tilbury boat trains were Class 27-powered,

The LMR used its Class 27s on a range of work. Here Nos D5377+5381 are on down coal empties near Sharnbrook on the Midland Main Line on 19 September 1969.
J. H. Cooper Smith

While based at Cricklewood, the class even penetrated onto the third-rail network. On 7 November 1962 No D5382 passes Gipsy Hill box on a Brent to Norwood Yard transfer freight.
Brian Stephenson

Moving north of the border, No D5407 was used on the final demolition train between Gatehouse of Fleet and Dumfries. It is seen here on Stroan Viaduct on 12 August 1968, a remote-looking spot, albeit with a caravan beside the loch.
The late Derek Cross

Another scene in South West Scotland finds No D5366 partnering a 5MT 'Black Five' 4-6-0 on a van train from Stranraer to Ayr or Glasgow on 19 March 1966. This train seemed to have been booked for such a pairing of motive power.
The late Derek Cross

During the 1960s the routes to the West Highlands saw Class 27s displace the final vestiges of steam, as well as the less successful NBL Type 2s. No D5359 turns off the Stirling to Perth main line at Dunblane on 2 March 1963 with an Oban-bound goods. Note the recess under the cab side window for fitting single-line token exchange equipment, which was only provided on Scottish examples. *The late Derek Cross*

and No D5380 was noted on this duty on 27 April 1962. This locomotive was later singled out for painting into two-tone green, as applied to later Class 25s, although one source also includes No D5382 in the re-liverying.

Rationalisation of motive power emerged from the National Traction Plan, and first Thornaby gave up its allocation to the LMR's Nottingham Division around 1966. Meanwhile, the LMR had itself been reorganising its fleet, with a gradual move from Cricklewood to the Leicester Division, then to the Nottingham Division during the late 1960s. Finally, during 1969 and 1970 the whole class was concentrated on Scotland, primarily at Glasgow Eastfield. The only casualty in the 1960s was No D5383, which was involved in an accident at East Langton on 20 August 1965.

In the race for further orders, it was inevitable that BR's own workshops would not lose out. Despite being a better product, BRCW's Type 2 was only selected for multiplication so long as the BR's facilities could not build locomotives fast enough to keep pace with demand. While the ER had decided to opt for the Brush Type 2 as its standard form of motive power in this category, this left no room for a third supplier within BR's dual sourcing policy. The Derby Type 2 thus became the standard for the LMR and future orders for the NER and ScR.

Length	50ft 9in
Width	8ft 10in
Height	12ft 8in
Weight	
With steam heat	73 ton 6 cwt
Without steam heat	71 ton 4 cwt
Fuel tank capacity (gallons)	500
Wheel diameter	3ft 7in
Minimum curve radius (chains)	5
Maximum speed (mph)	90

Engine
Sulzer 6LDA28B

Engine output (hp)	1,250 at 750rpm

Tractive effort (lb)

Maximum	40,000
Continuous	25,000 at 14mph

Gear ratio
60:17

BRCW assigned Works Nos DEL 190-258 sequentially to the class.

Above: Snow lingers on the hills on 15 April 1963 as a Class 27 eases into Callendar with the 12.05 Oban to Glasgow and Edinburgh, watched by the passengers of a land cruise excursion. *I. S. Carr*

Left: Even the Ballachulish branch train was formed of a Class 27 and stock as part of the early dieselisation of the ScR. A service, probably from Connel Ferry, the junction with the Oban line, enters the terminus behind No D5365 on 28 July 1962. *www.railphotoprints.co.uk*

Class 30 (later Class 31)

The Type 2 from the Brush Electrical Engineering Co Ltd (referred to as simply Brush, though the company's name has changed slightly down the years) was one of the designs ordered as part of the Pilot Scheme. A description of the factors that helped Brush win this order, and the use of an earlier export order to Ceylon (Sri Lanka), were described in *Diesel Pioneers*. Additional material has now become available about what became the ER's standard Type 2, and later the TOPS Class 30.

Although Brush was the main contractor for the 20 originally ordered, construction of the underframes to deck level and the assembly of the bogies was subcontracted to Beyer Peacock and W. G. Bagnall (which was part of the same group of companies as Brush). In all cases these portions went to the Loughborough factory, where all the superstructures were made, for installation of the electrical equipment, completion of erection, and load testing. In order to comply with BR's stipulated maximum axle load of 18¾ tons Brush had to spread the weight across two three-axle bogies of the Commonwealth design, but with only the outer two axles on each bogie being powered, resulting in the A1A-A1A wheel arrangement. This resulted in an overall weight of 104 tons 7cwt, something of an elephant when compared to the similarly powered Type 2s from BR and BRCW at around 75 tons.

A strength underframe was used, with cross-members supporting the steel-plate bodysides. The engine came from Mirrlees, Bickerton & Day Ltd (Mirrlees, later Mirrlees National and Mirrlees Blackstone) and was its JVS12T rated at 1,250bhp at 850rpm. A Brush TG160-48 8-pole traction generator was mounted on the engine, continuously rated at 823kW, 1,200A, 686V at 850rpm. A Brush TG69-24 Mk I 6-pole auxiliary generator, rated at 30kW, 273A, 110V at 450/850rpm, was used.

The traction motors were of Brush TM73-68 4-pole type, rated at 250hp each at 600A, 343V at 485rpm, and were connected two series-parallel and had three stages of field weakening. Gearing was 64:17 and maximum speed was 75mph, later raised to 80. An electro-magnetic system of engine control meant that, for operating in multiple, the locomotives were given the Red Circle code.

The BR Design Panel appointed E. G. M. Wilkes as design consultant. Before this, Messrs Cox and Barman (BR's Design Officer and the BTC Public Relations Officer) visited Brush in January 1956 to discuss external

The Brush Type 2 was the ER's standard Type 2, even though several other classes were allocated to the Region's depots during the early 1960s. This meant that a wide range of duties were diagrammed, from express passenger to mineral traffic. Deputising for an EE Type 4 on a Liverpool Street to Norwich express on 1 July 1961, No D5543 approaches journey's end.
David N. Clough

styling. By 26 March the general outline had been agreed and this was considered a major improvement on the original, though one is left wondering what the original must have been like! Some final details remained unresolved as late as April 1957, with the size of the front grille, location of the horns and driver's control desk under discussion.

Mr Wilkes visited Falcon Works on 11 September 1957, by which date four locomotives were nearing completion. A hand-over ceremony for No D5500 took place at Loughborough on 31 October. George Williams (head of BR's Design Panel) reported to Ted Cox the following day that Brush had got the lining-out colour wrong – instead of being light grey, it

The ER also used the Brush Type 2 on inter-regional workings, both passenger and freight. On 6 August 1964 a member of the class crosses the Ouse Viaduct bound for Brighton with an excursion from Enfield. *David N. Clough*

Fulfilling a secondary express passenger role, No D5555 curves through Haddiscoe with a York to Lowestoft service in June 1963. *David N. Clough*

was white! Mr Ferguson, the Chief Engineer for Brush, claimed that he had been told this colour.

For the record, the official paint scheme was standard green for the body, the roof was mid grey, the bogies black, buffer casings and beams red, drawhook black, and lining in light grey. The cab windows had two liveries; along the bodyside was standard green but around the cab was light grey, as was the top of the footplating. For the sake of completeness, even the location of the builder's plate was specified, which was to be central with the numbers on the cabside but set 4 inches lower. Lining out comprised two light grey bands, one at solebar level and the other just below the cab windows. Though not specified by the BTC, Brush chose light grey-green for the engine room.

Numbered D5500-19, the doyen of the class made a trial run from Loughborough to Chinley on 10 October 1957. Although officially shown in one source as the same as the King's Cross

dieselisation scheme, all the Pilot Scheme batch went to Stratford and spent their career on the GE Section, due to being non-standard in respect of the control system. Later batches adopted the BR standard electro-pneumatic system and consequently carried the Blue Star coupling code.

Although repeat orders of Pilot Scheme designs were given to several manufacturers during 1957, Brush appears to have lost out, perhaps because its unit cost for a Type 2 was significantly greater than other suppliers. However, possibly because of the haste to introduce diesels, possibly because the ER was pleased with early experience, repeat business did come. In sanctioning the order for 40 locomotives on 26 June 1958 at a total cost of £3,250,000, the BTC minutes record some confidence because the first deliveries of the Pilot Scheme had proved to be good.

The accompanying table sets out details of the various orders and shows that the ER was committed to the locomotives as its standard Type 2. On 13 August 1959 the BTC approved a further batch of 25 and noted that the price quoted by Brush of £2,025,000 represented a reduction in unit cost from the previous lowest tender. Regrettably, the actual dates of the last two orders are not available, but these were discussed by the BTC at a meeting held on 27 April 1961. Sanction for the first 10 was given, the cost per locomotive being £82,400, while a tender for the final 27 was to be called for. The fleet size thus became 263.

Date	Area	Quantity	Number series
16 November 1955	ER 2	20	D5500-19
3 July 1958	ER 1	40	D5520-59
8 December 1958	ER 1	20	D5560-79
21 April 1959	ER 2	35	D5580-5654
	ER 1	40	
14 August 1959	ER 1	25	D5655-79
26 January 1960	ER 3	46	D5680-99, D5800-25
N/a	ER 3	10	D5826-35
N/a	ER 3	27	D5836-62

Area 1 = GE Section and LTS; **Area 2** = King's Cross; **Area 3** = Sheffield

By the date of the first repeat order, Mirrlees had revised the engine by substituting two Brush HSBT turbochargers for the previous two of Brown Boveri manufacture, while increasing engine speed to 900rpm pushed up the rating to 1,365hp. Subsequently two further upratings were adopted, first to 1,600hp at 950rpm, then to 2,000hp at 1,000rpm.

For these 1,600hp locomotives the enhanced rating was achieved by further elevating the engine speed, and also a measure of oil cooling was provided for the underside of the piston crowns. Increased cooling capacity was necessarily gained by turning all radiator sections over to water-cooling, so a heat exchanger was introduced to cool the engine lubricating oil. There were also minor changes to the fuel injection equipment.

In the case of the 2,000hp engine, the uplift was achieved by the provision of charge-air coolers, and by elevating the engine speed yet again, to 1,000rpm. The diesel engine in question was serial number 5728.10, and it was recoded to a JVSS12T – note the additional 'S' in the model code for this engine.

Thus the first of the production series, No D5520, entered traffic rated at 1,365hp, while No D5545 of the same order was tried at 1,600hp. As this appeared to be successful, Nos D5655-70 were also shipped at that rating. Finally, No D5835 was the example selected for the 2,000hp trial.

Tabulated below are electrical machine continuous ratings for the 1,365hp and 1,600hp variants; regrettably those for the 2,000hp trial have not been published. The same models of equipment were used as in the Pilot Scheme series.

From No D5535 there was a change in traction motor gear ratio from 64:17 to 60:19 in order to raise top speed to 90mph. At one time, therefore, there were five sets of performance data for this standard class. The BR Diagram

Book, which has been made available for this book, omits the 2,000hp variant, but the accompanying table gives the statistics for the other four.

Variant	Maximum tractive effort (lb)	Continuous tractive effort (lb at mph)	rhp	Full-power range (mph)
1,250hp, 75mph	42,000	22,400 at 16.5	985	7.5-58.5
1,365hp, 80mph	42,000	22,400 at 18	1,076	8.5-64.4
1,365hp, 90mph	36,000	18,800 at 21.5	1,076	9.7-76.6
1,600hp, 90mph	42,000	21,240 at 22.4	1,270	9.3-75.5

During the building of the first production batch, BR requested the addition of a route indicator box. At this time Brush had subcontracted fabrication of the locomotive roof sections and the manufacturer was not able to meet the pace of assembly at Falcon Works. In consequence, there was no clear break in the number series between those without, and those with, indicator boxes; those delivered without boxes were Nos D5520-9/35/39/43/47/ 51/52/55/56/59/62. Nos D5671-5 had single-line tablet exchange apparatus fitted in a recess in the driver's doors. Two variations in livery were tried, when No D5578 emerged in Electric Blue (as applied to the 25kV AC electrics being built for the WCML), and golden ochre on No D5579.

Entry into service

First allocations went to the GE Section, with seamless production between the end of the Pilot Scheme and the start of the production series orders. Early in 1959 the Hawker Siddeley Chairman said that 25 of the current orders for 60 examples would be capable of more than 90mph. Just what was being considered is unknown, though it might have been the regearing referred to

Electrical machine	1,365hp	1,600hp
Main generator	900kW, 1,200A, 750V at 900rpm; 1,056kW, 1,320A, 800V at 950rpm;	900kW, 1,000A, 900V at 900rpm 1,056 kW, 1,100A, 960V at 950rpm
Auxiliary generator	30kW, 273A, 110V at 450-900rpm	30kW, 273A, 110V at 450-950rpm
Traction motor	275hp, 600A, 375V at 530rpm	317hp, 660A, 400V at 555rpm

Inevitably much time was
spent on freight turns,
such as witnessed here,
with No D5562 on a
partly fitted freight
traversing the down
slow line at Royston
Junction, near Barnsley,
on 31 July 1965.
J. S. Hancock

Inevitably much time was spent on freight turns, such as witnessed here, with No D5562 on a partly fitted freight traversing the down slow line at Royston Junction, near Barnsley, on 31 July 1965. *J. S. Hancock*

above from No D5535, or possibly the engine output to 1,600hp.

No D5545, the 1,600hp prototype, emerged early in October 1959, some weeks behind its numerical contemporaries. By now the class was deputising for Class 40s on the Liverpool Street-Norwich turns and was allocated to Ipswich, Norwich and March, as well as Stratford. In November Nos D5563/4 reportedly arrived at Hornsey, presumably for training purposes because Nos D5567-9 were the first allocated to the depot.

The GN line dieselisation scheme envisaged rapid electrification of the suburban network, following completion of similar work on the GE and LTS. Hence the diesels were to be used on local freight, both along the GN from the main yard at Ferme Park and to London yards on other Regions, replacing 'J50' 0-6-0Ts. The inner suburban timetable was to be covered by DMUs but augmented at the two weekday peaks by loco-hauled services. Here 'L1' 264Ts and 'N2' 0-6-2Ts were to be displaced, as also on main-line empty stock moves between King's Cross and Holloway and Hornsey. Finally 'L1s' and 'B1' 460s were to be displaced on outer suburban trains to Hitchin and Cambridge. Diesels would perform freight duties overnight and during the day between peak-hour turns.

By the time the first real influx of Class 30s came to Hornsey in February 1960, starting with No D5586, the NBL, EE, BR and BRCW Type 2s were already ensconced. Even so, pairs

of the new arrivals were tried out on a range of duties, including Nos D5587-91 on the New England to Ferme Park brick trains. By March of that year Nos D5565-9/86-99 were at Hornsey and appearing in pairs on the ECML as far as Peterborough. April saw the class displace the NBL Type 2s, which disappeared off to Scotland. By the summer, the BRCW Type 2s were also heading from King's Cross north of the Border. A similar displacement saw March depot give up its Class 24s in late 1960 as part of the creeping Class 30 takeover.

Meanwhile, in readiness for the advent of diesels in the Sheffield area, during the first week of February No D5567 was sent to Darnall, but outbased at Langwith Junction, for trials on colliery pilot and trip duties. On the 5th it worked from Mansfield Yard to Immingham, then returned to Hornsey. On 1 May 1960 the BTC announced that 114 of the 226 locomotives ordered to date were in traffic, a commendable rate of production in 18 months. The 1,600hp Type 3s, Nos D5655-70, began to appear in the autumn and went to March depot to power an accelerated timetable on the Cambridge line. It was not until No D5680 that Sheffield began to receive its first serious influx at the start of 1961.

Not content with a take-over in East Anglia, the ER sent the class far and wide. On 4 December 1959 No D5513 was used on a Shoeburyness-Southampton 'footex'. Another visit to the same destination came on 21 April

1961 when No D5616 headed a special from Barking to Southampton Ocean Liner Terminal. From the Summer 1960 timetable the class became regular performers on the 7.53am Norwich-Birmingham New Street service and the 3.55pm return.

Freight turns also brought visits deep into LMR territory from 1961 on the Purfleet to Tring cement workings, and Sheffield Darnall-based units appeared on freights from Rotherham up the Midland Main Line. Perhaps the most surprising of all, though, was a Darnall diagram, which included the 10.30pm Grimethorpe to Walton (Liverpool) merchandise service and the 10.05am return; Class 30s took up this duty in 1961 and it continued for four years until the service ended. The notion of a turn taking the class to Liverpool's north docks and Walton-on-the-Hill shed now seems remarkable. Not to be left out, from June 1961 Stratford began to use its allocation on the Thames Haven to Rowley Regis tanks as far as Didcot.

On 6 July 1961 Darnall's No D5684 had to cover for a Class 40 on the 'Sheffield Pullman', managing to arrive back at Sheffield Victoria 2 minutes early; such deputisations were not uncommon because Finsbury Park had only two of the Type 4s for two diagrams. From November the diagram was revised to a Brush machine, when Nos D208/9 moved to Stratford

for GE work and 1,600hp Nos D5655-7 migrated to Yorkshire.

In April 1962 No D5835, with its engine rated at 2,000hp, emerged from Falcon Works. As the first of Sheffield's final batch, it arrived at its home depot on the 24th but moved to Finsbury Park on 14 May, where it was put on the diagram assigned to the prototype 'Deltic' from King's Cross to Doncaster, after a spell on the Cambridge Buffet Car expresses. By September it had migrated to Stratford depot. No D5862 concluded production in October 1962, bringing the total to 263.

By now, the arrival of EE Class 37s in East Anglia curtailed some Class 30 passenger diagrams, while the following year the advent of Class 47s in Yorkshire put paid to some heavier freight work on which Class 30 had been seen in pairs. A development in mid-1965 saw No D5674 become the first to have cab-door-located tablet catchers for working the Highdyke branch.

Operational experience

By 1962 the former Great Eastern routes in East Anglia had diesels in the first four power classes and had largely dispensed with steam. The Brush Type 2s found wide deployment, not surprising since they were allocated to all the area's diesel depots. About the only diagrams on which they did not appear as a matter of course

Although several of the class were fitted with automatic token exchange gear for working iron-ore trains on the High Dyke branch, No D5652 is not so provided on 26 March 1964. The train is on the final section of the branch towards High Dyke Junction, north of Grantham, where it will join the ECML en route for the Scunthorpe steel complex.
Michael Mensing

Framlingham was the terminus of a short branch from Wickham Market, north of Ipswich, on the GE main line to Norwich. Although it lost its passenger service in 1952, No D5549 is on local freight duty in June 1962.
David N. Clough

were the Liverpool Street to Norwich expresses, where a Class 37 would now deputise if a Class 40 was unavailable. Cecil J. Allen made a return footplate ride between London and Ely, where the traction was from the 1,250hp Pilot Scheme series. Though the running was competent, extensive use of full power was needed and just over 70mph appeared to be the best that the nine-coach train could be worked up to on level track. Mr Allen concluded that the type was no better than a good 'B1' or 'B17' 4-6-0.

He also compared a 1,365hp variant to a 'B1' between King's Cross and Peterborough. Here steam was faced with a 410-ton trailing load, against the 340 tons of the diesel. No D5569 attained 56mph through Wood Green before steadily falling back to 48 up the 1 in 200 to Potters Bar, passed in 17min 50sec and a minute ahead of net schedule. This means that the equivalent drawbar horsepower was 910 and 1,015rhp, a little below the predicted figure. Meanwhile, the 'B1' had suffered a slight permanent way slack outside the terminus, but had attained 53 at Wood Green and was through Potters Bar at 47½ mph. This effort equates to 1,030edhp, 10% better than the Class 30, made during the start of the journey before the fire had bedded in. The 'B1' suffered two further pws checks thereafter, but touched 88mph after Hitchin and averaged 83.7 for more than 9 miles to Biggleswade, no mean feat with such a load. No D5569 was not pushed

beyond 86½ mph here and averaged 85mph over the same section. Ascending to the minor summit at MP 62, the 'B1' was allowed to fall to 43, whereas the Class 30 breasted the top at more than 60. Nevertheless both reached 81mph on the ensuing downgrade. Mr Allen estimates net times of 73½ minutes for diesel and 76½ for steam, and one must award the honours to the latter, though whether this can be regarded as a typical 'B1' performance, or one of the finest, remains open.

Mr Allen also published runs with both the uprated versions of the class. No D5656 was one of the trio of 1,600hp locomotives allocated to Darnall for the Sheffield to King's Cross duties. It had a special of 370 tons gross on the published run. After easing through the junction off the Sheffield line at Retford and surmounting the climb to MP 133¾ at 50mph, 87 was attained on the following descent and held on level track through Crow Park. There was a pws approaching Barkston South Junction, but on the 1 in 200 up to Stoke speed was held in the mid-50s and the summit was passed at 56. From Grantham, the rail horsepower was around 1,285, 80% of gross engine power, making for a fine run. Descending towards Peterborough, top speed was 97 at Little Bytham.

No D5835 of 2,000hp, and therefore a Type 4, had a 330-ton gross trailing load for a run between Peterborough and Grantham. Once clear of the restricted section to Werrington, the demands of the schedule would have called for full power and the train was worked up to 76mph through Tallington. Stoke Summit was topped at 66½ in 22min 25sec, against 24 minutes booked. There was no opportunity for great speed down to Grantham, reached in 27min 40sec, a little ahead of the 29-minute schedule. Climbing to Stoke, around 1,420ehp was being delivered, again a little lower than one might expect from a 2,000hp machine, and Mr Allen rated the effort similar to a Class 40, which, of course, was some 30 tons heavier.

The Queen was probably not amused on 11 January 1961 when No D5667, one of the 1,600hp variants, expired while hauling the Royal Train. Although only two months old and having run 10,000 miles, the failure of the lubricating oil pump shut down the locomotive.

The re-engining programme

The Mirrlees JVS12T engine had been used in the 1953 order from Ceylon, and this served to trial the unit in extended rail traction use. Hence the Pilot Scheme locomotives encountered very few initial problems and gave confidence in repeat ordering, so it was something of a shock when engine housing fractures began to show up in May 1962. A sample survey of the fleet quickly established that a serious problem existed. In fact, there were two defects, both attributed to the use of fillet welding during engine construction. Principal of the two was in the crankcase intercostals and also in the feet of the cylinder housing fabrication. It is, perhaps, unsurprising that all of the 1,600hp engines examined, and the sole 2,000hp-rated unit, were affected, whereas for the lower-powered variants only half the samples displayed cracks.

Following detailed examinations by the research sections at both BR and Mirrlees National, different causes for the two problems emerged. The cracks in the fillet welds were attributed to the engine firing load, while those in the bearing housings were attributed to inertia forces due to rotational speed. Either way, this explains why the higher-powered units suffered more.

A programme of modifications was proposed, with immediate action for No D5835. What is not entirely clear is the extent to which all the recommendations were implemented, though statistics on the number and type of fractures found during refurbishment by January 1965 point towards a modification campaign. A paper dated October 1964 by the BR Director of Engineering Research noted that the use of a securing bolt represented an improvement on the original design. This had been recommended by Mirrlees National in June 1963 and entailed through-bolting between the cylinder housing diaphragms and the crankcase intercostals, placing the cylinder housing feet in pre-compression.

On 23 July 1964 the BRB approved the purchase of 51 12SVT engines from EE at £15,750 each, one already having been fitted to No D5677 in the spring of 1964; the total contract price was £854,000. A digest of the meeting minute records that the Board asked for clarification of Brush's intentions regarding the remaining locomotives fitted with Mirrlees engines. The Board expressed doubts about the value of Brush's proposal to fit experimentally three locomotives with new Mirrlees J Mark III engines – in view of the time element, there appeared no advantage, as it was doubtful whether definite results would be forthcoming before the decision had to be made regarding the remaining locomotives. Further, it was up to Brush to back its own confidence in the new engine.

This suggests that the JVS12T engine refurbishment was not deemed to be a permanent solution because even Brush offered a substitute engine. Tantalisingly, the BR minute leaves open several unanswered questions. What intentions was BR expecting from Brush regarding the existing engines? Why was the BRB doubtful about the trial of the Mark III J engine? What was the time element that caused no advantage to the Board? If the refurbishment of the engines was proceeding, what caused the imposition of a time limit on replacing the overhauled engines? What caused the BRB to say it was up to Brush to have confidence in its own engine?

The Board next discussed the matter on 23 December 1965 as part of a proposal to re-engine a further 50 locomotives at a cost of £830,000. Mr Shirley and Mr Houchen were asked by the Board for an appreciation of the situation regarding the locomotives, assessing the advantage both in price and availability of

At the other extreme from 90mph passenger service, No D5521 has charge of a pick-up goods on the Fakenham line at Yaxham on 20 August 1969, by which time it had been repainted in BR Blue. *J. S. Hancock*

stepping up the rate of re-engining with EE, as compared with awaiting proving trials of the Mirrlees Mark III engines. One can only conclude that they reported in favour of the EE option because on 14 April 1966 the BRB sanctioned the re-engining of a further 112 locomotives with the EE model. Although the price quoted was £2,038,400, the Board asked that EE cut its price, in view of the size of the order.

Thus far 213 12SVTs had been ordered for 263 locomotives. A further 20 were purloined from the planned fitment of the same engine to the Metrovick Class 28s, in place of the Crossley units, which had received Board approval on 27 January 1966. Curiously, other BR sources noted this engine was too large for Class 28, so maybe the order was identified later as a mistake. The ordering of replacements for the remainder of the fleet, plus the obligatory spare units, has gone unrecorded.

The EE 12SVT engine was rated at 1,470hp at 850rpm and prompted a designation of Class 31. One explanation for the use of this rating was to permit retention of the existing cooler group. Based on the ratings of the eight-cylinder and 16-cylinder SVT engines fitted into Classes 20 and 40 respectively, one would have expected a rating of 1,500hp. Conversion was not rushed, with the Pilot Scheme batch left till last by virtue of the lower, 1,250hp, rating, and was not finished until 1969.

Otherwise, the class suffered with some engine control problems, while the fuel delivery system had never been satisfactory; the latter was investigated in late 1965 and an EE arrangement substituted. The foregoing issues cast a shadow over the type, but the remedies set it up for a long if undistinguished career during the following three decades.

Length	56ft 9in
Width	8ft 9in
Height	12ft 7½in
Weight	107 tons
Fuel tank capacity (gallons)	550
Wheel diameter	
Powered	3ft 7in
Non-powered	3ft 3½ in
Minimum curve radius (chains)	4½
Maximum speed (mph)	90

Engine
EE 12SVT Mark 2

Engine output (hp)	1,470 at 850rpm

Tractive effort (lb)

Maximum	35,900
Continuous	18,700 at 23½ mph

Gear ratio
60:19

Information is for re-engined locomotives. The 80mph variant had a maximum tractive effort of 42,800lb and a continuous rating of 22,250lb at 19.7mph.

Brush Traction Works Numbers
D5500-04	71-75
D5505-19	76-90

W. G. Bagnall Ltd Works Numbers for the underframes for Nos D5515-19 were 3127-31.

Brush contract numbers
D5500-19	04/45100
D5520-59	04/45800
D5560-79	04/45900
D5580-5654	04/46100
D5655-79	04/46300
D5680-99, D5800-25	04/46700
D5826-35	04/47200
D5836-62	04/47700

With all routes cleared, one wonders whether Alfreton box is switched out as No 5805 and its loaded coal train pass on the up fast line on 5 July 1969. *J. S. Hancock*

The SR argued a case for a diesel locomotive that was different from the types already being designed in the mid-1950s. Nothing for the Region had been included in the Pilot Scheme, or perhaps none of these initial orders was deemed suitable. While the intention was to extend third-rail electrification, which would include electric locomotives, some routes would not be so dealt with, bringing a requirement for diesel traction. The press release, issued at the time the order was placed, refers to use on freight and inter-regional passenger services.

The SR defined its requirements in a performance and equipment specification. Unlike the other Regions, it did not want steam train heating because its future procurement would be for electrically-heated rolling stock, while the 'Night Continental' stock for the through London to Paris service had electric train heating. Whereas the BTC had just resolved to continue with vacuum train braking, SR stock was to use air braking equipment, so both types were needed. The motive power was to be capable of hauling a 700-ton freight train up a 1 in 70 gradient or a 375-ton passenger or van train. The maximum speed was to be 85mph (the Regional upper limit at the time) and the design would have to have a wide route availability.

Assessing the above specification identified an installed horsepower somewhere between the Types B and C ordered under the Pilot Scheme. Nevertheless the SR's specific needs were accepted by the BTC and sanction was given for an initial order for 45 locomotives of around 1,600hp, becoming the first order within power category Type 3. There was an envisaged requirement of 98, which had been approved in principle. Following sanction, there was a gap of about a year before an order was placed, possibly due to the Works & Supply Committee approaching suppliers for bids. On 19 September 1957 the BTC sanctioned an extra 20 to the same design and noted that no order had yet been placed for the first tranche.

It was not until 5 December 1957 that BRCW received an order for the first 45 units, with deliveries due to commence during

The official picture of the first of the class, taken when brand new. *BR*

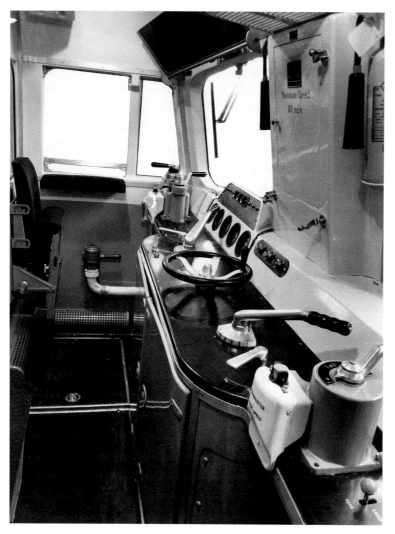

The cab controls, showing the dual driving position, unique among BR diesels of the era. *BR*

balance of 21 units to complete the proposed fleet of 98, but was concerned as to the need for these in the light of the order for electro-diesels, due for delivery from 1961. The SR was told to exercise great care and to be economical in its demand for expensive diesel locomotives and make do with a few, while retaining steam power. Consideration of the last 21 came up finally on 17 September 1959 as part of the 1961 building programme. The Supply Committee was asked to consider the matter, the cost being £1,645,980. Orders for the groups of 12 and 21 locomotives were placed on 25 May and 7 October 1959, but the redesign work on the 12 Hastings line examples pushed the anticipated delivery date of the first to February 1962, thus later than that for the first of the final series.

The design

Investigation by the Civil Engineer determined that a Bo-Bo bogie wheel arrangement would have wider route availability than a Co-Co. It appears likely that the design would be based around an existing contract in order to achieve as much standardisation and savings in cost and time as possible. Just why BRCW won the order is unclear, though the company was already collaborating with Sulzer and Crompton Parkinson in producing the Class 26. In a memo of 3 February 1958, R. C. (Chris) Bond, Chief Technical Officer, BTC, informed the SR's General Manager that external styling would follow that of the Class 26 in the interest of economy, though E. G. M. Wilkes was appointed as the design consultant for the project. On the 27th the head of the Design Panel informed Mr Wilkes that it was not possible to depart from the general outline of the Class 26.

The SR CME informed the BTC that two-character SR-pattern route indicators were to be provided and this eliminated the need for marker lights and headcode discs, as carried by other designs at the time. Between April and October there was much correspondence between the SR CME, the Design Panel and Ted Wilkes. The Region was unhappy with the shape of the driver's power control handle, with the anti-slip brake button sited under the handle. Whereas the Design Panel 'standard' was vinyl

September 1959. The next 20 were not ordered until a year later on 10 December, and at its meeting two weeks earlier the BTC had asked that the manufacturer not only keep to the promised delivery date but to improve on it, if possible. The urgency came from the desire to eliminate steam in Kent as quickly as possible, but the electrification scheme was running behind its scheduled completion date of 1959. Approval for an extension of the existing order by 12 was granted by the BTC on 21 May 1959, in order to replace 42 steam locomotives. These extra locomotives were for the Hastings line between Tonbridge and Battle, and involved redesign work to a slimmer profile to fit the 'O' loading gauge of the route.

Interestingly, the BTC noted the Supply Committee's recommendation relating to the

No D6500 is seen for the third time, undertaking a trial run from its home depot, 73C Hither Green, on 19 February 1960, just three weeks after acceptance by BR. *David N. Clough*

With steam in decline on the Bournemouth route during the run-up to electrification, the SR turned to using Class 33s in pairs on certain services, prior to receiving a small stud of Class 47s. During 1966 an unidentified pair comes through Wimbledon with the down 'Bournemouth Belle'. *David N. Clough*

The 8.45am boat train from Waterloo, bound for Weymouth Quay, departs from Southampton Central behind No D6520 on 24 June 1963. *David N. Clough*

The SR used its general-purpose diesels on a great deal of freight movements. Here a consist of Bedford vans is depicted between Redhill and Tonbridge on 24 June 1963, the trailing vehicle suffering with a hot axle box. *David N. Clough*

Class 33s were regular visitors to all the neighbouring regions on both passenger and freight duties. Interestingly, the LMR, not the SR, arranged for this photograph to be taken to illustrate the movement of a 2,000-ton oil train. Although there is no additional caption information, the working was probably from Fawley Refinery to Bromford Bridge in the West Midlands. *BR*

Type 2s but with two extra cylinders. Engine cooling was by means of a hydrostatically driven Serck-Behr radiator fan.

Attached to this was the generator set, comprising train heat, main and auxiliary machines in that order. The main generator was a slightly modified version of that being fitted in the BRCW Type 2, a Crompton Parkinson CG391B1 10-pole machine, rated at 1,012kW, 1,760A, 575V and with decompounding winding; this latter feature made it nearly impossible to overload the main generator at starting and contributed to drivers (stupidly) applying full power from rest. An 8-pole auxiliary generator, model CAG193A1, was rated at 57kW continuously, 518A, 110V at 450rpm.

A CAG392A1 train heat generator had an output of 170kW initially, but this was clearly inadequate – even a 10-coach set would require some 40 ETH units, equal to 200kW, and it was not practical to use two locomotives in multiple to provide extra train heat supply. The rating was therefore revised to 250kW, 315A, 800V at 550rpm continuously. To ensure a more stable supply when working with 4TC stock, an EE electronic voltage regulator was later fitted in place of the original device. With train heat in

for seat covering, the SR wanted its traditional moquette, and this relatively minor detail occupied quite a three-way correspondence between the Design Panel, Mr Wilkes and the SR CME.

Eliminating a steam heat generator meant that the same mechanical parts of this existing design allowed fitment of a bigger Sulzer engine, fulfilling the requirement for extra power. A Sulzer 8LDA28A power plant, rated at 1,550hp at 750rpm, was used, the same marque as that adopted for both the BR and BRCW

use, engine rpm was kept at a minimum of 550, but this was not ideal for getting a train on the move from rest, so when the driver called for traction power (as opposed to power for heating) the ETH was switched off automatically so that engine rpm could drop to 350, ensuring a smooth start. Once the driver demanded about three-eighths power, ETH was automatically switched back on.

Four traction motors of type C171C2 each had a continuous rating of 305hp, 440A, 580V at 499rpm, and again were similar to those fitted under the Class 26. The motor gear ratio was 62:17, and this permitted a top speed of 85mph. It was slightly higher than that used in the Class 26 and the change might have been to accommodate the higher required speed ceiling.

Unlike in the Class 26, cab-front gangway doors were not fitted. Instead the standard SR two-character route indicator blind was provided. Numbering was in the series Nos D6500-97, and livery was similar to Class 26, being standard locomotive green for the body, relieved by a light grey horizontal line, which wrapped round the entire body just below cab window height; the cab window surrounds were also light grey. The roof panels were mid grey and the buffer stocks were red.

Construction of the first order was concurrent with the last of the Class 26s, with No D5346 entering traffic on 30 October 1958 and No D6500 being delivered on 17 December. Commissioning at Hither Green involved haulage of trains on a circular route from there to Tonbridge, Dover, Canterbury, Faversham, Chatham and Dartford. The class was accepted for traffic on 30 January 1960, then Type 2 production was suspended to allow the works at Smethwick to concentrate on the Type 3 order, which was required as quickly as possible as part of the phasing out of Kent Coast steam. The Hastings-gauge batch were the last to be built, No D6597 completing the order when it entered traffic on 11 May 1962 without any break in production. All went initially to Hither Green.

Utilisation

With the need to replace steam to one deadline, but with the replacement third-rail electrification concluding with a later, delayed,

deadline, diesel locomotives had to fill the gap. This explains the exhortation in the BTC minutes for BRCW to improve on its promised delivery schedule for the first batch, if possible. As an interim measure, the SR was loaned a number of Class 24s, which could operate in multiple with Class 33s if required. Even after the No D6500s began to appear, they would see use in conjunction with Class 24s, the latter being required to provide steam train heating.

First duties for the 'Cromptons', as the Class 33s later became known, were from Charing Cross on routes in Kent, manned by footplate crews from Bricklayers Arms shed. With electrification in Kent complete, the class continued to be used on non-electrified routes in the county, notably on freight. With more in traffic, utilisation spread beyond the South Eastern Division to encompass both the Central and South Western Divisions.

Accepted by the Civil Engineer across virtually the entire Region, the design had been intended as a versatile traction unit for deployment on non-electrified routes, so it was inevitable that the majority of work would be on freight diagrams, once extension of the electrified network was complete. Although of medium power, they were marginally better than the SR's Class 5 steam fleet and as good as a 7P5F 'West Country' Pacific, when the latter was driven at the continuous firing rate of 3,000lb of coal per hour.

It was no surprise that other depots received allocations. Eastleigh began to receive a share

To facilitate the operation of through coaches from Waterloo to Weymouth after completion of electrification of the Bournemouth line, a number of the class were converted to enable push-pull operation of TC trailer coaches. This work was carried out during 1967 and the consequential cab-front clutter is evident in this view of No D6536. It is in charge of the Weymouth carriages of the 10.30 ex-Waterloo and is clearly working hard between Bournemouth and Branksome during the summer of 1967. *BR*

from September 1962, and had 27 by December 1964; the depot always held responsibility for the push-pull-equipped variants. Between July 1963 and October 1967 St Leonards took over all the Hastings-gauge sub-class, before reallocation back to Hither Green.

During November 1960 Nos D6556/9 went to Peterborough New England shed and London Clarence Yard respectively for driver training. This foreshadowed the diagramming of a pair of Class 33s on the Cliffe (Kent) to Uddingston (Lanarkshire) cement train as far as York from the following month; a North Eastern Class 40 then took the train forward, though there is one report of a Class 33 getting as far as Edinburgh.

As a precursor to similar off-Region activity, No D6503 went to Eastleigh for training purposes in April 1962, then Nos D6518/38 were loaned to Worcester for driver training in January 1963. While the former was to facilitate elimination of steam on oil flows from Fawley refinery to Bromford Bridge in the West Midlands, the latter was to obviate the need for a traction change at Didcot or Oxford. The use

of two locomotives permitted the train to comprise 54 tank wagons grossing 2,000 tons.

Such appearances on LMR metals presaged emergency deployments on inter-regional passenger services as far north as Birmingham New Street. Another off-Region duty worthy of mention involved haulage of a special train to Spalding, Lincolnshire, for the annual flower festival, and these forays commenced during the mid-1960s.

Although the first 20 Class 47s had an ETH facility, when trials began with rolling stock with this capability for the LMR, it was No D6504 that was borrowed during February 1961, running from Ferme Park carriage sidings near Hornsey, north London, to Craigentinny, Edinburgh. Since it was also the only diesel type with train air brake equipment at the time, when BR needed to test new vehicles for Freightliner traffic No D6553 was loaned to the Railway Technical Centre for that purpose during January 1964.

Introduction of 'merry-go-round' (mgr) operation for coal trains serving power stations

This strong composition features No D6580 bringing a cross-London freight out of Stratford yard and heading for home territory.
N. Gascoigne

in Kent brought a requirement for locomotives fitted with slow-speed control gear. Since the narrow-bodied examples were kept in the area, it was sensible to choose these 12 for modification. Completion of electrification to Bournemouth in 1967 meant diesel power was needed for through services between London and Weymouth beyond that point. The Bournemouth line EMUs comprised a four-car EMU tractor, either a 4REP or 4VEP, towing one or two 4TC sets, making up to 12 carriages in total. In order to minimise shunting of through coaches to and from Weymouth, it was decided to fit some Class 33s with push-pull equipment that would enable a locomotive to be driven from the cab of a 4TC set.

Tests of the viability of high-speed push-pull operation were carried out in July 1965, using No D6580 between Wimbledon and Basingstoke. A year later, in August 1966, the same locomotive ran some high-speed trials with new 4TC vehicles at up to 100mph. A number of technical obstacles had to be overcome. While BR locomotives used 110V for the control system, SR EMU stock used 70V. EMU stock only had a four-notch power controller – shunt, series, parallel and weak field, so instructions for power and braking sent by the driver in a 4TC cab had to be translated into commands capable of being understood and implemented by the locomotive. The 4TC auxiliary power demands for circuits such as lighting and braking also had to be met by the traction unit, because the rolling stock had no third-rail current collection equipment. Starting with No D6521 in September 1966, 19 Class 33s were modified and were easily identified by the addition of jumper connections and air pipes to the cab fronts at waist height. This ensemble led to the sub-class being nicknamed 'bagpipes'.

The new service commenced on 10 July 1967. At Bournemouth, one or both 4TC sets would be uncoupled and attached to a Class 33 for the continuation to Weymouth. On the return, the locomotive would propel the consist and recouple to the EMU tractor (usually a 4REP) at Bournemouth. With eight coaches, the locomotive would be right on its continuous rating speed during the steep climb at 1 in 50 up Upwey bank out of Weymouth. Push-pull operation then also became possible between Waterloo and Salisbury.

The class proved surprisingly accident-prone. No D6502 succumbed on 17 May 1964 when just under four years old, being in collision with No D6565 at Itchingfield Junction near Horsham. Meanwhile, No D6576 was withdrawn on 3 November 1968 due to accident damage at Reading. On 26 January 1967 the BRB sanctioned expenditure of £260,370 on reliability and safety modifications, including the fitting of replacement engine crankshaft dampers to 103 Sulzer 8LDA28A engines, which shows that there were originally five spares for the 98-strong fleet. The cost of this engine revision was £76,184, and it was noted that it would form part of ongoing negotiations with the engine maker regarding its liability. Eighteen months later a further £60,630 was authorised to be spent on additional reliability and safety modifications. Nevertheless, overall the class proved very durable.

Length	50ft 9in
Maximum width	
Standard	9ft 3in
Hastings line	8ft 8in
Height	12ft 8in
Weight	
Standard	73 tons 8 cwt
Push-pull	77 tons 6 cwt
Hastings line	74 tons 4 cwt
Sanding gear	Fitted
Fuel tank capacity (gallons)	800
Minimum curve radius (chains)	4
Maximum speed (mph)	85

Engine
Sulzer 8LDA28A

Engine output (bhp)	1,550 at 750rpm

Tractive effort (lb)

Maximum	45,000
Continuous	26,000 at 17.5mph

Gear ratio
62:17

Class 35

Whereas the WR's first area for dieselisation had been west of Newton Abbot, the second area was to cover Bristol and this was approved by the BTC on 28 November 1957. It was not, however, until 8 January 1959 that the BTC earmarked a capital sum for the programme and awaited the WR Board's recommendation whether the new locomotives, which were to be of Type 3, should have electric or hydraulic transmission. While several Type 4s, and numerous Type 2 designs had already been ordered, the only other Type 3s ordered thus far had been for the SR.

On 9 April 1959 the BTC authorised £3.6 million for 45 diesel-hydraulic Type 3s, with the order going to Beyer Peacock (BP) on 5 June 1959. Nominal allocation, however, was 32 locomotives for Area 1 (west of Newton Abbot) and 13 for Area 2 (west of Bristol), with deliveries commencing during July 1961. On 20 July 1960 a further 50 were ordered for the Bristol area at a cost of £4,050,000, while the final six were ordered during December 1961. It is said that the WR envisaged that the type would replace 'Hall' and 'Grange' Class 4-6-0s, which totalled 333, and this might be why it is alleged that BP was told the eventual class size would be of a similar number.

E. J. M. Wilkes was appointed as the design consultant for what was to become the classic BR diesel design. Swindon was the sponsoring drawing office and assigned Lot Numbers 449, 455 and 457 to the three orders. Replicating the policy for the Swindon-built Type 4 'Warships', nose-end gangway doors were not to be provided. From the correspondence it is evident that the external styling was Mr Wilkes's inspiration. Within five days of No D7000 being exhibited for the first time, George Williams, the head of the Design Panel, wrote to Wilkes with general congratulations but a few criticisms. The reverse angle of the front end, the contouring at the top of the nose and the curvature round to the cab sides and the front-end slope of the roof were novel. In truth, these features were refined further by Ted Wilkes in his work on the Class 47, when the criticisms were addressed. Mr Wilkes abhorred the clutter of the buffer beam and with these locomotives, which became known as 'Hymeks', added an upper cowling.

It was also Mr Wilkes who proposed a two-tone green livery, with white for the cab window surrounds. A cast badge for the bodyside was

This undated view of No D7000 at Swindon Works is probably not long after entry into traffic during June 1961. Note that the horns were mounted at buffer-beam height on the first examples. *G. H. Marsh*

turned down by the Traffic Advisor, so transfers were to be used instead, although cast alloy numbers were used. The livery did not meet universal approval. Christian Barman, PRO to the BTC, wrote to the head of the Design Panel on 19 August 1960 stating that having the lighter green for the lower part of the body would show up brake dust, in spite of this livery having been selected for the Class 55 'Deltics', though with the dark/light colours in different proportions. Mr Barman clearly did not like BR Standard Green, because he considered that this was not the time to try and revive the scheme. Finally, he predicted possible criticism in adopting differing liveries between the different hydraulic designs (see the section on Class 52).

When the first of the class, No D7000, was exhibited at Marylebone in May 1961, the livery also attracted criticism from J. F. Harrison, by then the BR CME. He hadn't liked it on the 'Deltics' either and wanted the Design Panel to revert to the use of two stripes, as employed on the Brush Type 2 (Class 30), hardly a progressive stance! Clearly the size of the light green area, as well as its shade, were issues, and a revised colour was substituted quickly on both the Type 3 and 5. Even Ted Wilkes, whose idea it was, accepted that on such a large expanse as the bodyside, the colour contrast was too great. The head of the Design Panel objected to the forward-staggered line at the rear of the cab, something that he noted Mr Wilkes had abandoned on the prototype locomotives *Falcon* and *Lion*. Liveries were always a very tetchy topic because everyone had their own views, few of which ever coincided.

BP had entered into a joint venture with Metropolitan Vickers for construction of the Class 28 Co-Bos, Nos D5700-19, ordered as part of the Pilot Scheme. Like NBL, the company was basically a metal-basher, manufacturing neither diesel power plants nor electrical machines, and, again like NBL, by the 1950s had recognised the need to move into building modern traction locomotives, as traditional markets for its steam products diminished. Bristol Siddeley at Ansty, near Coventry, had acquired a licence to build Maybach engines, while J. Stone of Deptford could similarly build Maybach's Mekydro transmissions. The three companies formed a

collaborative venture to bid for orders from BR, using the name Beyer Peacock (Hymek) Ltd. Put in the context of a desire to dieselise quickly, with the BTC recognising that new players would have to be brought into locomotive construction in order to expand workshop capacity, it is clear why the new venture won the order for WR Type 3s.

Whereas weight constraints brought about the use of a German stressed-skin body design on the 'Warships' and the 'Westerns', the latter being the other hydraulic design concurrent with the 'Hymeks', BP had no such limitation and was able to use a traditional strength underframe. In a further difference from the two Swindon-inspired hydraulic Type 4s, which opted for a bogie of German design, BP chose one of Commonwealth pattern with a Bo-Bo wheel arrangement. Fully loaded with supplies, the resultant locomotive weighed 75½ tons.

On 22 April 1962 No D7030 has been three days in traffic and is at Cardiff Canton, its home depot. Note the location of the horns now atop the cab roof and the addition of a small yellow warning panel on the cab front. *R. J. Henry*

By way of contrast, this official view of No D7067 illustrates the application of Corporate Blue. *BR*

Services between Paddington and Worcester/Hereford had a long association with the 'Hymeks'. On 16 May 1964 No D7059 hurries through Sonning Cutting at the head of the 11.10am from Worcester Shrub Hill. *Brian Stephenson*

This was good, being some 30 tons less than the EE Type 3 (Class 37), and thus absorbed less power moving the locomotive. It was, however, also bad in an era when most of the freight rolling stock was unbraked, especially the mineral wagons used in the steeply-graded South Wales valleys.

The Maybach engine fitted was the MD870, which had 16 cylinders and intercoolers as well as being turbocharged. It was offered at a British rating of 1,920hp at 1,500rpm, but was set at 1,740hp at 1,500rpm for use in the 'Hymeks'. For some reason the rating is often given as 1,700hp, but the engine rating plate quotes the higher figure. A Mekydro K184U hydraulic transmission, with four gear stages, was coupled directly to all four axles.

At full power the transmission changed gear at 26, 42½ and 70mph, and this provided a good performance characteristic, with transmission efficiency over 80% as high as 100mph, well above the service maximum of 90. A governor prevented excessive speed while under power and drivers fought shy of the inconvenience of resetting this by keeping speed to the permitted maximum, unless the locomotive was known to have a governor that was set incorrectly. Maximum tractive effort was 46,600lb and the continuous rating was 33,950lb at 12½ mph.

Nos D7000-44 were built with Stone Vapor train heat generators, while the remainder had a Spanner Mark IIIa. Nos D7000-2 also had minor differences; although built with external warning horns at buffer-beam level, these were later revised to the standardised mounting on the cab roof – no doubt Ted Wilkes would not have been amused! The driver's warning light display was mounted vertically on the pillar between the windscreens, whereas the later builds had a more conventional location on the driver's desktop. The Yellow triangle multiple unit coupling code was unique to the class.

From No D7020 small front-end yellow warning panels were applied. When BR Blue became the standard livery, at least three – Nos D7004/7/51 – did not retain white window surrounds, unlike the rest. The following table sets out the BP order and works numbers.

Order	Works Nos	BR Nos
1711	7894-8	D7000-4
1712	7899-7908	D7005-14
1713	7909-38	D7015-44
1714	7949-73	D7045-69
1715	7974-7998	D7070-94
1715	7999-8004	D7095-7100

Into service

No D7000 was exhibited at Marylebone, the BR HQ, from 10 to 14 May 1961, with the official hand-over at Paddington on the 16th, two months early. Having been constructed at BP's Gorton plant, a proving run was made from the nearby Ashburys carriage sidings to the Peak District via Chinley. A trailing load of seven cars was chosen in order to allow the locomotive to accelerate through the transmission ranges. Swindon Works then carried out its own assessment before allocation to a depot. Hence No D7000 was not taken into stock officially until the 31st, a fortnight after the Paddington ceremony. No D7001 made its Peak District trial trip on 20 June, but was not added to stock until 19 July. Bristol Bath Road received deliveries up to No D7055, then Cardiff Canton got Nos D7056-68. Thereafter both depots received further deliveries, as did Newport, Newton Abbot and Old Oak Common. During the 1960s Bath Road, Canton and Old Oak Common had the major allocations.

In mid-summer 1961 Nos D7000-2 went new to the partly complete Bath Road depot for training purposes, the 8.10am Bristol to Portsmouth being worked as far as Salisbury for this purpose. On 19 October No D7004 hauled the eight-coach up 'Bristolian' to Paddington and managed an early arrival, even though the timing was for a 2,200hp 'Warship'. New deliveries to Swindon appear to have been trialled on a variety of services, including fish trains from there to Oxford and Banbury. November 1961 saw Cardiff and Radyr drivers sent to Bristol to be trained because Canton

depot was not ready; appearances on Bristol to Cardiff trains were used for the purpose.

From January 1962 Class 35s took over the 4.50pm Penzance to Manchester from Bristol Temple Meads as far as Hereford, and came back with the 12.45am return. Other work took the type as far as Shrewsbury. No problem was experienced keeping to time, and drivers reported that the new arrivals were nearly as good as the Class 42s and had a superior ride. Around this time they powered the 9.50pm Swindon to York as far as Leicester Central and the 10.22pm York-Bristol balancing service. Nos D7008-9 were sent to London during February for training use.

Being a mixed-traffic design, freight work was included in the diagramming. One such was daily from Westbury to Minehead, while another Westbury duty was the Kensington Olympia to Weymouth milk. Expanding use in South Wales brought appearances on parcels traffic to Milford Haven. Bath Road also put one on the Stoke Gifford to Tavistock Yard freight.

March 1962 saw the introduction of three diagrams between London and South Wales, including the 'Welsh Dragon' to Cardiff and the 'Pembroke Coast Express' to Swansea. From June Canton had a sufficient allocation to cover all Class 1 turns to Paddington, which were

Reported as the first visit of a 'Hymek' to the SR Central Division on 25 August 1963, No D7045 passes East Croydon with an excursion from High Wycombe to Brighton. *David N. Clough*

No D7088 is signalled for the Golden Valley route to Swindon as it departs from Gloucester Eastgate, trailing a lengthy London-bound van train on 27 July 1963. Sister No D7033 sits on the right, while the railway to Gloucester Central (now abandoned) diverges to the left. *David N. Clough*

rostered for a Class 7 steam locomotive, typically a 'Castle', and with a booked load of 13 vehicles a Hymek was expected to keep time. This illustrates the capability now seen in the BP Type 3s, whereas on delivery the WR saw them as replacements for its Class 5 steam power.

Summer 1963 was expected to see the class displace the 'Castles' on the Paddington to Worcester route, although the start actually came with the Winter timetable. The change-over came in part because of displacement from some work in South Wales, as a result of the arrival of Class 37s. Crew training at Worcester was under way by June, but by November these changes were reversed because of major but short-lived availability problems with Class 52s. A similar cascade came the following year, when Class 47s replaced Class 52s on the Paddington to Wolverhampton route; the redundant Type 4s migrated to front-line Paddington to South Wales work, allowing the release of Class 35s for lower-profile activity in the London area and the West Country. One example was an appearance on the Reading to Redhill route.

Of course the above was all done against a background of technical difficulties, although by the end of 1963 these were largely resolved. This was fortunate because an axle failure on a 'Warship' at the start of 1964 caused all of the type, and the Class 52s, to be stopped for examination. Yet again Class 35s came off the

Worcester road and back onto Class 1 work from the capital to South Wales. By May matters had returned to normal and the 'Hymeks' were going beyond Worcester to Hereford. This was to be a preserve of the type until its demise, while Cardiff to Portsmouth also proved a long-term stomping ground.

One duty on which the class was well known was banking trains up the Lickey incline from Bromsgrove. When steam was to be displaced in 1964, it was rumoured that 'Hymeks' would be the replacement, but Class 37s appeared instead. It was not until 29 August 1967 that No D7011 arrived for crew training. Initially three locomotives, drawn from Nos D7021-5, were deployed, later reduced to two. To avoid a gear change during banking, with the inherent transitory cutting of power, the examples in question had the first gear range locked out.

Really only Cornwall never witnessed regular sightings, for the class even penetrated the surviving part of the Somerset & Dorset route, while serving the Mendip coalfield at Radstock. Perhaps the great might-have-been was the scheme drawn up to fit electric train heating equipment, proof that the WR had faith in the type's longevity.

Despite being intended for secondary passenger work, for whatever reason in 1962 the WR's largest steam passenger type, the 8P 'King' Class 4-6-0s, were withdrawn from the London to South Wales route and substituted with 'Hymeks'. Actually, most of the timetable had been in the hands of Class 7 steam power – 'Castles' or 'Britannias' – but the WR had envisaged that the BP Type 3 would supersede its Class 5 coal-burners.

A popular myth in enthusiast circles describes Class 35s being flogged unmercifully on 13-coach trains on 8P timings. As is often the case with such views, this is wide of the mark here. Diesel engines are designed to run continuously within the manufacturer's rating – it is cycling from idling to full power, back to idling then full power repeatedly that causes problems. Thus on the South Wales expresses the 'Hymeks' were working in a near-ideal condition, at or near full power for long periods, which is not flogging a diesel engine. Additionally, the schedules were so ridiculously slow that, even with a full timing load, a Class 35 did not need to be fully extended continuously.

In his train running column in *Trains Illustrated*, then *Modern Railways*, Cecil J. Allen admitted to being sceptical whether a Type 3 could time the South Wales expresses until evidence to the contrary arrived. He published a run with a 12-car trailing load, which ran easily after Swindon because the train was gaining on its booking. From Newport, the 133.4 miles to Paddington were, however, still covered in even time – about 133½ minutes net, against a schedule of 154. Flogged to keep time? Not at all!

Far more demanding was the substitution of the 'Hymeks' on the route when the timings had been drawn up based on a Type 4 diesel. In March 1964 Mr Allen published a journey when No D7030 had the usual 10 coaches, weighing 360 tons gross. Speed peaked at 81mph on level track by Maidenhead and was sustained around 76-77 on the gentle rise between Reading and Swindon. The latter was passed 4½ minutes to the good in 66min 28sec. On what Mr Allen considered to be an exceptional run by a 'Castle' with a coach more, it accelerated to 72mph after passing Reading but was unable to sustain 70 thereafter to Swindon.

The diesel touched 83mph after Badminton, then there were checks approaching the busy traffic centre at Stoke Gifford. Combined with a signal stop at Magor, arrival at Newport was 2 minutes in deficit, but still a highly creditable performance in putting in a gross time of 126 minutes, which should be compared to the up run described above.

Assessing the performance by No D7030 does not suggest a predicted all-out 'Hymek' effort. Whereas one would expect around 1,350 to 1,400rhp on the basis of a claimed 80% transmission efficiency from a 1,740hp diesel, between Ealing Broadway and Slough the figure was less than 1,000, while up the Vale of the White Horse towards Swindon the figure was only 1,150. Even taking more conservative figures of the usually quoted 1,700hp output and transmission efficiency of 75%, rail horsepower should still be 1,300. Looking at other published data, it seems that No D7030's run was a typical performance.

A short, but interesting, emergency piece of haulage was timed by Michael Oakley when a 'Warship' failed on a Plymouth to Newcastle train. With a trailing load of just over 500 tons, No D7070 accelerated away from Puxton box to 70mph by Nailsea on level track before hitting the rising grades to Flax Bourton.

Technical issues

With only a small number in traffic, in November 1961 reports circulated of an under-design in the engine cooling arrangements due to insufficient water. Then, in May 1963, serious transmission failures in service necessitated new gearboxes. On 25 August 1963 J. F. Harrison, as

Appearances on SR metals were also made on the Acton to Norwood transfer freights. No D7030 comes past Streatham Hill Carriage Sidings during April 1970. *David N. Clough*

the BR CME, submitted a report to the BRB outlining various problems with the main-line diesel fleet. His report says that Maybach, which made both the engine and transmission, was called in and expressed the view that the problem lay in the control equipment (the command box), coupled with an over-high horsepower rating. In retrospect, this seems surprising because Mekydro knew at the design stage that the proposed horsepower would be less than Maybach's recommended engine rating. The BR CME, however, disagreed with Mekydro and felt the cause to be excessive torque developed when starting trains in low gear. He thought resolution lay in a revised rubber coupling in the drive train.

To assess these opposing views, half the class (those with odd numbers) were derated to 1,350hp, while the other half (even-numbered locomotives) had first gear locked out. Mr Harrison was able to say that it was quickly established that high horsepower was not the cause, and he planned to return the class to its nominal rating within weeks. What was needed, though, was how to address the excess torque that was occurring at very low speed.

Mr Harrison continued that he believed that certain minor modifications were needed to the

command block and that this work could be carried out quickly and simply; in fact, for the fleet as a whole, he gave a date of January 1964, and this would permit reinstatement of first gear. Experimental work was commissioned from the BR Research Department, reporting to a committee chaired by Mr S. O. Ell, who headed the Swindon Locomotive Testing Unit.

A paper describing the work of the Research Department survives in the National Archive and says that the principal failures were of the so-called No 5 transmission shaft and/or gear teeth in the main gearbox. Although the failures were first thought to be due to a single event, such as wheelslip, it was established that the true cause was many thousands of repetitions of shock loads, which caused high stresses. Maybach acknowledged that its calculations for Shaft 5, when the transmission input was 1,800hp (for Class 35 it was 1,590hp), was at the limit of tolerance, and proposed stiffening the shaft. The Research Department work, however, led to a redesign of both the shaft and the gear teeth at its extremity. Interestingly, it was concluded that neither of the temporary steps put in place while testing was carried out – derating to 1,350hp or locking out first gear – was found to alleviate the true cause.

A busy scene at Bromsgrove: three Class 37s form the usual complement of Lickey bankers, arranged into a pair in multiple and a single locomotive depending on the demand of each train. No D5285 has descended the incline and waits while the brakes on its wagons are unpinned. No D7048 meanwhile has the relative luxury of a fully fitted train and is thus able to proceed on its journey along the up slow line.
Anthony A. Vickers

On 12 December 1966 Mr Ell presented a paper to the Institution of Locomotive Engineers in which he described the 'Hymek' troubles. The original engine rubber coupling was replaced by one that was half as stiff on 36 examples as a first attempt to overcome the troubles. Mr Ell then identifies the various shafts that caused trouble, and the transmission/dynostarter shaft was the one failing most frequently. In short, there was more than one problem.

Mr Ell says that investigation determined the presence of severe vibration torques in the lower half of the speed range and that this peaked at 1,380rpm. Such torques stress materials way beyond the tolerances built in by designers and must be reduced. 'Tuning' the system suppressed this condition in reducing engine-transmission torsional stiffness by one-third and increasing three times the 'lumped' inertia of the transmission, and was achieved by the simple expedient of inserting an additional coupling at the transmission end of the shaft. Drawing on similar experiences with the 'Western' Class, using the same coupling between transmission and dynostarter reduced to 40% the level of critical vibration.

Allegedly due to the above problems, Nos D7077/9/80/1 were held back at BP's Gorton works from May until December 1963, although deliveries of other new builds up to No D7091 continued as normal throughout the second half of the year. Then, between 14 and 16 December, the locomotives that had been held back were all accepted into traffic. No D7100 completed the class on 5 February 1964.

During the autumn of 1964 availability dropped due to Swindon Works being forced to cut its parts stock levels. Of course, one question is why such high stock levels were necessary, since it implies that components needed changing frequently.

In retrospect, the class was the best diesel-hydraulic because, after the early vicissitudes, it settled to very reliable and versatile service. Quoting Mr Ell from his paper referred to above, 'The D7000 Class has earned an excellent reputation and has established a relatively high mileage per casualty on mixed traffic duties.' Average annual mileages were no match for the Type 4s, but this was due to the nature of the work assigned. In the Type 3 classification, the WR had two very competent designs, the other being the Class 37. The latter was, however, cheaper to operate and had the edge in reliability and availability. Nevertheless, had the WR plan for fully-braked freights been realised much earlier, the 'Hymeks' would have been ideal on the Welsh valleys traffic and would have been multiplied accordingly. In any event, it was still the WR's standard truly mixed-traffic Type 3.

Length	51ft 8½ in
Width	8ft 10 in
Height	12ft 10³⁄₁₆ in
Weight	75 tons 8 cwt
Sanding gear	Fitted
Fuel tank capacity (gallons)	800
Minimum curve radius (chains)	4
Maximum speed (mph)	90
Engine	
Maybach MD870	
Engine output (bhp)	1,740 at 1,500rpm
Tractive effort (lb)	
Maximum	46,600
Continuous	33,950 at 12½ mph
Gear ratio	
N/a	

Class 37

Section, while Nos D6730-41 were for the NER's Area 1 (Blaydon).

At a date that has gone unrecorded, the need for diesel traction within the Type 3 range was recognised and a new category of between 1,500hp and 1,750hp created. Even then, why was the range confined as it was? The diesel plans of the SR have already been dealt with (see Class 33), while the WR made it clear that it wanted a locomotive in this range. No doubt around the same time plans were evolved for a diesel-electric of similar output.

Again, what is unclear is why an English Electric design was chosen. What must be remembered is that BR was taxing the workshop capacity of any and every locomotive builder at the time, and the BTC minutes record a desire to find new entrants into the building sector. In any event, the first reference to a diesel-electric Type 3 in the BTC minutes came on 8 January 1959, when the purchase of 42 examples from EE was authorised; the order was placed on the 27th. Nos D6700-29 were destined for the GE

The design, which was to become the standard Type 3, was similar externally to the company's Class 40, already under construction. This included the 'traditional' nose ends, which incorporated gangway doors, flanked by a two-character route indicator box on either side. Of interest is that EE engaged E. J. M. Wilkes in 1962 to produce a revised body style. Although the revised outline was discussed with BR in 1963, with a view to adopting it on future orders, the proposal proved stillborn. The livery replicated that of the Class 40, being green, with light grey roof, red buffer-beams and black undergear. The matter of the grey roof is a moot point because some sources do not mention it, but one colour photograph clearly shows a new locomotive so turned out. Half-height yellow warning panels were added to the cab fronts from either No D6720 or No D6732 (again, sources differ), while many of the class also received full yellow ends during repaints before BR Blue livery was adopted. Round buffers were preferred to the oval pattern seen on the Class 40.

A new design of bogie with three axles, all powered, was selected. Development work on the SVT diesel enabled EE to offer it in Mark 2 charge-cooled form, with charge-air cooling, and this provided a rating of 2,025hp at 850rpm. In

From new, Class 37s quickly displaced Stratford depot's 7MT 'Britannia' 4-6-2s on the 'Hook Continental' boat train from Harwich Parkestone Quay to Liverpool Central. At first, the diesel was replaced by a Woodhead electric at Sheffield Victoria, but later diesel traction worked through to Manchester Piccadilly. In September 1961 No D6714 is seen here climbing away from Retford. *J. S. Hancock*

one of the many perverse decisions made by the BTC's engineering supremo, the actual rating adopted was 1,750. Two turbochargers of either type HP 200ZINT or HP 210 were used.

In traditional EE philosophy, a shaft from the free end of the engine drove the radiator fan, while main and auxiliary generators were bolted onto the crankshaft at the other end. The main generator was the 10-pole EE 822/10G, rated at 1,107 kW, 1,800A, 615V at 850rpm. With successive builds, EE made some minor modifications to the main generator and this gave rise to different model codes, principally the EE 822/13G and EE 822/16J.

An 8-pole EE 911/5C auxiliary generator was used, rated at 66kW, 600A, 110V at 850rpm. Six EE538/A 4-pole traction motors were connected in three series-parallel pairs, each rated at 240hp, 600A, 300V. Two stages of field weakening were fitted, permitting full engine output to be available between 10 and 79mph. With a Clayton RO 2500/3 steam generator and fully fuelled, the overall weight was 105 tons.

Vulcan Foundry was contracted to build the locomotives and No D6700 entered service at Stratford, East London, on 2 December 1960. Following a visit to the USA by the BTC Chairman, the original plan of modernising a large number of steam sheds was abandoned in favour of concentrating the new traction at a few strategic depots. Thus, by the time No D6730 emerged in late 1961 the NER had revised its plans and Blaydon (on Tyneside) was no longer to be a maintenance facility. Instead, Nos D6730-41 went to Hull.

Service experience

Even before the class doyen had made its debut, EE had received a repeat order on 5 February 1960 for 37 units. Nos D6742-54 were destined for Sheffield, with Nos D6755-78 allocated to Thornaby. BTC approval for 17 of the class was given on 27 April 1961 at £89,400 each for the Hull area. On 13 December another order was authorised, this time for 23 at a slightly lower unit price of £89,300, but no decision was taken on regional allocation.

By 12 July 1962 there was debate as to the relative merits of Types 2 and 3, with disagreement within the NER area board. Even

so, the BTC resolved to augment its commitment to the EE Type 3 by procuring a further 100, this time at £89,250. No D6819 was not only the first of the order but inaugurated abandonment of nose-end gangway doors, the adoption of a central four-character route indicator box, and was the first of the class to be assigned to the WR.

In December 1963 the BRB considered a report by Mr Ness, which set out the relative benefits of ordering Type 2 or Type 3 diesels. The former were cheaper, but not necessarily significantly so. By contrast, the latter were deemed more versatile and could be delivered sooner. Based on this analysis, sanction was given for a further 70 Class 37s, which were split between 20 ordered in January 1964 and 50 ordered in February, the latter at £86,858 each.

This view of an unidentified locomotive having its engine lowered into position within Vulcan Foundry is very interesting, and gives a clear impression of the impressive size of the engine and generators, topped by the turbochargers. Note the absence of hard hats in an era when Health & Safety requirements were less onerous. *EE*

This brought the total order to 289, but the Board minutes are silent on when the remaining 20 were procured. To fulfil delivery deadlines, EE apportioned construction between Vulcan Foundry and RSH. When the number series reached No D6999, the final nine became Nos D6600-08, the latter arriving on the WR on 9 November 1965. Before this series went into production, questions were asked as to whether the fitment of a steam generator was necessary because many of the South Wales examples were used only on freight work. Additionally, the question of regional allocation was discussed and it was decided that all should go initially to the WR, with reallocation thereafter in the light of an emerging national traction plan, even though such transfers would not be popular with recipient Regions. One of the Regions was to be the LMR, though this never materialised.

The accompanying table summarises construction and Works Number details.

Numbers	EE contract number	EE rotation numbers	VF Works Numbers	RSH Works Numbers
D6700-41	CCL 1031	2863-2904	D579-620	
D6742-68	CCM 1114	3034-60	D696-722	
D6769-78	CCM 1114	3061-70		8315-24
D6779-95	CCN 1239	3206-22		8325-42
D6796-6818	CCP 1267	3225-47	D750-72	
D6819-28	All CCP 1304	3264-73		8379-88
D6829-38		3274-83	D803-12	
D6839-58		3314-3333	D813-32	
D6859-68		3337-46		8390-99
D6869-78		3347-67	D839-42	
D6879-98		3357-76		8400-19
D6899-6918		3377-96	D843-62	
6919-38	CCR 1320	3405-24	D863-82	
6939-58	All CCS 1362	3496-3515	D927-46	
6959-6999		3519-59	D948-88	
6600-08		3560-68	D989-97	

On the GE Section the class was regarded truly as mixed-traffic. It deputised for the non-availability of a Stratford Class 40 on the Liverpool Street to Norwich Class 1 turns, and also appeared on the Cambridge line. In fact, No D6700 made its service debut on 9 January 1961 on the 5.56pm Liverpool Street to Cambridge. During February and March trials were conducted on coal trains on the Cambridge line to assess the relative merits of the two EE types based at Stratford. The Class 37 had a lower maximum axle load and higher power-to-weight ratio than its larger cousin, and by the summer had replaced 'Britannia' Class 'Pacifics' on the Harwich boat trains, which included the double-home turn as far as Sheffield Victoria on the through service to Liverpool Central.

The arrival of examples at Darnall from June 1962 opened up new operating possibilities. The York to Bournemouth service, which was routed via the former GC line, picked up a Class 37 as traction as far as Banbury. No D6743 made the debut for the type at King's Cross on 4 August, heading the 7.05am from Sheffield. Having ordered 100 of the design, trials were staged in the South Wales valleys to assess the suitability for dealing with braking the unfitted coal trains, which were beyond the capability of the much lighter Class 35s. On 2 October 1962 No D6743 was loaned by Darnall for the purpose, going up the Rhondda to Stormstown Junction and the Rhymney Valley two days later. A long association with the area was thus ushered in.

No D6784 led the way to Gateshead in February 1963, where the depot's allocation was first put to use dieselising traffic flows between Newcastle and Carlisle. Meanwhile, the ER opted not to change to electric traction at Sheffield Victoria for the Harwich to Liverpool boat service, so Class 37s became the only daytime diesels to operate through the Woodhead Tunnel. An initiative to name some GE examples saw the fitting of plates to Nos D6703/4/7 during 1963. Unimaginatively, the names were *First East Anglian Regiment, Second East Anglian Regiment* and *Third East Anglian Regiment* respectively, but the plates remained covered until removal a few months later, when the scheme was dropped.

At the end of April 1963 Nos D6819/29/31 debuted at Cardiff, with Nos D6821/33 at Landore. The new arrivals mirrored practice with earlier diesel types in being trialled between Swindon and Gloucester. Nos D6834/5 in multiple were tried on a rake of 21-ton brake-fitted coal wagons from Eastern Valley Hafodynyrys Colliery to Llanwern steelworks. During early June the class was on crew training at Pontypool Rd, and by August forays were being made along the Carmarthen to Aberystwyth line. On 18 July 1964 No D6938 became the first diesel used on Lickey banking duties, with two more to follow. Some idea of the spread of use in South Wales can be gauged from observations made by David Rapson over the weekend of 4/5 April 1964:

Saturday

Pontypool Road (86G)	D6826
Aberbeeg (86F)	D6829/44/917
Neath N&B	D6886
Neath (87A)	D6853/90
Danygraig (87C)	D6869
Swansea East Dock (87D)	D6908
Llanelly (87F)	D6870/85/909
Carmarthen (87G)	D6823/84
Landore (87E)	D6821/38/52/ 54/61/64/93/ 905/07/26
Briton Ferry	D6825/928
Tondu (88H)	D6862/73/911
Cardiff Canton (86A)	D6819/32/41/ 56/92/94/900/ 04/10

Sunday

Radyr (88B)	D6830
Barry (88C)	D6820/59/91
Newport Ebbw Junction (86B)	D6827/42/46/ 47/48/60/66/ 68/71/72/74/ 75/82/99/901/ 02/03/20
Severn Tunnel Junction (86E)	D6886/89/900

Gerard Fiennes was the WR General Manager in 1965 and was keen to speed up his Region's passenger services. His role in securing the ordering of the Class 55 'Deltics' will be explored under the section dealing with that design; he tried to borrow one of these 3,300hp machines for a high-speed trial but was rebuffed, due to alleged unavailability, so instead he turned to the WR's own resources in the shape of two Class 37s in multiple. Canton's Nos D6881/2 took part in a Paddington to Plymouth journey on 3 June 1965, hauling a

nine-coach rake of XP64 stock and a dynamometer car.

With the exception of one minor pws and two slight delays caused by tardy action by signalmen, the trial ran unchecked both out and back. Passing Westbourne Park at 50mph, speed built up to 88 at Southall and 98 by Slough, which was maintained until easing to 76 for the permanent restriction through Twyford. The Berks & Hants route was no speedway at the time, with numerous interruptions to sustained 90mph running. Taunton, 142.75 miles, was covered in 107min 15sec, against 109 minutes booked. Climbing to Whiteball at a minimum of 64½ mph involved a combined value of 2,750rhp. The 173.5 miles to Exeter occupied 132min 10sec, or 131 minutes net, more than 4 minutes early and giving an average of 78.8mph. Climbing the South Devon banks, minima of around 40mph were sustained. Adjusting for the brief stop at Exeter St David's, the overall net time for the 225.55 miles to Plymouth was 192.25 minutes, 70.4mph.

Returning from Plymouth, speed fell to 34 climbing Hemerdon (2,350rhp), but reached an 85mph maximum near Exminster before easing through Exeter. After the restricted section below Tiverton Junction had been negotiated, a rousing effort was made up to Whiteball, where speed was still 76½ mph, worth 2,650rhp. Along the near-level road towards Bristol, 97mph was touched at Highbridge, with an easing back thereafter. Hurrying along the last leg towards Paddington, speed was sustained at 100mph east of Swindon, helping to produce a

Another official view, probably at Stratford depot, contrasts the front end of Class 40 No D200 with Class 37s Nos D6723 and 6717.

Above: Sheffield Darnall depot deployed Class 37s on various services on the ex-Great Central main line. No D6976 takes a local linking Nottingham Victoria with Sheffield Victoria, pictured at Kirkby & New Hucknall in March 1963. *J. S. Hancock*

Below: Further south on the ex-GC line at Rugby Central, No D6751 pauses with the York to Bournemouth working on which the class was the booked power. *Ian Allan Library*

together with two rakes of stock, the XP64 set and a set that was repainted into the new blue and grey corporate colours. One roster started and finished at Swansea, with a return run to Bristol from Paddington in between, while the other made two return journeys from Paddington to Bristol. Two sections of track, between Southall and Rushcombe and between Pangbourne and Challow, were passed for 100mph. An overall time of 105 minutes from Bristol to Paddington was scheduled, inclusive of a stop at Bath, from where the average was 73.9mph. The balancing speed on level track after Slough appeared to be around 98mph with a 10-car consist.

This high-speed scheduling proved short-lived and had ended by September 1966. One can speculate that the WR's General Manager, Gerry Fiennes, was instrumental in its inception, and his departure to the ER was a factor in its demise. Possibly the BR Board was unhappy at the use of two Type 3s in this way. One outcome of the curtailment was that the WR gave up quite a number of its fleet, some going to Scotland for the first time.

In the mid-1960s EE began to experiment with electronic control of the main generator, and Stratford-based No D6818 was modified with a KV10-B field supply unit. An interesting development involved No D6700 during the first three months of 1968, when it went to the Derby Research Centre for the fitment of push-pull equipment in readiness for trials with five modified coaches. These took place between Edinburgh and Glasgow, the intended route for such a service. Another trial took place during March and April 1968, this time examining train air braking; the former Midland route between Derby and Matlock was the venue, and No D6868 was one of two class members loaned for the purpose. The LMR was, however, not best pleased at having to sort out fuel dilution on the locomotive before the trial could start!

Really only on the GE Section did the class put in any quantity of express passenger mileage during the 1960s, where use as deputies for Class 40s on the Liverpool Street to Norwich expresses extended their potential fully. Cecil J. Allen reported a number of examples of such running and never felt that the type showed up as a match for the schedules. In truth, they were

time from Bristol of 87min 3sec. Such running had never been seen before on WR metals. Predicted rhp for two Class 37s is around 2,500, so Nos D6881/2 were clearly well up to rating. One cannot, however, reflect that a pair of Class 37s weighed 215 tons, while a 3,300hp Class 55 'Deltic' weighed 99 tons and had a predicted rhp of 2,640, nearly 100hp more for 117 tons (three coaches) less than the two Type 3s. It should be remembered that the class had the same bogies, traction motors and motor gearing as the Class 50 and 55, both of which were passed for 100mph.

A report states that pairs of Class 37s were introduced on some Paddington to Bristol services in late May 1965; it was not, however, until 18 April 1966 that a new high-speed timetable was introduced. Class 37s from the range Nos D6875-92 were used in multiple,

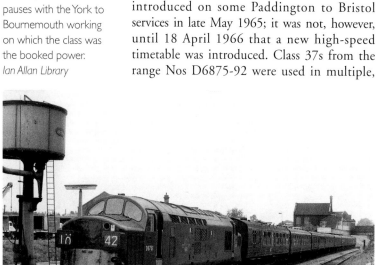

fully extended and this left no margin to cope with delays.

No D6715 had the standard nine-coach consist on one trip, which was heavily checked as far as Ipswich but put up a net time of 69 minutes for the 68.8 miles, well inside the 73-minute net schedule. Continuing to Norwich, there was the usual fast running on the downgrades, with a maximum of 88. Net time for the 46.25 miles was 44 minutes, just the net schedule.

In the up direction, No D6729 had a coach more, grossing 360 tons, and sustained 34mph on the 1 in 84 curving exit from Norwich. Two pws checks spoiled the run to Ipswich, but even so Mr Allen estimated a loss of more than a minute on the 43-minute booking. Matters worsened, with a further three track slowings by Marks Tey and a signal stop, plus two other slowings before London, so assessing power output and haulage potential was problematic. In the early stage, accelerating away from Norwich, an indifferent 1,030rhp might suggest a below-par locomotive. Examining other runs on this length of line has, though, also revealed some poor efforts, and one starts to question the gradient profile.

Finally, in this survey of contemporary performance, Darnall-based examples took a hand for a time on the 'Sheffield Pullman' diagram to King's Cross. With a load augmented to eight vehicles, grossing 335 tons, No D6747

Below: On 16 June 1962 No D6736 is two months old and sports its radiator grille mesh cover, an item later removed from all the class. It is heading a partially fitted up freight across the Plain of York, near Beningborough. *Gavin Morrison*

With a Class 37 at each end, a load of either coal or ore is taken into Llanwern steelworks from the South Wales main line. *Ian Allan Library*

One of the first order for Class 37s, No D6718, passes Enfield Lock on 6 April 1968 heading the 15.40 Kings Lynn to Liverpool Street service. *P. Paye*

put in a creditable effort. Restarting from Grantham, Stoke was passed at 53mph, with the average rhp from rest being 1,200, thus in line with expectations in such circumstances. Top speed down to Peterborough was then 92mph and the time of 26min 41sec was inside schedule for the 29.1 miles. Some restrictions applied at that time over the Fens, but this was followed by speed in the mid-80s from Tempsford to Biggleswade. The minimum to Stevenage was 76mph and the passing time for the 58.65 miles to Hatfield was 49min 43sec, nearly 2 minutes adrift of the net schedule, which suggests that the extra two cars over the normal consist proved too much to handle. After Hatfield delays ruined the remainder of the trip.

In late 1962 EE retained E. G. M. Wilkes (who had hitherto been commissioned by the BTC as a design consultant) by private arrangement to advise on revising the design of the Type 3. Various changes were considered by EE, but meanwhile the BTC had its own agenda for modifications. Clearly the shaped driver's doors had caused problems, which had not been found on similar doors on other locomotives. One variation introduced was a widening of the door from 18 to 20½ inches. The WR was consulted about this too in the spring of 1963 because it was to receive the next batch ordered. Regrettably, the radical flat-front redesign schemed out by Mr Wilkes was not adopted on later builds.

Perhaps the only major area of trouble came from the bogie, a new design that was to become an EE standard and was also used on Classes 50 and 55, and which had been developed from the EE prototype 'Deltic'. Around April 1961 fractures were found in the EE Type 3 bogie frames, which were also beginning to be fitted to the first examples of the Class 55 then also under construction at Vulcan Foundry. The ER had planned some service revamping on the GE Section, commencing with the Summer timetable, and the BTC decided to give priority to modifying the Class 37s over the new Class 55s in order not to disrupt the planned schedules.

A report by the Director of Engineering Research dated September 1964 describes fatigue failures in the bogies. Problems had clearly flared again with this item during the first half of the previous year, because a meeting had been held on 24 May 1963 between the BRB's CME and the Research Department to discuss fatigue cracking of the bogie transoms. During the previous year, strain gauge tests on No D6708's bogie highlighted an under-design in one area, but, for practical reasons, EE rejected the Research Department's proposed solution. Instead, the company counter-proposed fitting a bridge piece to add strength, and the same bogie was stress-tested with the modification in February 1964. The result was that stress levels at the critical point were reduced from peaks of 12.9 ton/sq in to 3.7, and EE's modification was thus accepted.

No D6983, new to stock on 13 May 1965, was in collision with No D1671 at Bridgend on 19 December that year; both locomotives were withdrawn and cut up nearby.

Undoubtedly the Class 37 was one of BR's best main-line diesels in terms of reliability and availability, just giving way, perhaps, to the Class 20 as being the most successful. In the 1960s availability was consistently above 80%. Despite the engine being unproven in a charge-cooled version, and the use of some new electrical equipment, the design worked very well straight from the drawing board.

Length	61ft 6in
Width	8ft 11⅝in
Height	12ft 10½ in
Weight	
With steam generator	105 tons 13 cwt
Without generator	101 tons 4 cwt
Sanding gear?	Yes
Fuel tank capacity (gallons)	800
Minimum curve radius (chains)	4
Maximum speed (mph)	90
Engine	
EE 12CSVT Mk II	
Engine output (bhp)	1,750hp at 850rpm
Tractive effort (lb)	
Maximum	55,500
Continuous	35,000 at 13.6mph
Gear ratio	
53:18	

Class 40

This view of the Class 40 production line inside Vulcan Foundry is undated, but the bodyshells are all cut to accept nose end gangway doors. *EE*

When the options for traction in the Type C (later Type 4) category were under consideration, an invitation to EE was, perhaps, inevitable, since its power train in the Southern Railway prototype No 10203 had proved generally successful. What emerged was, essentially, No 10203, packaged within an EE body design that incorporated nose ends as well as Bulleid's 1Co bogie (Percy Bollen was actually the designer). The order for ten units, Nos D200-09, was delivered during 1958 and split between the ER's GE and GN lines.

The 16SVT Mark II diesel engine had an EE 822/4C 10-pole main generator, rated at 1,313kW, 1,800A, 730V at 850rpm. Overhung from the main generator was an 8-pole EE 911/2B 43-48kW auxiliary generator. From new, EE 526/5D six-pole traction motors were supplied, three per bogie, and connected in three series pairs in parallel across the main generator, being continuously rated at 212hp at a nominal 600A, 300V at 362rpm. The radiator fan was directly driven by a shaft from the free end of the engine. Blue Star multiple-working equipment and sanding gear were included, and livery was standard BR green, with a grey roof and a light grey band between these two colours. The underframe and bogies were in black, while red was used for the buffer-beams and bogie fronts.

No D200 went to Stratford, East London, on 14 March 1958 and made its public debut on 18 April on a train to Norwich, being the first Type 4 example. Unlike almost any other design, BR had gained service experience by the date of the first repeat order, and the following table sets out details of how the class was eventually multiplied to a total of 200.

Before the first repeat order had been placed, the wily Chairman of the BTC, Sir Brian Robertson, voiced his concerns about the suitability of the Class 40. In his opinion, these locomotives were insufficiently powerful to meet the demands for haulage of heavy trains at high speed. He also claimed that the type was too expensive to work in multiple. These views were aired at the BTC Board on 26 June 1958, but he was prepared to pass the question back to the regional boards. Clearly they were content, for more were ordered, as set out above. At the time the final order was sanctioned, Chris Bond (Chief Technical Officer) said future orders would be for 2,500hp machines.

Not for the first time, Sir Brian was right. Experience on the GE alongside 'Britannia' Class 7 'Pacifics' showed no advantage of diesel over steam, when the latter was in good order and driven hard. Unsurprisingly, the ER turned down any further allocations, arguing that the type was under-powered to replace its Class 8 Pacifics on the ECML. In fact, the Region

Ordered	ER	LMR	NER	ScR
16.1.55	D200-09			
14.7.58		D210-36	D237-39	
28.11.58			D240-9	
20.4.59		D255/67-69/87-304	D250-54/56-59/70-86	D260-66
27.7.59		D305-24		
5.2.60	D345-72*	D325-44	D385-99	D373-84

Although ordered for the King's Cross and Sheffield areas, the ER declined to take them and the locomotives went instead to the NER. All bar Nos D305-24 were built at Vulcan Foundry, the remainder coming from RSH.

quickly cascaded the GN stud, based at Hornsey, to diagrams to Sheffield, then reallocated the five locomotives to Stratford for GE utilisation. Nevertheless, BR wanted to phase out steam quickly and workshop capacity forced it to order further Class 40s for top-flight passenger duties, notably on the WCML.

At the time of the July 1959 order, EE intimated an intention to uprate the engine to around 2,500hp, and this was reaffirmed during a visit to Vulcan Foundry around August 1960, but nothing came of it. RSH took a share of construction in order to allow Vulcan Foundry to concentrate on the Class 55.

Train heating generators were certainly an issue, their frequent failures causing indifferent availability in the early years. Initially a Stone Vapor OK4625 model was installed, but later a Clayton RO2500 Mk 1 was tried. No D248 had

a Clayton generator and went to Hornsey from new, while No D255 was kept close to Derby to enable easier evaluation of the electric train heating equipment installed. From No D325, two-digit route indicator boxes were sited on either side of the nose-end gangway doors. A decision to abandon these doors – little used and a great source of cab draughts – saw Nos D345-99 emerge with a four-character route indicator panel, a modification retro-fitted to Nos D260-66 on the ScR during 1965.

When nearly new, the LMR opted to name 25 examples, commemorating Merchant Navy passenger liners, and Nos D210-12 were dealt with at ceremonies at Liverpool Riverside station during 1960. On 8 August 1963 No D326 was at the head of the up 'West Coast Postal' when the train was stopped north of Cheddington by thieves who stole a seven-figure haul of used

To mark the last delivery of the class, EE made up a headboard for No D399. The locomotive is outside Vulcan Foundry and the date is probably late August 1962. Although in monochrome, the ex-works livery can still be discerned. Note the mesh covering the radiator grille, which was eventually removed from all the class. *EE*

Right: Although the ER was not keen on the Class 40 because of its low installed power for top-flight passenger work, the locomotives were a common sight on the ECML on parcels and fitted freight trains. This illustration post-dates entry into traffic of all 200 examples, but no details of the locomotive, train, date or location are available. Nevertheless, the ensemble makes a fine sight as it tracks north along the ECML with a fully fitted freight for the North East. *EE*

Below: The LMR received a large allocation of the class and deployed the type on its Western Lines – essentially the routes of the old LNWR. This atmospheric scene in 1961 shows a completely different Rugby station from the one to be found today.
Michael Mensing

bank notes being conveyed for destruction, an event that in the annals of history became known as the Great Train Robbery.

Service experience

Despite shunning the type for ECML use, during the initial allocation to Hornsey the ER got between 4,000 and 4,500 miles per week per locomotive, two-and-a-half times that of a King's Cross-allocated 8P 'Pacific'. The last duties from a GN depot were two diagrams incorporating the 'Sheffield Pullman', ending in October 1961 when Nos D208/9 migrated to Stratford.

In contrast, the NER happily turned out Gateshead and York examples on Class 1 turns along this route. In fact, from the summer of 1960 a diagram for a Gateshead machine on the King's Cross to Edinburgh car/sleeper became the first diesel to work throughout between the capitals.

The LMR began to receive its first deliveries during May 1959 at Camden. By August footplate staff from Carlisle were lodging in London in order to train on the new arrivals, so that through running into Scotland could be diagrammed. Three months later Class 40s had displaced Stanier 8P 'Pacifics' on the principal WCML services. From 24 April 1960 Euston to Holyhead trains switched to the diesels, and even the Midland Main Line witnessed occasional visits. That summer Crewe-based locomotives ventured to Perth with the 'Royal Highlander', filling in with trips to Aberdeen during the daytime layover period. West Midlands sheds, such as Aston and Monument Lane, were also trained around this time.

In anticipation of diesel traction replacing steam on the Newcastle to Liverpool services, on 18 February 1960 NER-based No D245 was used as part of a trial, hauling 12 coaches between the cities. On 2 January 1961 the new order took over, and seven days later No D253 made the debut for diesel-electric traction on the WR when it worked the 12.48 York to Bristol throughout. Meanwhile Neville Hill turned over the 'Queen of Scots' Pullman between Leeds and Glasgow to one of its locomotives.

Of course, a lot of work was done hauling freight. When the Cliffe to Uddingston bulk cement train was dieselised in late 1961, an NER Class 40 took over from the brace of Class

33s at York. The Summer 1961 ECML timetable had no booked turns for the class, so they were bound to be more evident on parcels as well as freight. A further dent in Class 1 activity came in January 1965 with the loss of the Liverpool Street to Norwich expresses in favour of Class 47 haulage. The following month the LMR began a similar cascade, when Class 47s took over the daytime Euston to Perth train, while from that summer none of the principal WCML work was rostered for Class 40s.

The NER's Nos D253/6-9 were loaned to Haymarket during February 1960 for training purposes, in advance of the arrival of the ScR's allocation, the first two of which arrived the following month. The Region preferred to use its examples on routes emanating from Edinburgh, which encompassed both passenger and freight, the latter notably handled over the Waverley route, while Class 1 passenger activity included the Aberdeen road.

Performance on the GE Section was reviewed in *Diesel Pioneers* and showed a competence at adhering to the 2-hour Norwich expresses while offering no advantage over the steam power displaced. Cecil J. Allen felt that diesel had the advantage getting away from stops but was marginally inferior at high speed.

Shortly after the Newcastle to Liverpool services were dieselised on 2 January 1961, Mr Allen made a footplate run with the usual

From January 1961 the class took over the Newcastle to Liverpool passenger workings. On 9 March of that year, No D274 traverses the now-closed Heckmondwyke loop with the 9.45am from Newcastle. The location is Birstall, the summit of the climb, mostly at 1 in 70, from Farnley Junction, where the route diverged from the alternative line via Dewsbury, which was less sharply graded. *Gavin Morrison*

10-coach consist of 337 tons tare, 355 gross. Adverse weather provided extra drag on the train as it powered across the Vale of York. From Darlington full power was used, save for an easing to 64mph over Wiske Moor troughs. Despite level track or slightly favourable grades, top speed was only 86½ mph at Tollerton, and the time to York was 37min 33sec, 1½ minutes down on the booking. The next part of the run of particular interest was the ascent from Huddersfield to Standedge Tunnel, mainly at 1 in 105. Here 40mph was attained and held, giving 1,400 rhp, a little lower than predicted. Overall, the impression gained was that the new

schedule represented the best achievable with the type, which were displaced by Gateshead Class 46s within a couple of years.

On the WCML the EE Type 4 lingered longer on front-line duties, largely due to the decision not to roll the initial electrification forward to Glasgow, once the southern half of the route was complete. Although no match for a Stanier 8P 'Pacific' when the latter was well extended, schedules between Euston and Glasgow were liberal and Class 40s coped quite well. When Mr Allen pitted diesel against 7P 'Royal Scot' in his columns, to the slight advantage of the latter on the principal climbs, correspondents commented that the 'Royal Scot' was clearly unusually good and well above the norm.

Examining running north of Preston, typically maxima of 72 to 74mph were attained on the level to Lancaster with 430 tons gross. Passing Carnforth at 78mph, full power produced 51 at Oxenholme and 37 over Grayrigg, and such an effort was worth 1,350rhp, again below the predicted 1,500. Recovering to around 68 past Tebay, Shap summit would be topped at 27mph. The non-stop schedule from Crewe was 125 minutes, which included 5 minutes of recovery time, for 109.6 miles, 52.6mph average, and the Class 40s could keep this easily, despite several interruptions to the running. Continuing to Carlisle, maxima in the mid-80s were the rule.

The typical Class 40 performance just outlined would cover Crewe to the border city in a net time of 138½ minutes for the 141 miles, whereas the timing allowed was 156 minutes gross, 150 net of recovery time.

Despite No 10203 serving as a prototype, the Class 40s did not prove trouble-free. The 1Co bogie was a constant source of problems, giving a hard ride and its bulk and lack of secondary suspension making it prone to stress fractures. Privately, it has been admitted that EE was punished more severely than BR's own workshops, which used the same bogie design under the 'Peaks', in being called on to rectify or replace faulty items.

The original EE526 traction motor also proved prone to flashover. While having 6 poles gave smoother torque, one engineer described the commutator as behaving like a razor blade in causing excessive brush wear. The LMR experienced many motor flashovers, to the extent that in 1963 BR approached EE to set up a formal examination facility at Rugby to isolate the cause. Meanwhile, the NER declined to acknowledge a problem, though this was rather dishonest. Various alternative types of motor brush were tried in an effort to reduce wear while maintaining good commutation, but eventually the original type was deemed the best.

EE offered a 4-pole motor in substitution and this coincided with an order for further Class 20s for the LMR, so most of the Region's Class 40 got new motors while its discarded 6-pole motors were refurbished by EE and re-used in the Class 20s. The new motors were of type EE551/A, rated at 253hp, 365V, 600A at 410rpm. As a result modifications to the Class 40 control gear were needed on account of changes to the field weakening arrangements, and to help maintenance staff the control cubicle was painted blue, while a blue line was added under the bodyside locomotive numbers to identify those with the EE551/A motors. With a higher field strength in weak field than the EE526 motors, the replacements were less prone to flashover at high speed, while having only 4 rather than 6 poles also reduced the risk of flashover. The main generator also did not prove trouble-free, with flashovers causing concern.

No D322 was the only casualty during the

Even in June 1965 the local freight facilities at Corbridge appear derelict as No D253 passes on a Newcastle to Carlisle fitted freight. *J. S. Hancock*

1960s. On 13 May 1966 it was at the head of the 20.40 Euston to Stranraer train when it was in collision with a runaway tank train on rising gradients approaching Acton Grange Junction, south of Warrington.

Despite the problems outlined above, the Class 40 generally proved durable and reliable. In fact, during the 1960s the design could claim to be the most successful Type 4, at least in terms of availability, though it was eclipsed in annual mileages by the 'Warship' Class 42, which will be considered next.

Numbers	EE contract number	EE rotation numbers	VF Works Numbers	RSH Works Numbers
D200-09	CCF 0874	2367-2376	D395-404	
D210-39	CCK 0994	2666-95	D427-56	
D240-09	CCK 0994	2716-24	D457-66	
D250-09	CCK 0994	2772-81	D467-76	
D260-304	CCK 0994	2782-826	D497-541	
D305-14	CCK 0994	2725-34	8135-44	
D315-24	CCK 0994	2850-9		8145-54
D325-99	CCM 1115	3071-45	D621-95	

Length	69ft 6in
Width	9ft
Height	12ft 10 ⅜in
Weight	133 tons
Fuel tank capacity (gallons)	730
Wheel diameter	
Powered	3ft 9in
Non-powered	3ft 0in
Minimum curve radius (chains)	4½
Maximum speed (mph)	90
Engine	
EE 16SVT Mk II	
Engine output (bhp)	2,000 at 850rpm
Tractive effort (lb)	
Maximum	52,000
Continuous	30,900 at 18.8mph
Gear ratio	
61:19	

No D378 accelerates its train past Bushbury MPD during 1962.
Michael Mensing

Western Region requirement

Authors invariably claim that, initially, the BTC is reported only to have been willing to authorise the ordering of Type 4 diesel-hydraulics on condition that a private-sector manufacturer would carry out the work. NBL already had manufacturing rights for the German MAN engine, so submitted a tender, which resulted in the ordering on 16 November 1955 of Nos D600-04 as part of the Pilot Scheme. On learning what NBL proposed as a design, pressure by the WR finally saw the BTC relent in January 1956 and authorised Swindon Works to construct three locomotives. The BTC minutes, however, provide a different view because on 26 May 1955 it acceded to a WR request for the ordering of Maybach equipment to facilitate the building of three locomotives. Careful consideration, though, was to be given to publicising this. Clearly, the WR's plans were quite independent of what NBL was formulating.

The two designs could hardly have been more different, with the NBL offering using two MAN engines and Voith transmissions in a locomotive weighing 117 tons, whereas Nos D800-02 from Swindon used two Maybach engines and Mekydro transmissions in a locomotive that weighed 78½ tons.

Nos D800-02 were a direct derivative of German Federal Railways' V200 class and offered a high power-to-weight ratio in line with the WR's expectations for diesel-hydraulic

Classes 42 & 43

traction. To achieve this, the WR entered into a licence agreement with Krauss-Maffei (KM) for mechanical parts. Initially, however, it was agreed that the first six engine and transmission sets for three locomotives would be built by Maybach, with Swindon using Krauss drawings to produce a scaled-down V200 to fit the British loading gauge.

In order to advance dieselisation on the WR, a further batch of 30 machines (Nos D803-32) was authorised from Swindon (Lot number 437) on 28 February 1957. On 17 July 1958 a further 33 (Nos D833-65) of the same design were ordered from NBL under Swindon Lot number 443, NBL Order number L100; the manufacturer allocated Works Numbers from 27962 to 27994. Finally, on 9 April 1959 the BTC authorised Swindon to build an extra five (Nos D866-70) as Lot number 448 under the Bristol Area 2 dieselisation scheme at a cost of £560,000. Prior to the last-mentioned, the BTC Board minutes for the meeting held on 26 June 1958 refer with dismay to the rising cost of the

No D805 was less than a year old when caught in June 1959 at the head of the 7.55am Plymouth to Paddington service at Teignmouth. Note the WR-pattern three-character headcode and disc indicators. *David N. Clough*

This study of No D817 on 27 August 1962 is interesting in several respects. First, the locomotive has a four-character route indicator box, and is probably deputising for an unavailable Class 52, the class that had recently taken over passenger duties on the Paddington-Wolverhampton Low Level-Shrewsbury-Chester route. The train, the 2.10pm Paddington to Birkenhead, is approaching Wellington and has shed part of its consist at Wolverhampton, leaving just seven vehicles.
Michael Mensing

NBL order, commenting that it would not have been placed if this had been appreciated. The Board noted that NBL's costs had risen more steeply than Swindon's, the minutes quoting £1,615,950.

The engine used in all the Swindon-built Type 4s was the 12-cylinder 'V'-form Maybach MD650. In the Pilot Scheme series, this was rated at 1,035hp at 1,400rpm, but from No D803 the rating was raised to 1,135hp at 1,530rpm. There were four ranges in the transmission, with changes at 24, 40 and 67mph under full power. The slight increase in engine rating became possible because the Mekydro K104U transmission was revised in order to be capable of an input power of 1,035hp instead of 966hp. Maybach manufactured the engines, totalling 63, in order to provide three spares; ten were disassembled and shipped for assembly in the UK. Mekydro did the same with 63 transmissions. Each locomotive had two engine and transmission sets.

NBL's 33 locomotives, although based on the Swindon body design, were fitted with two MAN/Voith power trains in keeping with that company's licences, and the equipment was installed in its 117-ton Type 4s. The same uprated versions of engine and transmission were used as were being fitted to NBL's Type 2s, Nos D6306-57. Surprisingly, subtle differences existed between the MAN engines for the latter, so the nominally identical engines could not be used interchangeably between the two classes. Not only did the company have to learn the

difficulties of construction using the stressed-skin method, but it also had to arrange the Voith transmission for a 90mph top speed. The same basic transmission as that being fitted to its No D6300s was employed, which had three stages, but the Type 2s had only a 75mph top speed.

Swindon found translating the V200 bodyshell into a British size quite a challenge. Construction employed the stressed-skin technique, which made use of the body superstructure for load bearing; this reduced the amount of weight and was the fundamental difference between the Swindon design and NBL's Pilot Scheme offering at nearly 40 tons heavier. External styling won plaudits when compared to that of, for example, the purposeful noses of the Type 4 outputs from both BR's workshops and EE. Four-character route indicator panels were incorporated from new from No D813 onwards; the previous examples had three panels to match prevailing WR train numbering practice. In fact, other differences existed between locomotives up to No D812 and the remainder from Swindon, and at first the two could not operate in multiple.

Internally, each of the two engine and transmission sets was mounted symmetrically on either side of the centre point, with the train heat generator in between. The transmission output gears were on the bogie centre lines, which meant that the cardan shafts were short. Nos D803-12 and 866-70 were fitted with a Spanner Mark Ia train heat steam generator, Nos D813-17/19-65 had a Stone Vapor, while No D818 had a Spanner Mark IIIa.

The Krauss-Maffei bogie had been designed with no central pivot. Instead there was an arrangement of links, whose geometry was arranged to provide rotation about a virtual central pivot. The available space could thus be occupied by the intermediate gearbox cardan shafts to the final drive. In Germany, a line speed of 75mph caused no problem in ride quality, but in Britain 90mph running found the bogie wanting. The driving wheel diameter was a small 39½ inches. Not long after entry into traffic, ride quality was deemed dangerous at high speed and the whole class was restricted to 80mph in 1960, pending investigation. A redesign of the bogie solved the problem, and 90mph was reinstated as top speed in 1963.

Both the Swindon and NBL fleets used Brown Boveri electrical control gear, thus ensuring full flexibility in the multiple operation of locomotives, with the exception of the Pilot Scheme batch. Initial experience with the German V200 locos highlighted that six power notches on the driver's controller was insufficient. Thus, although the Pilot Scheme batch replicated early German design, Nos D803-32 had seven power notches. In fact, around 1962 engine rpm at each notch setting was also amended, so idling became 620rpm as against 600. From new, a seventh power notch was added to raise rpm to the revised upper limit of 1,530. The NBL MAN-engined fleet also had seven power notches, though the likelihood of engine overheating caused many drivers to avoid using the top position.

Nos D803-70 were assigned the White Diamond multiple-unit coupling code. Such operation was seldom used and over the years many locomotives had the external jumpers and cabling removed, having been the source of earth faults. In 1968 this equipment was reinstated on a number of the Swindon-built examples, including Nos D808/12/14/19/21-29/31/2/66-70.

Testing and later modifications

No D801 was put through controlled road trials and these confirmed the predicted performance curve. A maximum drawbar pull of 48,000lb was recorded at 7mph, while the continuous rating speed was determined to be 11.8mph, at which drawbar pull was 43,800lb. At the same speed the slightly more powerful No D803 series produced a pull of 45,000lb. Transmission efficiency peaked at a very good 82½ in each transmission range, while a theoretical maximum speed of 120mph meant efficiency remained high at the maximum permitted 90mph.

The results of these trials were used to construct revised schedules over all the principal routes. Among other things, it was found that a 'Warship' could maintain the 240-minute timing of the 'Riviera' with a 10-coach load. On the Birmingham road, an 11-coach consist was the limit on the 2-hour timetable, with the provision of a generous 12 minutes of recovery time. This led the WR to equate a 'Warship' to a 'Castle' class steam locomotive.

In its batch, NBL came up with a reasonable compromise to provide a suitable performance characteristic. With only three stages, transmission efficiency was high in the top range, but the low-speed characteristic was inferior to that of the Mekydro variant. Continuous rating was now at 14mph, with a drawbar pull at that speed of 37,000lb. Nevertheless, by about 18mph there was only a slight inferiority against the Mekydro-equipped locomotives. With new rolling stock having air, not vacuum, braking equipment, in 1968

The 'Warships' had a long association with cross-country services from the West of England to the North West and the Midlands. With the former, routing was via the Severn Tunnel and Hereford, with traction being changed at Shrewsbury or Hereford. In the case of the latter, the diesel-hydraulic would be replaced at Bristol. On 24 April 1964 No D860 passes Church Stretton with a Manchester to Plymouth service.
The late Derek Cross

From 6 September 1964 the 'Warships' displaced steam on the Waterloo to Exeter route, though only Class 42s were permitted to run east of Salisbury onto the SR. During July 1967 No D804 negotiates the flying junction at Worting, west of Basingstoke, with a down express. *David N. Clough*

consideration was given to fitting the No D800s with the capability to operate such trains. The sleek design, which had won praise back in the late 1950s, now backfired because there was insufficient space to accommodate the components. Another proposal to install electric train heating equipment also foundered. Some work was, however, carried out on No D870, including the fitting of jumper cables to connect to coaching stock.

The class had a complicated livery history. When new the locomotives were BR standard green; light grey was used for a horizontal line between the cabs at waist height, with mid grey for the removable roof panels. Red was chosen for the buffer-beams, with the underframes, bogies and drawhooks being black. Tyre sides and wheel hubs were polished. Cab fronts gradually sported yellow warning panels, then full yellow ends. In January 1962 No D845 and ex-works Nos D859-65 were observed with cab-front yellow warning panels, but of different styles. Thirty-two 'Warships', just under half the class, received maroon livery, which was applied by Swindon between September 1965 and October 1966. Eight failed to survive long enough to have Rail Blue applied.

All the production series locomotives carried Royal Navy warship names, and under the TOPS numbering system those from Swindon became Class 42, while those from NBL were Class 43.

Service experience

No D800 of the Pilot Scheme batch made its inaugural run on a service train on 15 July 1958 at the head of the down 'Cornish Riviera Express'. No D803, the first of the production series, emerged from Swindon in March 1959 and, like all the subsequent 'Warships', was allocated initially to Laira. This fulfilled the dieselisation plans for the Region, which were to start with the elimination of steam in Devon and Cornwall. Swindon continued seamlessly with its total of 35 units, until No D870 was accepted into traffic on 25 October 1961. The works took roughly a year to build each example and No D870 took around 400 days.

Meanwhile, NBL delivered No D833 on 6 July 1960, six months late, though it had made a light engine run from that company's works in Glasgow to Kilmarnock on 5 May. No D865, the last of the batch, entered traffic on 23 June 1962, though the order should have been completed the previous September. NBL reputedly took around half as much time as Swindon to build a locomotive. Trial running as far as Dumfries on the Glasgow & South Western line seems to have escaped a photographic record. While the Class 42s were only ever allocated to either Laira or Newton Abbot, many of the NBL Class 43s spent around a year at Old Oak Common during the late 1960s. Completion of the West Coast electrification brought a downgrading of the Paddington to Birmingham route, which thereafter only had a semi-fast timetable from 1967. Class 43s were assigned these diagrams and several class members were loaned to depots in the Birmingham area for crew training, including Bescot, Oxley and Tyseley. This use proved relatively short-lived, and the following year Class 47s were substituted. While at 'the Oak', diagrams on Worcester and Hereford services were added to the type's repertoire.

In addition to usurping steam on passenger turns between London and the West Country, the 'Warships' were soon deployed on the Bristol road. By 15 June 1959 there were sufficient Class 42s available for the 'Bristolian', the prestige service between the capital and Bristol, to be accelerated. When No D809 took the eight-coach train of 300 tons gross, Cecil J. Allen was aboard and was impressed with the run. By Southall speed had reached 80mph, before the slowing for bridge reconstruction at Hayes. Recovery to 92 beyond Maidenhead was cut short by observation of the 70mph restriction that applied at that time through Twyford. Beyond Reading speed settled to 86½ mph up the 1 in 754 between MPs 53½ and 70. Top speed was 95mph down Dauntsey Bank, and Temple Meads was reached in 93min 48sec, or 91 minutes net, an average of 78mph, against a schedule of 100 minutes.

In the up direction on the same day, No D804 had a coach less, so the booked load for the train was 260 tons gross. A log timed by Rev R. S. Haines showed the obvious superiority of the diesel-hydraulic over the classic steam performance by 'Castle' class No 7018 in falling from 50 to only 48mph on the 1 in 75 of Ashley Down bank, as opposed to a fall from 40 to 34 by the 4-6-0. Of course, the steam driver could not thrash his machine so soon from a cold start in order not to wreck the fire, a constraint not imposed on the diesel. Once on the South Wales main line at Stoke Gifford, No D804 pulled hard up the 1 in 300 grade to Badminton, topped at 77mph, whereas No 7018 had managed a very creditable 71. Two other contemporary runs with 'Warships' turned in the same speed at this summit.

Downgrade on the 1 in 300 to Little Somerford, the diesel-hydraulic touched 102mph, matched by the 'Castle'. Wootton Bassett Junction imposed a reduction to 60 on both trains, after which No D804 touched 102mph twice, whereas No 7018 (being driven against a 105-minute schedule and in standard fashion) attained 90. Passing Steventon in 47min 29sec, No D804 was 2 minutes up on schedule and 3½ minutes ahead of No 7018. This was just as well because it suffered a 15mph permanent way slack before Didcot, but recovered well to 95 by Goring. Two further slacks after Reading rather spoiled matters. Although the actual time was 92min 52sec, Mr Allen estimates a net time of just 87 minutes, an 81mph average. No 7018 ran unchecked throughout in 93min 50sec, probably a record for steam.

For several years the WR Civil Engineer had passed certain lengths of track for speeds 'as high as necessary'. The advent of the 'Warships', with exploits such as those just described, brought the imposition of a Region-wide 90mph ceiling.

In July 1960 Mr Allen published a contemporary journey on the down 'Riviera' when No D812 had the customary 10 coaches, grossing 370 tons. WR punctuality at the time was the worst of all the Regions, and it was

By the date of this picture, 20 June 1970, the Class 43 was very much in decline. No D866 has been rostered for this Newcastle to Penzance train at Sampford Peverell, near the current Tiverton Parkway station. *David N. Clough*

reported that drivers had failed to adjust their technique in the transition from steam to diesel. There were many instances when late-running trains were not being pushed at full power and a programme of training was implemented eventually to ensure drivers used all available locomotive power. On a steam engine the driver would have to take into account the strain imposed on the fireman in pushing his locomotive beyond its continuous capacity towards its upper limit.

On the trip with No D812, after the bridge slack at Hayes, the train attained nothing higher than 75mph before Reading, where it was more than 5 minutes late. At this juncture, of course, one has no idea of what events on the footplate might have brought this about. Possibly the locomotive was underperforming, possibly the driver knew he had sufficient opportunity to recover the loss without working his locomotive flat out. Nevertheless, the same driving style persisted, with only 75mph being attained on the long downgrade from Patney, and Heywood Road Junction was passed still 4 minutes late.

If the driver had been aiming for a gradual recovery of time, his plan was thwarted by a signal stop of more than 9 minutes at Charlton Mackrell, waiting for a freight to clear. Thus Taunton was reached in 150min 21sec, more than 14 minutes behind time. From 71½mph here, speed rose to 75mph at Norton Fitzwarren, thereafter falling steadily on the steepening climb to Whiteball to 44mph. A quick calculation points to this representing a normal full-power performance.

Interest now focused on performance over the South Devon banks, and on the climbs to both Dainton and Rattery Mr Allen noted slight slipping by the locomotive. Minima on the climbs were 24½ and 35½ mph respectively. Plymouth was finally reached in 249min 20sec, against a schedule of 240 minutes. Mr Allen estimated a net time of 221¼ minutes for the 225½ miles, whereas the schedule time net of recovery allowances was 230 minutes. No D812 therefore had plenty of time to spare on the prevailing schedule with a 10-coach load, the maximum that an 8P 'King' class 4-6-0 was allowed unassisted west of Newton Abbot.

Brian Basterfield logged Class 43 No D855 with an 11-coach train from Bristol to Exeter. On the level track before and after the call at Weston-super-Mare, 80mph appeared to be the balancing speed. Climbing from Taunton, 58mph was attained before steepening grades brought speed down to 41 at Whiteball, a comparable performance to that of No D812. In 1962 the same recorder timed No D825 on the 9.10am Liverpool to Plymouth train from Shrewsbury. 'Warships' had just replaced 'Castles' on these duties, and on top of the substantial 13-coach train of 480 tons the driver had to contend with a late start. Demonstrating both the generous scheduling and also the superiority of the diesel on prevailing steam timings, No D825 gained 14 minutes on the 74-minute booking to Hereford.

Comparing No D812's performance on the down 'Riviera' with a routine (rather than special) effort by a double-chimney 'King' class 4-6-0 on the same schedule showed diesel and steam to be evenly matched over a long run. Granted, the maximum output of an 8P 'King' was above that of a 2,200hp 'Warship', but such endeavours were short-term because of the limit of the fireman's ability to shovel coal at the required rate for long periods.

In 1969 David Adams timed No D816 on the 11.30 ex-Paddington, when the load was one coach less than on No D812's run. By now some of the permanent speed restrictions had been lifted or eased, notably that at Twyford. A signal check before Old Oak Common provided some impetus to the driver. Southall was passed at a very creditable 80mph, Slough at 93 and the ensuing level track saw a peak of 94. Even so,

No D807 would have given way to a diesel-electric at Temple Meads. It brings the 08.55 Newquay to Newcastle down Whiteball bank during June 1970. *David N. Clough*

arrival in Reading was 2 minutes behind time. Up the Kennet Valley speed was kept around 75mph before Newbury, with a subsequent 79 maximum before surmounting Savernake summit at 61. No restraint was shown downgrade towards Westbury, with 97mph (compared to 75 by No D812) before Heywood Road Junction. Arrival into Westbury was in 50min 15sec, less than a minute ahead on the net schedule. Nearly a minute was lost to Castle Cary, from where the driver went really hard to achieve an average of 86.4mph to Cogload Junction. This saw the Taunton stop reached in 39min 49sec, against the 39 minutes booked. One can only speculate that the schedule was for a 2,750hp Type 4 because No D816 certainly performed to a very high standard.

During 1968 the WR revised the West Country timetable, which was based on the deployment of two Class 42s working in multiple in order to accelerate the schedules. In addition to the principal named services, such as the 'Cornish Riviera Express', the diagrams also embraced the overnight sleeper workings. Invariably, a riding technician was aboard in order to monitor events in the engine room and address issues as they arose. By 1969, however, apart from the 'Cornish Riviera Express', double-heading was abandoned and 'Westerns'

were substituted on trains of shorter length. Drivers enjoyed the rapid acceleration and hill-climbing from a 4,470hp combination, however. The 1968 schedule for the down 'Riviera' came down to 3¾ hours for an 11-coach load and the inclusion of stops at Taunton and Exeter, while an extra 15 minutes was pared the following year by eliminating the call at Taunton.

From 1962 the 2,700hp 'Western' class began to appear and displace the 'Warships' on the premier duties. With deliveries of the more powerful design completed by the end of 1963, augmented by new BR/Brush Type 4s, the 'Warships' began to be redeployed. Starting on 5 March 1962 they displaced Newton Abbot 'Castles' on the through services between the West Country and the North West, taking the type to Shrewsbury and Crewe; these diagrams continued until May 1964, when South Wales-based Class 47s took over. Presaging this, on 26 February one of the type had taken the 8am Plymouth to Manchester train forward to Shrewsbury to start driver training. At the time, traction changes were invariably made at regional boundaries, such as Shrewsbury and (for trains from Birmingham) Bristol. Thus the 'Warships' were frequently allocated to cross-country trains from the West Country as far as Temple Meads.

This study of Class 42 No D866 illustrates well the essentials of the BR Blue colours, though there were variations in the style and location of numbers and emblems. The working is an empty stock service from Bristol to Paddington. *David N. Clough*

In 1963 regional boundary changes brought under WR control the former Southern Railway routes west of Salisbury to Plymouth and beyond. On 10 March 1964 No D827 performed a trial run between Exeter and Salisbury with a 12-car load. Subsequently, driver training of Southern crews commenced, so that 6 September witnessed a complete revamp of the Waterloo to Exeter route, with a 'Warship'-hauled 2-hourly semi-fast service replacing the previous steam-hauled timetable.

The Southern refused to have the less reliable Class 43s, and the Region's drivers were not trained on the variant. Additionally, No D830, which had twin Paxman engines in place of the Maybach type, was barred from the SR. Some commentators claim that No D818, with its different train heat generator, was also barred, but it was actually a very regular performer. If an NBL example was put on a Waterloo-bound duty, it was removed at Salisbury. Interestingly, the SR made liberal use of Class 42s on internal passenger and freight turns.

Use on freight trains started very gradually, not least because the low weight of around 80 tons meant the locomotives had inadequate brake force to cope with unfitted freights. Of course, the WR had envisaged that all services would be fully fitted, so a low locomotive weight would not be an issue. With more powerful Type 4s commandeering the top passenger turns as the 1960s wore on, so the 'Warships', notably the Class 43s, found greater employment on parcels and freight services.

Service experience and rundown

Regrettably, all the 'Warships' proved troublesome to a greater or lesser degree. Space does not permit a full exposition of the issues here, but in the drive train the cardan and dynostarter shafts failed frequently as a result of a flexible coupling failing. Both engine variants had weaknesses, and the electrical and control apparatus were a source of trouble.

The Maybachs suffered cylinder-head failures and cooling system problems. Being more complicated than the MAN units, they were also more difficult to maintain, which could have caused under-maintenance and contributed to the problems, certainly during the early years before depot staff gained a high level of competence.

The MAN engine was considered technically inferior, though simpler to maintain. As a matter of course, the sophisticated Maybach engines required pre-heating before starting; oil cooling

Of course freight activity comprised a fair proportion of the mileage of the class, especially latterly. No D859 bustles along the up slow line through Sonning Cutting trailing the Severn Tunnel Junction to Hither Green on 5 July 1970. *David N. Clough*

of the piston crowns necessitated the oil to be thin (warm) enough to pass through tiny passageways to avoid component damage. During the severe winter of 1962/3, the Maybach-engined locos were unable to be pre-heated, so had to be sidelined. The less-sophisticated MAN engines did not have pre-heaters, so the Class 43s were able to be turned out for traffic.

However, inadequate cylinder oil supply in the MAN variants caused piston overheating and failure, which is why drivers eventually opted not to use full power. As with the No D6300s, poor design of the exhaust system resulted in frequent leaks, which was reflected in a drop in turbocharger efficiency and meant fumes permeated everywhere, even into the driving cabs. Many photographs of a Class 43 at work bear testimony to the footplate crew having the cab windows open because otherwise the smoke choked their eyes and throats. In an attempt to improve matters, and with the Railway Technical Centre fully committed with resolving issues on other engines, in 1965 the British Internal Combustion Engine Research Institute was engaged to examine the MAN engines and propose improvements. By late 1967 a programme of work was put forward, but alas too late in the day.

Despite all the problems, availability during the mid-1960s was reasonable, even for the NBL batch, which was generally above 60% and superior to the 'Westerns'. Meanwhile the Class 42s achieved at least 70%. Typical annual mileages of between 80,000 and 100,000 compared very favourably with the BR Type 4 (Classes 45 and 46), and when No D800 was withdrawn in 1968 it had covered nearly one million miles in ten years. These figures support the component exchange maintenance philosophy of removing defective engine and transmissions for separate repair, keeping the locomotive in traffic by fitting an overhauled unit. Laira could achieve such a change in a day, which comprised three shifts.

The Pilot Scheme trio succumbed first in 1968 and several Class 43s were withdrawn the following year. Spare Type 4s on other regions in 1971 and 1972 enabled the whole class to be withdrawn, with all the Class 43s going first, while most of the Class 42s survived longer.

Final regular duties are reported to have centred on stone traffic from Merehead Quarry, and the last survivors were dispensed with in December 1972. No D832 was appropriated by the Railway Technical Centre and was reinstated for Departmental use during the 1970s before being sold for preservation. Another of the December 1972 casualties, No D821, also found its way into preservation.

Length	60ft
Width	8ft 10in
Height	12ft 10½ in
Weight	
Class 42	78½ tons
Class 43	80½ tons
Fuel tank capacity (gallons)	800
Wheel diameter	3ft 3½ in
Minimum curve radius (chains)	4½
Maximum speed (mph)	90
Engine	
Class 42	2 x Maybach MD650
Class 43	2 x MAN L12V18/21B
Engine output (bhp)	
Class 42	2 x 1,135hp at 1,530rpm
Class 43	2 x 1,100hp at 1,530rpm
Tractive effort (lb)	
Class 42	
Maximum	48,600
Continuous	46,900 at 11½mph
Class 43	
Maximum	49,030
Continuous	37,000 at 14mph

The diagrams quote a height of 13ft 0¾in over open ventilators.

BR Diagram bDH/4101/2 (the Spanner-boilered D803s) shows maximum tractive effort as 48,600lb, and continuous at 46,700lb at 10.7mph.

DH/4101/3 (the Stone Vapor-boilered D803s) shows maximum tractive effort as 48,200lb, and continuous at 46,700 at 10.7mph.

Class 44, 45 & 46

The Pilot Scheme order (Class 44)

It was natural that BR's workshops would be given an order within the Type C, later Type 4, category. Derby Works' drawing office had handled the design of the LMS prototypes Nos 10000-01, as well as the Fell locomotive No 10100, so it was sensible to assign design work on the new large diesel there as well. At that time the railway-owned works were under the control of the relevant Region, and J. F. Harrison was the CME of the LMR. Mr Harrison was of the view that the Sulzer LDA28 engine was superior in engineering quality to British builds and envisaged the LMR's diesel requirements being met by locomotives of two classes, one with a six-cylinder and one with a 12-cylinder engine.

The choice of prime mover for the Derby Type 4 was therefore the twin-bank Sulzer 12LDA28-A, rated at 2,300hp at 750rpm, and Crompton Parkinson (CP) was chosen for electrical equipment. The CP CG426A1 main generator, continuously rated at 1,546/1,531kW, 1610/2640A, 960/580V at 1,080rpm, was coupled to the engine output shaft, and the CP CAG252A1 auxiliary generator, unusually operating at 220V, was overhung from it. Six CP C171B1 traction motors continuously rated at 305hp, 440A, 580V at 450rpm were mounted on the three innermost axles on each bogie. Control gear was of Allen West manufacture. As with EE's Type 4, the choice of bogie fell on the one produced for the prototypes Nos 10201-3, of 1Co wheel arrangement, where the leading axle was unpowered.

Styling included the traditional nose ends, which had gangway doors, and a large bodyside grille provided engine room air. Subsequent to construction, the styling came in for a great deal of adverse criticism from within BR and its design consultant, the latter referring pointedly to Derby's lack of co-operation. One feature that irritated Chris Bond, the BRB's Chief Technical Officer, was the lack of a window in the cab doors. Livery followed standard practice, with a mid grey roof, standard Locomotive Green for the body, black for the undergear and red for the buffer-beams, which were mounted on the bogies. The cab handrails were polished aluminium at first, later light grey, and the latter colour was also used for the bodyside grille and for a stripe above solebar height, which extended along the body between the cab doors.

Assigned Nos D1-10, the doyen was exhibited at Marylebone station on 21 April 1959, but not taken into stock until 11 August. By this date EE had turned out 32 of its Type 4s, even though the initial orders had been placed by the BTC on the same date! No D10 represented the end of the Pilot Scheme order on 6 February 1960, concurrent with No D259, the 60th delivery from EE.

Names were applied, taken from mountains in the North of England and Wales, leading to the class being dubbed the 'Peaks'. The reign of the type, Class 44 under TOPS, on passenger work was short, because as soon as sufficient of the production series of both EE and Derby Type 4s were in traffic the Class 44s were downgraded to freight duties, operating off Toton, Nottingham. During these first few years, however, most of the mileage was accumulated on the WCML, not the Midland Main Line, as often reported. This utilisation was in line with the order being against dieselisation of LMR Area 8, the Western Lines. In fact, the class was a frequent visitor to Perth on both daytime and overnight trains coming off the Caledonian route.

Classes 45 and 46

Overall, the Class 44 was not particularly successful initially and modification to the traction motor gearing and field weakening was necessary, while reliability was indifferent. It is rumoured that the true locomotive weight was more than 140 tons, though this was never admitted officially. Nevertheless, as the BR design of Type 4 it was bound to be multiplied. The BTC minutes record approval on 8 January

1959 for an order to CP for 137 sets of electrical gear. This was also the date on which orders were placed with Derby and Crewe Works for Nos D11-147. On 17 December a further tranche was ordered, this time with Brush electrical equipment, because CP was fully committed supplying against orders for Types 2 and 3. The ordering and planned allocation of the 'Peaks' from No D11 onwards can best be summarised in the following table:

Nos D	Ordered	Works	Allocation
11-44	8.1.59	Derby	108 to
45-124	8.1.59	Crewe	Midland
			Lines, 6 to
			Longsight
125-137	8.1.59	Crewe	Camden
138-147	8.1.59	Derby	Camden
148-185	17.12.59	Derby	Edge Hill
186-199	17.12.59	Derby	Thornaby
1500-13	17.12.59	Derby	Thornaby

With only a handful of Class 44s in traffic, the BTC had sanctioned a total of 214 units, the largest commitment for any design at the time.

By the late 1950s Sulzer had developed its LDA28 diesel into its 'B' model, which incorporated a degree of charge-air cooling, thus lifting output to 2,500hp at 750rpm. BR wished to test this uprated version. No D2 had received an 'A' series engine (whether this was set at standard or the new higher rating is not known), but it seized during running within the Works' test house and was replaced with a 'B' series version from the order for the Class 45, set at 2,500hp. All this caused No D2 not to emerge until September 1959, so whether it was intended to be a prototype, or received the uprated engine by accident, cannot be determined. It was, however, derated officially from 23 February 1963.

Around May 1961 the order to CP was cut by ten to embrace locomotives up to No D137. For Nos D11-137, (Class 45) the same CP CG426A1 main generator was installed as in the Class 44. It was rated at 1,637/1,660kW (note that the ratings usually quoted are for the Class 44) and had a decompounding winding that prevented excessive currents being generated. The auxiliary generator was a CP CAG252A1 with a continuous rating of 90kW, 410A, 220V at 650rpm. Six CP C172A1 traction motors were provided with a continuous rating of 337hp, 445A, 615V at 660rpm. Motor gearing was always 62:17, unlike the Class 44, where it was regeared from 62:17 to 57:22. Full engine output was available between 12 and 82mph. Engine cooling was by Serck radiator panels, with the radiator fan powered by a roof-mounted CP electric motor. Train heating was from a Stone Vapor OK4625 generator.

By the time No D55, one of the final examples to be built, was ready to leave Crewe Works on 9 September 1962, the day before it was commissioned, the route indicator panels had migrated to sit side-by-side because nose-end doors had been dispensed with. A small warning panel was also added to the cab front. *John K. Morton*

Brush equipment in the Class 46s was substituted for that of CP. The Brush TG160-60 main generator was rated continuously at 1,650 kW, 2,100A, 785V at 1,080rpm, and overhung from this was a Brush TG69-28 auxiliary generator, rated at 47½ kW, 432A, 110V at 468-1,080rpm. Six Brush TM73-68 Mk III traction motors were fitted, each continuously rated at 331hp, 700A, 392V at 527rpm, with a gear ratio of 62:19. Full engine output was available between 11.2 and 85mph.

Two other technical differences between the 45s and 46s need to be mentioned. Unlike the other 'Peaks', Brush opted to drive the radiator fan by a hydrostatic arrangement. Unusually, the CP-equipped 'Peaks' had a 220V auxiliary power system, due to their having an electric radiator fan drive, but this was revised to the standard 110V supply in the Class 46s. Also different was the installation of a Spanner Mk IIA steam generator from No D166, which accounts for a slight difference in weight between Class 46 members. Another difference was that the power circuit was connected in series-parallel, unlike the all-parallel arrangement in the Class 44s and 45s.

At the end of 1960 the LMR changed its policy on the fitment of nose-end gangway doors and corridor connections being a requirement. This policy shift seems to have come about because the inter-locomotive connection facility was virtually never used, while on one occasion the connection tore during the negotiation of tight pointwork. Only Nos D11-15 had a full set of gangway equipment. Route indicator boxes or route indicator displays reflected the change of policy. On 19 May 1961 the CME responded to an enquiry by the Design Officer and set out the position as follows. Nos D11-30/68-107 were to have two two-digit boxes mounted on either side of the nose-end gangway doors, while, with the policy change, Nos D31-67/108 upwards were to have two two-character boxes situated centrally on the nose end. The reason given was that this gave the best outcome in relation to the delivery of boxes and the state of construction of nose fronts at the time it was decided to eliminate gangway doors. Finally, a single four-character box was fitted.

Distinguishing the two types of 2,500hp Derby Type 4s was not too easy at the start. One external difference was the shape of the battery box, which arose because the 110V control system of the Class 46 demanded fewer battery cells than the 220V system of the Class 45.

A number of both classes received regimental names, and their livery replicated that of the Class 44, except for the addition of small yellow warning panels during 1961. Among Derby-built examples, the addition of the yellow panel seems to have come at some point between Nos D42 and D49 and from about No D144, proving that the works was building both classes concurrently. At Crewe the panel was added between Nos D124 and D129. Sanding and multiple-unit operation equipment were included.

Neither the allocation of construction nor completed locomotives followed the plan outlined in the above table. To speed up production, Crewe built Nos D50-67 after completing its original allocation of Nos D68-137, and Derby assembled the remainder. Save for No D57, No D193 proved to be the last 'Peak' when it emerged in January 1963; the order was curtailed in order to use the remaining 20 sets of Brush equipment in Class 47s then under construction. No D57 was delayed because its engine was the 'C' variant of the 12LDA28, uprated to 2,750hp at 800rpm. Again, the idea was to use the locomotive to prove the modifications, but it was so delayed that the first Class 47s were nearing completion before No D57 turned a wheel. The locomotive entered traffic on 22 June 1963, having been reset to 2,500hp by Derby beforehand.

Service experience

Derby's No D11 went into traffic on 1 October 1960 for WCML duties, based at Willesden. Crewe wasn't far behind with its first output, No D68, which also went to the WCML five days later. Earlier in the year the BTC had announced that 38 of the class, Nos D148-85, would go to the ER, but almost coincident with the arrival of the first deliveries it was announced that the Region would instead receive the first of a new standard Type 4. A further change in planned allocations came at the start of 1961 when the LMR decided that Nos D68-82 would go to the former Midland routes instead of the WCML.

On being completed No D34 was despatched to Corkerhill shed, Glasgow, for training purposes. This involved trips to Ayr, from where it departs on 6 June 1961, in charge of a Glasgow-bound parcels train. *The late Derek Cross*

Planning for dieselisation of the Midland Division had commenced in 1957, and covered St Pancras to Carlisle (via Leeds) and Manchester Central, together with Derby to Bristol. Longer-distance service diagrams for all traffic were planned, and 122 Type 4s ordered. Of these, 22 were to be based at Leeds Holbeck and 10 at Bristol.

The first four diagrams were to be between St Pancras and Manchester Central with effect from 16 January 1961, extended from 6 February by five more turns between London, Manchester Central and Leeds, with one locomotive based at Holbeck. By 17 April deliveries facilitated 23 diagrams.

Early experience showed excellent timekeeping by the diesels on existing schedules and led to re-prioritisation of the transition from steam. Instead of putting diesels onto fast freights out of London, in conjunction with the WR, the elimination of steam was agreed between Derby and Bristol. However, inauguration of the diesel diagrams on 8 May had to be deferred due to the WR not having sufficient trained crews. Extension to the NER was also complicated because York and Gateshead crews were being trained on Class 40s and 55s at the time.

Through working from Leeds to Carlisle and Glasgow/Edinburgh was delayed because gauge clearance of the Class 45s had not yet been granted, while training of sufficient Edinburgh staff was also an issue. The Summer 1961 timetable was confined to through Leeds to Glasgow runs, as well as extension of Bristol to Derby diagrams to Sheffield and York. On 3 July, however, operation commenced between Leeds, Glasgow or Edinburgh with the daytime trains, and the 'Devonian' between Leeds and Bristol, together with other services on the latter route. With effect from the Winter 1961 timetable, from 11 September, through Bristol to Newcastle locomotive running commenced for the first time, by which date there were 59 Class 45 turns, divided between the LMR (32), NER (19) and WR (8). Sufficient power was to hand to permit fitted freights between Birmingham and Bristol to go over to Class 45 operation.

The foregoing shows that eliminating steam on Class 1 duties robbed freight

The Class 45s quickly began a long association with the routes of the former Midland Railway and its satellite, the Glasgow & South Western. On 29 May 1967, two years after being named, No D99 passes Kibworth North, north of Market Harborough, on a Leeds to St Pancras duty. *J. H. Cooper-Smith*

The Bristol-Derby-York axis quickly witnessed Class 45 power. In this instance, however, No D131 would have come on to the northbound 'Pines Express' at Bath Green Park, as the Bournemouth to Manchester through service reversed direction there. Kings Norton, in Birmingham's south-west suburbs, has changed since this March 1962 photo.
David N. Clough

operators of the use of Type 4 resources. In 1961 Class 45s had taken over some Anglo-Scottish services, working throughout on the Harpenden to Greenhill car carrier and the 'Condor' Cricklewood to Gushetfaulds mini-container services.

Dynamometer tests with No D13 established that the design was well suited to freight use. Conducted during February 1961 over the former GN route from Woodhouse Junction to Ulceby on unfitted, partially fitted and fully fitted freights, weighing up to 1,528 tons, the maximum tractive effort recorded was 65,000lb, well above the nominal maximum of 55,000lb quoted officially. The Derby Type 4s were not only participating in the dawn of long through inter-regional locomotive running: on 4 June 1962 No D108 worked a special 1,300-ton test train of steel ingots, with dynamometer car, between Darlington and Severn Tunnel Junction, as a trial first through diesel working.

Around May 1961 it was announced that the order for the Class 45 was to be cut by ten, while an undated decision was made to curtail Class 46 production at No D193. The 20 sets of Brush electrical equipment would be used instead in the proposed new standard Type 4, which was being designed by BR and Brush. Why more Class 46s were not cancelled is unclear, because the last few did not emerge

until January 1963, by which time the first half-dozen Class 47s were already in traffic. A visitor to Derby Works during late May 1961 found Nos D34-44 in various stages of construction, but also No D138, the first Class 46; this was waiting for equipment from Brush and was to serve as a test bed to prove the electrical machines, ahead of the squadron production of Class 46.

No doubt suitably 'fixed' to ensure that a product of a BR workshop was involved, on 20 June 1961 No D34 became the 1,000th main-line diesel. Nevertheless, the class was far from a shining example, suffering poor availability caused by fracturing of the fabricated water tanks and traction motor flashovers, probably due to running at well above the official 90mph maximum.

Three further dynamometer car trials are worthy of mention. On 20 and 21 September 1961 No D40 was used to assess Type 4 capabilities on the Lickey Incline. A 16-car train was restarted successfully, while runs were also made with freight stock. The upshot was that a Type 4 with up to 12 coaches was no longer required to stop for banking assistance.

Although the ER had spurned the 'Peaks', on 4 November 1961 D29 of Holbeck appeared on the 5.25pm Leeds to King's Cross service. Later that month No D25 was noted on a

10-coach train with a dynamometer car to assess whether the type could match Class 55 timings on the fastest duties in emergencies, and No D154 ran trials for the same purpose during February 1962. The ECML Summer 1963 timetable included 'Peak' diagrams as Class 40s were displaced.

Whereas the Class 45s were always really Midland Division engines, the Class 46s were shared by three Regions during the 1960s. Nos D138-165 went to MML depots but, as the decade grew to a close, the LMR rid itself of the type, mainly to the WR as replacements for the 'Warships'. Meanwhile, Nos D166-93 enjoyed a long association with Gateshead, whence diagrams took them to the West Country, King's Cross, Liverpool and, for a time, Inverness on the car/sleeper service from York.

There is no doubt that the 2,500hp 'Peaks' were markedly superior to the EE Type 4s in terms of road performance. On the MML they

eclipsed everything that had gone before in terms of hill-climbing and sustained running at 90mph. On 1 in 200 gradients, minima of 74-75mph were achieved with up to 385 tons. The challenging 1 in 100 grades of the Settle & Carlisle route also presented no problems; hauling a typical nine coaches, it was not unknown for Ais Gill to be cleared southbound at 61mph. Runs on the WCML have proved elusive, save for No D2, while rated at 2,500hp; on a run up from Carlisle with a 12-coach consist, the initial acceleration to Southwaite appeared laboured. Thereafter the locomotive really got going and peaked at 72mph before Penrith, a rate that would not have disgraced a 2,700hp Class 50.

Technical problems

Some of the in-service issues have already been touched on. In August 1963 Freddie Harrison, then Chief Technical Officer to the BRB,

The Class 46 was, for most of its life, mainly assigned to the Eastern and North Eastern Regions, though the Western took an allocation on the withdrawal of its 'Warships'. On 8 August 1964 No D192 eases the Edinburgh to King's Cross car carrier into Newcastle.
J. S. Hancock

Class 46s displaced Class 40s on the Newcastle to Liverpool turns from the Winter 1962 timetable, commencing on 11 September. By 15 April 1967 the Micklehurst Loop between Diggle Junction and Stalybridge had closed, as evidenced by the removal of the signal arms controlling movements off the line. No D183 approaches Diggle Junction box with a Newcastle-bound express.
J. S. Hancock

Coincidentally on the same day as the picture of No D183, No D169 prepares to depart from Leeds Central with the up 'Yorkshire Pullman'. Note the application of blue livery and the addition of the small bodyside grille during refurbishment.
Gavin Morrison

presented a report on the reasons for poor availability in the main-line diesel fleet. Whereas on 3 November 1962 (when not all the 'Peaks' had been built) Sulzer Type 4 availability was 69%, by 15 June 1963 this had dropped to 64%. By comparison, the EE Type 4 achieved 77% and 78% respectively. Mr Harrison commented that, while initial experience had been satisfactory, save for attention to turbocharger blade failures and cracked water tanks, two new problems began to emerge. The turbo-blade issue was resolved by lacing the blades with damping wire, though this campaign change took 18 months to complete.

With the majority of the 'Peaks' based on the LMR, cylinder liner wear began to appear, which was traced to the LMR (unlike other Regions) not adopting proper coolant water treatment. Additionally, high crankcase pressures were observed, and this was diagnosed to a failure to change engine oil sufficiently frequently, while the suitability of the BR standard lubricating oil was called into question. A programme of engine top-end

overhauls was put in place, though interestingly it seems that BR shops could not conduct a complete overhaul at that time and engines were being sent to Vickers Armstrong at Barrow, Sulzer's UK licensee, for repairs. In consequence, the LMR cut daily diagrams to 50% of its fleet.

Engine seizures began to affect all three types of the 'Peaks' during the early years, remedied by improvement to the lubrication of the synchronising gears that linked the crankshafts from each of the two cylinder banks to the drive output shaft. Within 18 months of Mr Harrison's submission to the Board, fatigue cracks began to appear in the engine block and sump in a number of Sulzer-engined Type 4s of all classes. Rephasing the crankshaft and also adding extra balance weights to the shaft solved the problem, with no need for derating of the engine output of the 'Peaks'.

It is clear that the 2,500hp BR Sulzers had a significant number of design defects, albeit generally minor, that could impact on reliability. Thus as early as 1965 a refurbishment and modification programme for the Class 46 was implemented, encompassing some 200 modifications. To provide continuity of work at Falcon Works on completion of Class 47 construction, Brush negotiated a four-year contract for Sulzer-fitted locomotive overhauls, and Class 46s were dealt with under this arrangement, together with some Class 45s. The remainder of the Class 45s, starting with No D60, were refurbished at Derby, commencing in 1967. During the programme a small grille was added to the Class 46s below the main bodyside grille, and this distinguished the two types. In order to cut down on engine room dirt, filters were added on the inside of all the bodyside grilles.

In summary, the 1960s was not a good decade for the Derby Type 4s, when they showed up as inferior in terms of both availability and reliability compared with their EE equivalents. Nevertheless, the 2,500hp 'Peaks' had a profound impact on services during the decade. Implementation of long-distance passenger and freight diagrams across routes from St Pancras to Glasgow and Bristol to Newcastle fell on their shoulders, and the extra power they provided put them in a different league from the steam motive power they displaced. With the major issues resolved, the stage was set for a successful future into the 1970s.

Length	67ft 11in
Width	9 ft 1⁹⁄₁₆ in
Height	12ft 10½ in
Weight	
Class 45	135 tons 17 cwt
Class 46	137 tons 9 cwt*
Fuel tank capacity (gallons)	840
Wheel diameter	
Powered	3ft 9in
Non-powered	3ft 0in
Minimum curve radius (chains)	5 (original)
Maximum speed (mph)	90

Engine
Sulzer 12LDA28B

Engine output (bhp)	2,500 at 750rpm

Tractive effort (lb)

Maximum	55,000
Continuous	
Class 45	30,000 at 25mph
Class 46	31,600 at 23.3mph*

Gear ratio

Class 45	62:17
Class 46	62:19

* *The BR Operating Manual gives 34,080lb at 21.6mph continuous tractive effort and 138 tons 13 cwt (Nos D138-165) or 138 tons 11 cwt (Nos D166-193) maximum weight.*

Class 47

At the BTC meeting on 11 February 1960 the Technical Officer, Traction & Rolling Stock, R. C. Bond, explained the reasons for inviting new designs and tenders for the Type 4. The BTC approved the recommendation, on the understanding that all Type 4s to the new design would be equipped with engines (English Electric or Sulzer) of 2,500hp, as Type 4s of 2,000hp were not a type on which it was intended to standardise. This appears to be the sanction for inviting the railway industry to produce new designs for evaluation as the future standard Type 4, with a technical specification (DE/M/5) provided for guidance. It prompted the production of *Falcon* by Brush, *Lion* by BRCW/AEI/Sulzer and 'DP2' by EE.

The BTC minutes are then silent on the placing of any orders for Type 4 until 21 December 1961.

In late 1960 a number series of D1200-59 for a new design of Type 4 was announced, while the ER stated that it would receive these and would not now take the BR/Sulzer 2,500hp Type 4 Nos D148-85 (later Class 46). Eventually, however, the allocated number series began at D1500, possibly because the WR was still planning to build several hundred of its 2,700hp diesel-hydraulic Type 4s.

Following a tendering process that involved NBL, EE, BRCW and Brush, on 28 February 1961 the latter was awarded a contract to build twenty examples of the new design.

This was kept very quiet because BR declined to comment about press speculation at the time.

By May 1961 the bodyshell for No D138, the first of the BR/Sulzer Type 4s to be fitted with Brush electrical equipment, as opposed to the machines of CP manufacture fitted to Nos D1-137, was complete. This was well ahead of numerical sequence, as the works was still constructing Nos D34-44, but this locomotive was required as early as possible in order to assess

First-series No D1505 was reputedly the first Class 47 to visit the Leeds area, where it was used for training. It is stabled at Neville Hill on Sunday 24 March 1963, when it would have been in original livery. *Gavin Morrison*

Perhaps the route most synonymous with the class during the 1960s was the ECML. No D1771's driver is keen to be part of the picture as his train eases round the tight curve at Retford with the down 'Sheffield Pullman' from King's Cross on 14 June 1965. *J. S. Hancock*

the Brush equipment ahead of its application in the new standard Type 4. There was still no official announcement about the project, however.

The CME wrote to George Williams, BR's Director of Industrial Design, on 24 April as follows:

'An order has now been placed for 20 *2,750hp* Type 4 Brush. Except for a slight difference in length, these locomotives will externally be very similar to *Falcon*, which they are already building at their own expense and to your designs. In view of the short delivery period already agreed for *Falcon*, it should apply to these as well.'

On 9 May Mr Williams commissioned Wilkes & Ashmore to advise on the styling of the new design.

Just how BR viewed the private-sector prototypes can be judged from the content of a letter from Ted Wilkes to George Williams concerning *Falcon*, written on 16 October 1961:

'Everyone concerned felt that BR were not interested in this loco. It was a private enterprise project by Brush. In our case, Brush have commissioned all our work and paid for everything. Consequently because Brush, and not BTC, were our clients, we have to be careful not to get

mixed with BTC over our design recommendations to Brush. They have been so co-operative that we have been able to impart the BTC point of view without it appearing to be BTC's instructions.'

Nevertheless, Mr Wilkes was also commissioned by BRCW to assist with the styling on *Lion*, and the same letter from Wilkes to Williams makes it clear that the writer had to tread a delicate path because of being engaged by BTC as well. It was therefore unsurprising that there were strong similarities between the external appearance of *Falcon*, *Lion* and the new standard Type 4, which became Class 47 under TOPS. Bear in mind also that Mr Wilkes had also schemed out the external styling for the Class 35 'Hymeks' and note the 'family' resemblance.

A photograph in the National Archives' files of a Bedford 'E' Series van was used to illustrate Mr Wilkes's ideas for the styling of the class. However, as was so often the case, engineering considerations overrode aesthetics. In January 1963 Mr Wilkes expressed his views: 'In our experience the setbacks have been … Brush Type 4, where engineering and dimensional requirements proved unusually awkward.' He elaborated:

'The appearance on the Brush Type 4 cab floor windows is lower. The Brush Type 4

From January 1964 the class took over on the Wolverhampton Low Level to Paddington route at the LMR's behest. No D1685 passes Hatton during the summer of 1964 with the 2.10pm to Paddington. *David Adams*

has a double disadvantage of a roof that is 6 inches deeper and 25 inches shorter than the *Falcon*, and this is the main reason for the failure to match up to the *Falcon*'s appearance. The value of the yellow warning patch cannot be denied and the first loco was the Brush Type 4. A yellow patch and broad green band were considered together and are a marked improvement, but it makes it appear very narrow at the front end.'

In other correspondence Mr Wilkes expresses a preference for the appearance of the 'Hymeks' over *Falcon*.

Some confusion appears to have crept into other writings about how these prototypes influenced the design of the standard Type 4. In fact, design development of these four offerings was concurrent, rather than consecutive, with both *Falcon* and No D138 emerging during October 1961, *Lion* (the BRCW prototype) and 'DP2' (from EE) in May 1962 and the first Brush/Sulzer in September of that year.

As noted in the section covering the 'Peaks', during construction of those locomotives Sulzer had developed its 12LDA28 engine to enable it to produce 2,750hp at 800rpm – the 'C' version. Essentially, the extra 10% output over the 'B' version was achieved by an increase in maximum engine rpm, backed up by larger intercoolers, strengthened connecting rods and piston assemblies, and a modified water-cooling circuit. The crankshafts from the two cylinder banks drove an output shaft that was geared at 1:1.44, giving a maximum rpm of 1,152 when the engine crankshaft rpm was 800.

Although nominally a 'standard' design, gradually changes were made so that there were a considerable number of variations within the fleet. Three major variations came to exist in terms of the electrical equipment. BR decided to cancel construction of the last 20 Class 46s (allocated numbers D194-9 and D1500-13), which had been ordered in 1959 as part of the series commencing at No D148, and decided to use the Brush electrical equipment instead in the new Type 4, a decision that led some to dub the pilot order as the '46½s'. In fact, the generator set was different from that in the Class 46 because the frame incorporated a train heat generator, though this applied only to the initial order, Nos D1500-19.

For the remainder, there were differences in the equipment, dependent on whether the traction motors were connected in series-parallel or all-parallel across the main generator. The generally accepted view is that using an all-parallel motor configuration offers better suppression of wheelslip, but means that the main generator has to be larger to cope with current at double the value encountered in the series-parallel locomotives. The following summarises the electrical machine data for an engine rating of 2,750hp:

Series-parallel locomotives Nos D1500-19

Main generator

Frame size	TG 160-60 Mk 2 8-pole
Continuous rating	1,798kW, 2,130A, 844V at 1,150rpm

Auxiliary generator

Frame size	TG 69-16 Mark 1 6-pole
Continuous rating	26.4kW, 240A, 110V at 1,150rpm

Train heating generator

Frame size	TG 160-16 Mark 1 8-pole
Continuous rating	320kW, 400A, 800V at 690-1,150rpm

Traction motors (6)

Frame size	TM 64-68 Mark 1 4-pole
Continuous rating	368hp (274kW), 710A, 422V at 776rpm

**Series-parallel locomotives
Nos D1520-74, D1682-1701/07-14**

Main generator

Frame size	TG 160-60 Mark 4 8-pole
Continuous rating	1,798kW, 2,130A, 844V at 1,150rpm

Auxiliary generator

Frame size	TG 69-28 Mark 3 6-pole
Continuous rating	55kW, 500A, 110V at 1,150rpm

Traction motors (6)

Frame size	TM 64-68 Mk 1A or 1B* 4-pole
Continuous rating	368hp (274kW), 710A, 422V at 776rpm

Newton Bros wheelslip detection inductor alternator

Type F.793 65VA, 155V, 0.8 PF, 180-440Hz

* *The Mk 1B motor differed in that the bracket carrying the pick-up for the Western Region AWS equipment was mounted on the motor frame.*

**All-parallel locomotives
Nos D1575-1681, D1715-1999, D1100-11**

Main generator

Frame size	TG 172-50 Mark 1 12-pole
Continuous rating	1,805kW, 4,260A, 423V at 1,150rpm

Auxiliary generator

Frame size	TG 69-20 Mark 1 and Mark 1A 6-pole
Continuous rating	50kW, 455A, 110V at 1,150rpm

Traction motors (6)

	50kW, 455A, 110V at 1,150rpm

Exciter inductor alternator

	Type HFA 4/15
Continuous output	4.2kVA, 150V, 517Hz at 1,150rpm

Class 47s had radiator panels mounted above the cantrails, and so were more susceptible to freezing conditions than other designs. The remedy was to fit shutters on the air intakes to the radiators, and this was also a major cosmetic change. These shutters were thermostatically controlled and hydrostatically operated, except on Nos D1500-19, which had no hydrostatic pump; their shutters were operated by an air cylinder supplied from the control air reservoir.

Significant changes were made to the design during construction, and the following table sets these out:

From **No D1529**	Omission of ETH and change of brake equipment. Introduction of revised cooling arrangements in consequence, featuring Serck-Behr hydrostatic cooling fan drive
From **No D1682**	Change in axle design
From **No D1715**	Change from series-parallel to all-parallel connected traction motors, to improve reliability and reduce maintenance
Nos **D1631-81** and from **No D1758**	Dual train brake equipment
From **No D1782**	Introduction of 'Universal' boiler compartment enabling any one of three makes of boiler to be fitted
Nos **D1520-1841**	Electro-pneumatic starting contactors
From **No D1842**	Electro-magnetic starting contactors
From **No D1862**	'Static' field divert control
Nos **D1758-1856, D1862-1920, D1977-99/1100**	Slow Speed Control (ssc); Nos D1894-1897 had automatic ssc
Nos **D1913-51, D1962-1111**	'Static' AVRs
No D1880	Sulzer 'static' engine governor coupled with 'static' load regulator

The 'Peaks' used a traditional strength underframe, and to ensure an acceptable route availability the weight of some 135 tons was carried on two 1Co bogies. Part of the saving in weight achieved by the D800-series 'Warships' came from the use of stressed-skin body construction techniques, as used in aircraft, with the locomotive superstructure being load-bearing. This method of construction had been followed by Brush in *Falcon* and was also used in the new Type 4. In consequence, a three-axle bogie could be used, with each axle powered, and these factors combined to give an overall weight of around 117 tons. A Commonwealth-pattern bogie was used.

Developments in traffic requirements and technology occasioned a number of changes and trial fitments. Selective fitment of train air brake equipment was prompted by the start of liner trains, though, short-sightedly, all builds from 1965 were not so equipped, bringing costly retro-fitting later. Electronics ('static' devices) began to be used within the control system; during the 1960s such components were used for slow speed (later automatic slow speed) control, field divert control and for automatic voltage regulators.

As built, only Nos D1500-19 were able to supply both steam and electric train heating. To ensure a regular loading on the train heat generator, it was used additionally to power the radiator fan drive. The two traction motor blower motors were also supplied from the ETH generator, and were in series. By these means it was ensured that the ETH generator would not lose its commutator skin during the anticipated

long periods of otherwise no-load running.

Other class members did not have this generator, so a hydrostatic radiator fan drive was employed. Not all the locomotives were built with a train heating capability; so far as can be determined now, Nos D1782-1836/1875-1900 were not fitted from new, while those that were had a Spanner Swirlyflow Mk III steam generator. As noted above, the compartment for this equipment was redesigned on later builds to accept other manufacturers' generators, and TOPS records show the fitment of Clayton Mk II and Stone Vapor 3625 alternatives.

Passing mention must be made here of the use of a Sulzer 12LVA24 engine in the last of a batch of locomotives ordered in September 1962. These five examples, Nos D1702-6, were classified as Class 48 under TOPS and were test bed machines, produced to evaluate the new engine. A description of this development can be found in *Diesel Pioneers*.

The choice of livery was, no doubt, the source of much debate. Earlier sections of this book have reported on the differing views of senior officers. Freddie Harrison favoured a stripe along the lower part of the bodyside to relieve the Locomotive Green. The green/yellow (BR's description of the colour) used for the lower bodyside on Classes 35 and 55 did not find universal favour, not least because it dirtied quickly with brake block dust. In the event, the Class 47 was blessed with what many regard as the smartest colour scheme of any BR diesel

class, using Locomotive Green but broken on the bodyside by the use of a band of Sherwood Green, a colour that preservationists have found difficult to replicate faithfully in recent years. In 1964, when the planned Rail Blue livery was to be exhibited for the first time, No D1733 was selected for repaint.

Even before any locomotives had been built, the Works & Supply Committee recommended the ordering of further batches. Although each order was tendered competitively for what Brush wanted to be known as the Hawker Siddeley Type 4, it was Brush and BR's Crewe Works whose bids were accepted until the fleet size reached 512. Order details are as follows.

Date	Builder/Order Number	Construction Numbers	Loco Numbers
26 February 1961	Brush 04/47500	342-361	D1500-19
1 January 1962	Brush 04/47800	413-442	D1520-49
1 January 1962	Crewe/301		D1550-82
4 September 1962	Crewe/400		D1583-1661
4 September 1962	Brush 04/48100	444-468	D1682-1706
4 September 1962	Brush 04/48300	469-543	D1707-81
22 July 1963	Brush 04/48900	544-603	D1782-1841
22 July 1963	Crewe/400		D1842-61
24 March 1964	Brush 04/49000	624-709; 610-623 respectively	D1862-1961
24 March 1964	Crewe/400		D1962-91
July 1964*	Crewe/400		D1992-99/ 1100-11

* Date approved by BRB

Before the advent of the Class 50, the Brush/Sulzer Type 4 held sway on WCML front-line duties north of Weaver Junction from 1965. On 6 April 1968 No 1959 powers the 13.05 Euston to Blackpool round the curve at Winwick Junction, hard by Vulcan Foundry. *J. S. Hancock*

Examining the BTC and BRB minutes sheds some light on the procurement process. On 21 December 1961 the Technical Officer reported the acceptance of Brush's tender for supply of 30 Type 4s at a current price of £111,750 each (excluding train heating) and subject to price variation. In addition, an order was to be placed with Crewe Works for 33 Type 4s to the Brush design of mechanical parts, the choice of power equipment to be decided after competitive tenders had been received. He added that every effort must be made from design onwards to reduce teething problems, as in the past. This statement was surely going to haunt him for the next few years.

On 12 July 1962 the minutes record dissent among the Regions as to the relative merits of Type 3 versus Type 4, but approval was given for 99 locomotives from Crewe at £105,239 and 100 from Brush at £108,850 each. The next orders came in May 1963, with 20 for Crewe at £108,700 and 60 for Brush at £110,344 each; one source claims the 20 for Crewe were switched from Brush, but the BRB minutes do not reflect this. On 12 March 1964 further authorisation came for 50 from Crewe at £113,543 and 100 from Brush at £114,783 each; Crewe's order was subsequently limited to 30 and the remaining 20 deferred, but the full quantity was agreed on 23 July.

All Regions received allocations, but neither the SR nor the ScR got new examples, though the latter *was* due to receive nine from Crewe, based on the December 1964 planning document. Problems with Class 52s led the WR to request the reallocation of Nos D1500-19, once the ER received Nos D1520 upwards.

Naming locomotives fell out of favour as the 1960s progressed, but in 1965 the WR obtained authority to adorn 17 of its fleet, some honouring past Great Western Railway luminaries or locomotives, others honouring figures from mythology. Prior to receiving its first allocation of Class 47s, on 18 April 1963, Stanley Raymond, the WR's General Manager, wrote to Freddie Harrison and George Williams about the proposed livery. He said that the Region had recently adopted maroon for its locomotives and wanted the Class 47s to appear thus too. Mr Harrison responded quickly to say that he could trace no authority for the choice of maroon for the WR's diesel fleet and that the Director of Industrial Design was not in favour of the colour.

Until completion of the Bournemouth electrification in 1967, a few Class 47s were drafted to the SR to assist the Bulleid 'Pacifics' as these became overdue for works attention. No D1926 brings the 'Bournemouth Belle' through Winchfield on 1 July 1967. *J. S. Hancock*

Later, the need for agreement among senior personnel caused a blip in the introduction of the Rail Blue livery. On 20 January 1967 No D1958 was inspected in this guise at Derby Works and three days later the Director of Industrial Design wrote to the Chief Engineer (Traction & Rolling Stock) in approving tones, but also commented thus:

'It would be preferable if in future these locos carry a 2ft rather than 2ft 6in symbol. The latter looks too large for the space under the cab window, and neater to use smaller size.'

The following day the Chief Engineer wrote to the Mechanical Engineer Design, Derby, to confirm that the Director of Industrial Design had signed off on the livery, which had already been applied to several examples, and henceforth the scheme should be applied universally to the class.

Crewe's last locomotive, No D1111, entered service on 18 February 1967. Final deliveries from Brush were widely spaced, No D1959 entering service on 4 February 1967 and No D1960 on 11 July; finally, No D1961 went initially to Derby Research Centre from 20 January until 3 April 1968, in connection with the fitting of ETH equipment, as new rolling stock was being heated in this way. The new scheme bore no resemblance to the DC scheme used in Nos D1500-19 as it employed a dual-wound 3-phase brushless alternator and accompanying rectifiers. A new ETH/auxiliary machine included a winding to supply the 110V auxiliary machines and to charge the batteries. Voltage regulation was on this auxiliary winding, so train supply voltage could vary significantly. Consequently, the old DC auxiliary generator was eliminated. Details of this machine are as follows:

Class 47s also worked onto the SR on inter-regional expresses. The 'Pines Express' from Manchester enters Parkestone on 29 July 1966 behind No D1692. *Gavin Morrison*

It was finally decided that the diesel engine idling speed would be permanently elevated from 325rpm to around 385rpm, irrespective of whether ETH was on or off. The scheme was adopted for a programme that saw an increasing number of the fleet converted over the years as train steam heating was eliminated.

Into service

On 6 September 1962 No D1500 was sent to Crewe for weighing; it was taken into stock on the 28th and spent time at Finsbury Park for training purposes. When built, No D1502 went to Gateshead for the same purpose, and thus a very long association between the class and the ECML passenger diagrams began. During October No D1500 worked a 385-ton train between King's Cross and Doncaster on a 2hr 20min schedule before going to the WR at the beginning of November, where it was put on the usual Swindon trial diagram of the 6.35am Cheltenham to Paddington train, but then went back to the ER.

Frame size BL 100-30 Mark I 16-pole

Continuous ratings, AC side

300/65kW, 328/73kVA, 0.91/0.89PF, 700/88V line, 270/480A line, 470rpm, 62.6Hz

300/65kW, 320/71kVA, 0.93/0.92PF, 650/85V line, 285/480A line, 1,150rpm, 153.3Hz

DC continuous rating 'through the rectifier'

300/65kW, 353/590A, 850/110V, 470/1,150rpm

Back on Western metals on 5 January 1963, full dynamometer car trials were conducted. The routes selected included both the South Devon banks and the Lickey Incline; a 571-ton train was started on Dainton's 1 in 38, while a restart was managed on the 1 in 37¾ of the Lickey with 637 tons trailing. The trials established a maximum tractive effort of 71,700lb, though the value usually quoted in official rating data is 55,000. Transmission efficiency was excellent at 82%, with 2,250 rail horsepower being maintained between 30 and 80mph, the latter being the main generator unloading point.

Subsequently, trials were carried out on the ER with freight rolling stock. Among these was the use of No D1513 on 28 March 1963 in the Scunthorpe area, as a prelude to the use of the class on activity associated with steel production. At the head of a 1,500-ton consist of iron-ore wagons, the train was restarted on the 1 in 96 grade near Appleby, producing a wheel-rim tractive effort of 70,000lb. The Class 47s offered a marked improvement over the prevailing steam power, and the limiting factor became the ability to brake trains on downgrades, rather than haul them uphill. In fact, a significant amount of mileage by the ER's fleet was run on non-passenger services, though it went largely unreported; for example, on 23 May 1963 No D1503 was noted at York on an empty fish train.

The trials with No D1513 brought the introduction of, for the era, complex diagrams associated with the production of steel. Before

Tinsley Depot was opened, Wath shed was involved in these, and a sample Class 47 turn from 1963 illustrates train operation between High Dyke (Highdyke in railway use, the start of an ironstone branch south of Grantham), Frodingham (for the Scunthorpe steel complex) and the major yard at Colwick (near Nottingham):

Depart	Service	Arr
02.35	Wath-Frodingham	04.30
05.54	Frodingham-Barnetby	06.44
08.21	Barnetby-Highdyke	12.19
13.55	Highdyke-Colwick	15.00
16.00	Colwick-Highdyke	17.07
19.15	Highdyke-Barnetby	22.55
23.59	Barnetby-Frodingham	00.45
02.00	Frodingham-Wath	04.08

Another duty came from 4 May 1964 when Darnall substituted one of its 'D1500s' for a Type 2 on the Scunthorpe to Cardiff and Margam steel traffic as far as Washwood Heath, where it was replaced by a Canton equivalent. The longest through working for any BR motive power started around June 1965 when WR class members began working the 540-mile Milford Haven-Thornton Junction block oil train, while at about the same time mgr trials were conducted in the Sheffield area with No D1794.

It soon proved other than plain sailing on the freight front. Obtaining a very good tractive effort/speed curve entailed two compromises. The maximum speed was limited to 95mph, whereas 100 would have been preferable, and achieving this top speed, with the performance characteristic, produced a continuous rating speed of 27mph, which proved rather high for freight-train operation. Use on mgr trains on the ER caused the main generator to be operated for significant time periods beyond its continuous rating over certain sections, which resulted in the component burning out. Train weights therefore had to be tailored to ensure that speed was within the performance envelope. On the WR the same issue meant that loadings could not match those of the Class 37 over some lines.

Of course, other Regions were also receiving the type in quantity. From 13 January 1964 the Brush Type 4 displaced the Class 52 on Paddington to Wolverhampton duties. On 26 March 1964 No D1722 became the first into the West Country on a service train, the 11.50 York to Bristol, extended to Paignton. The class also had a diagram on the up 'Bristolian', while displacement of diesel-hydraulic traction on the North & West route commenced during July.

Following trials with No D1531 in August 1964 between Liverpool Street and Norwich, seven machines were allocated for GE Line duties from January 1965. The following month LMR-based locomotives took over the Euston to Perth trains, while the ScR appropriated them for internal duties between Glasgow and Aberdeen during the layover time. Polmadie crews began training in March and within a couple of months all the principal West Coast Anglo-Scottish services had gone over to this form of traction.

While on the West Coast route it is opportune to examine some performance data published in *Modern Railways* in October 1965. Two runs with No D1848 on 11-car formations, grossing 410 tons, were featured, the Crewe-based locomotive only having been in traffic a couple of months at the time. The second run was, remarkably, unchecked between Crewe and Carlisle, covering the 141 miles in 120 minutes against a schedule of 146 minutes.

Accelerating from the slack through Preston, the 90mph line speed had been reached by Garstang on level track. A further spell at this rate was put in between Carnforth and Oxenholme before Grayrigg bank was tackled, topped at 58mph. Attaining 82 through Tebay,

both the runs cleared Shap at 50mph, while a Class 40 with a similar load would have managed nothing better than 30mph at the summit. Down to Carlisle the maximum was 89 at Plumpton. Excellent though these efforts were in a contemporary context, the rail horsepower on Grayrigg and Shap was only around 1,900, which begs the question as to the engine rating, more of which in a moment.

O. S. Nock made a footplate ride on No D1861 over the same course but with a load grossing 465 tons. Again, at the time of the journey in 1966 the locomotive was only a few months old, having gone to Crewe on allocation in August 1965. Top speed between Preston and Lancaster was 88mph, and 85 between Carnforth and Oxenholme. Although these rates were lower than No D1848, No D1861 also climbed Grayrigg at a minimum of 58mph. A pws after Tebay ruined the ascent of Shap, with an acceleration to only 35½ mph before a minimum of 35, but 90mph was touched after Penrith. While on Grayrigg the rhp was 2,200; a sustained 35mph on Shap was worth only 1,900. Examining the effort on the lower reaches of Grayrigg, Milnthorpe to Oxenholme, speed fell from 85 to 71mph, equating to 2,200 rhp. Based on the dynamometer car trials, this is the level of performance predicted for a 2,750hp locomotive.

Equipment problems

A report produced by Freddie Harrison for the BRB in August 1963 covering problems with locomotives makes no mention of any of the issues to be described below. It therefore seems likely that these only manifested themselves subsequently. The problems that beset the 12LDA28-B power units in the 'Peaks' have already been described; fatigue cracks at several locations in the crankcases of these engines were addressed by removing part of the gusset plate containing the sharp change of shape, at which point the stress was concentrated. In all, 184 crankcases already fitted to, or destined for, 12LDA28-C engines had to be modified as well, of which 101 were already in service in Class 47s.

Other cracking then manifested itself on the girder carrying the thrust bearings. Loading on the girder was related to crankshaft end thrust and caused by resonance, and cushioning the forces involved proved difficult. Both Nos D1733

By the date of this photo, 15 June 1968, full yellow ends had been adopted. No D1822 illustrates this guise, seen here with down empty MGR wagons, approaching Alfreton station in the Erewash Valley.
J. S. Hancock

For the three-month period given in the report, there were 12 cases of fatigue cracking in the engine frame, while corrosion fatigue in engine water jackets, due to bad or incorrect maintenance, amounted to four cases. Other engine defects (fractures in oil sump casings, fractured cylinder liners, water leaks and other minor matters) had been found on nine engines. Engine failures were attributed to one of three causes: design (56%), bad manufacture (32%), and bad maintenance (12%). The bad manufacturing was being addressed during overhauls by cutting out and re-doing defective welding. As to the design defects, it is worth quoting the report's comments:

'Design weaknesses lie basically in the light structure of a complicated engine crankcase carrying two crankshafts in parallel. The design, to be successful, requires first-class workmanship, and did not take into account the unforeseen effects of crankshaft resonances. These have overstressed a main member of the structure carrying the shaft thrust bearings, and have so been the cause of a large number of fatigue cracks.'

It is worth noting here that transmission resonance had also been an issue in several of the diesel-hydraulic classes and had been addressed by this date (see the Class 35 section).

The engine was not the only source of trouble. Failures of electric traction equipment (generators and traction motors) had arisen in 38 cases, with control systems accounting for a further 15 cases and mechanical parts eight. Two stages of traction motor modifications had been carried out. There had been fires and fractures on the bogies, while condensation in the control cubicle had led to unsatisfactory operation.

In hindsight, a couple of matters seem incredible. The ordering of Class 17s in 1961/2 followed traditional BR practice of the dual sourcing of equipment in a total order for 117 locomotives, yet there was no similar approach with the Class 47, ordered alongside the 'Claytons'. As part of the tendering process for 199 Class 47s, sanctioned by the BRB in July 1962, EE submitted a tender in May, which offered several options, including the basic Class

and D1821 were taken by the BR Research Department for various tests, which determined that increasing the longitudinal float of the crankshaft in its bearings provided the solution. Establishing the cause of the girder cracking was exacerbated by the discovery that some cracking in the crankcase transverse-girders was due to substandard welding during manufacture. More was to come, with two more forms of structural failure: one was cracking in the sides of the lubricating oil sump, while the other involved cracking in the internal cooling water feed pipe, which was integral within the engine block. Rectification of the former involved cutting out and re-welding part of the block.

It has been said that some of these problems were an inevitable consequence of a combination of uprating the engine while keeping key components as lightweight as possible because of BR strictures on weight. At this time (1965) BR was still in the throes of the Mirrlees engine problems in the Class 30, which were also stress-related, and a decision was taken to impose design specifications laying down maximum stresses in critical areas.

A report produced for the BRB by Mr Harrison's department on 8 October 1965 provides some relevant statistics for the previous three months. By this date 402 Class 47s had been delivered and availability had been 75%, better than stated in a similar report of 5 April, when 297 examples were at work and availability was 'usually below 70%'. A quarter of locomotive non-availability was due to unplanned repairs.

47 design, with either Sulzer or EE engine and Brush or EE electrical machines. Unsurprisingly, the lowest-priced option was a design that was EE-equipped, at £98,347 for an order of 100, considerably lower than Brush's accepted quote of £108,850. One must conclude that someone in BR was determined to order Brush and Sulzer equipment in the new standard Type 4, without dual sourcing. Freddie Harrison has been identified as the main proponent of Sulzer engines and he was, by then, in a position to influence decisions.

Before a long-term solution was agreed, some Class 47s had their engines derated, a highly unpopular development with the Regional General Managers, and Freddie Harrison, as Chief Officer (Traction & Rolling Stock), came in for considerable flak. On 3 June 1965 he wrote to the General Managers in the following terms:

'Re meeting of 19 May, it was stated that two engines have already been derated and that a further ten made up of five 12LDA28Bs ("Peaks") and five 12LDA28Cs (Class 47s) will be downrated for trial purposes before modification is approved. Following further discussion with Sulzer, make clear to all, other than the two already done, no more until instructions given from this office.'

On 15 July the Operating Officer wrote to the Movements Manager, ER, enquiring about the results of a trial run with derated No D1507

between King's Cross and Newcastle, and seeking his views about the practicality of these maintaining existing running times. He refers to seven engines having suffered girder cracking. The General Manager, LMR, reported that a revised rating of 85% would add 7 and 12 minutes to passenger schedules, dependent on load, adding that only between 30 and 40% of each journey was made on full power. For Freightliners between Maiden Lane and Gushetfaulds, 850-ton loads would need an additional 7½ minutes, and 600 tons 6 minutes.

On 16 September the BRB told the ER and NER to base schedules on 85% of rating, irrespective of the engine troubles. The ensuing months brought considerable correspondence, which culminated in Mr Harrison saying that a rating 'of the order of 2,300hp' was, indeed, being considered, and pointing out that 85% of 2,750 was 2,340. In August 1966 a memo was sent to the Movements Manager stating that Nos D1930 and D1932 had been modified to 2,340hp. A recent decision had been taken by the BRB to apply this to a further 100 examples – Nos D1862-D1961 – and tests were to be carried out showing loss of time. Some of these locomotives had yet to be built.

The Regional General Managers continued to express discontent during 1966. In 1963 the Board policy had been to aim for the scheduling of the principal Class 1 services at an average speed of 75mph. The General Managers now concluded that this was impractical without the use of double-heading, when slowings from track work and the need to meet increasing demand were factored in.

An array of signals at Gloucester Midland Junction frames No D1738 as it heads for South Wales on a freight from the north on 13 March 1965. Class 47s were deployed quickly on the freight movements along this corridor.
www.railphotoprints.co.uk

During December 1965 the BR Chairman met the Chairmen of the three companies responsible for the production of the design (Hawker Siddeley for Brush, Sulzer and Vickers Armstrong), and left them in no doubt as to the seriousness of the situation. The BRB might have to take further action, but he had been given a verbal undertaking that the consortium intended to provide the BRB with reliable engines and was now working out a method to enable services to be kept running in the meantime. By the start of 1966 a rehabilitation programme had been agreed and was scheduled to be completed by June the following year.

Matters had progressed by the Board meeting of 25 January 1968, when it was reported that agreement had been reached with Sulzer regarding the rehabilitation of 12-cylinder engines at an *additional* outlay of £1,981,000. This included the Board's share of the cost of the programme agreed with Sulzer and totalling £1,179,000. The Board was assured that on completion of the work at the end of 1969, the Type 4's Sulzers should be satisfactory in service with reasonable life. There is extensive correspondence in the National Archive about BR's claim arising out of the whole debacle – debacle because it was not just the technical problems but also availability and performance – but the above gives a summary of the degree of seriousness with which matters were treated. Board approval the previous January to procure 98 new Sulzer engine blocks was cancelled.

Remedial work carried out on the engines has already been referred to. As part of the permanent solution, reducing the crankshaft thrust stresses to an acceptable (to BR) level involved reducing maximum rpm to 750. Effecting this change was achieved by the simple expedient of substituting a spring in the governor, a task carried out by depots with an allocation of the class. This then gave an engine output of 2,580hp and a main generator unloading point of 75 rather than 80mph. Not only was there a drop in rail horsepower to around 2,080, but performance in the upper speed band was also inferior to the characteristic at the higher rating.

The rotational balance of the crankshafts required alteration, so the number of crankshaft balance weights was doubled, while the angle between the two crankshafts was increased to the maximum that could be accommodated. One locomotive, possibly No D1773, was modified fully and tested. With successful results achieved, a campaign modification programme was put in place to deal with the remainder of the fleet. Commencing in March 1966, this involved using the 17 spare engines as a 'float', with locomotives going to Vickers' Barrow works for power unit removal and replacement.

Sulzer is a highly reputable company and thus wanted the matter remedied satisfactorily. History shows this to have been the case. These events, though, undoubtedly coloured the minds of BR's engineers because no further diesels were ordered from the company.

The Class 47 demonstrated a road performance superior to any other Type 4 during its early years. In derated form it seemed rather emasculated, a shadow of past glories. The one minor downside was a top speed of only 95mph, due to Brush being unwilling to agree to anything higher. As has so often been said in this book, if only a proper trial had been conducted! But it was a mix of the headlong rush into dieselisation, the clamour for more power, and personal preferences among key people that caused a major problem.

Length	63ft 6in
Width	9ft 2in
Height	12ft 9⅜in
Weight (boiler fitted)	116 tons 18 cwt
Sanding gear	Not fitted
Fuel tank capacity (gallons)	810
Minimum curve radius (chains)	4
Maximum speed (mph)	95

Engine
12LDA28C
Engine output (bhp)

Original	2,750 at 800rpm
Derated	2,580 at 750rpm

Tractive effort (lb) (No D1520 upwards)

Maximum	62,000
Continuous	30,000 at 27mph

Gear ratio
66:17

Background to the order

As explained in *Diesel Pioneers*, in response to a call by BR on 15 January 1960 for a new Type 4 design of around 2,700hp, EE had designed a prototype, carrying the number DP2. Unveiled on 25 May 1962, the locomotive had basically a Class 55 bodyshell and a Class 40-type engine, which had been through a development programme and had charge-air cooling. This had the effect of raising power from 2,000 to 2,700hp at 850rpm. It ran trials on the LMR initially, moving to the ER in July 1963. DP2 acquitted itself very well until being involved in a serious accident on 31 July 1967, which resulted in its withdrawal and eventual cannibalisation to recover components reusable in the Class 50.

Although none of the prototype Class 47 batch – Nos D1500-19 – had emerged from Falcon Works, BR invited tenders for further 2,700hp diesels, to which EE responded on 16 May 1962. This offered three alternatives. Alternative 1 comprised essentially a Class 47 but with EE electrical machines. Alternative 2 was essentially based on the company's prototype locomotive DP2. Alternative 3 was the same as Alternative 2 but substituted a Sulzer engine. Although Alternative 2 was 10% cheaper than the tender submitted and accepted by Brush, the other options were dearer. With Mr Harrison, the CME, favouring Sulzer products, he clearly persuaded the Board to go for the Brush/Sulzer proposal.

With no prospect of WCML electrification being extended through to Glasgow, consideration had to be given to whether there was a need for the provision of additional large diesels for duties north of Crewe. A paper dated 5 April 1965 sets out the pros and cons of Class 47 versus Class 55 to fit the bill, showing sample timings for both classes. Despite the Brush/Sulzer locomotives having an availability 'usually below 70%' at the time, whereas the EE 'Deltics' were attaining better than 80%, the BRB decided to send out enquiries for more Type 4s.

On behalf of the CME, Mr J. Ratter submitted a paper to the BRB on 8 October 1965, setting out the pros and cons of ordering more Class 47s or opting for a production series based on DP2. Of course, by now, the fatigue cracking issues with the Sulzer Type 4 engines

Around the turn of the year 1967/8, No D403 reverses out of Crewe Works before setting off on a commissioning trial to Carlisle. *EE*

The class quickly took over all the express passenger diagrams north of Weaver Junction. No D431 comes through Lancaster with the 13.10 Lancaster to Euston service on 9 September 1968. *Leslie Riley*

25 August 1967, and although the initial price had been £120,930, when adjusted for inflation and design changes the final figure was £128,000. Deliveries were to start in July 1967 and conclude the following June.

The design

Although EE and the LMR would have been content with a fleet of DP2s, forces within BR had other ideas for what was seen as the future standard Type 4. For a start, the new Type 4 was to be equipped with dual braking, electric train heating (ETH) and dynamic (rheostatic) braking. BR then asked for the inclusion of the facility to operate up to three locomotives in multiple, slow-speed control for working 'merry-go-round' trains and finally equipment for push-pull train working. A joint BR/EE decision resulted in the fitment of inertial primary air filtration and a 1,055-gallon steel fuel tank, whereas that of the Class 47 was of 810-gallon capacity. Although sanding equipment for extra adhesion had fallen out of favour, the new Type 4 had sand reservoirs and internal piping installed, together with an external filler cap, should sanding come back into vogue in the future. No provision was made for train heating by steam. Not unexpectedly, these changes affected the size and weight of the design, which turned the scales at 117 tons, as opposed to 105 tons for DP2.

In order to meet the revised BR requirement, EE had little option but to use electronics within the locomotive control system. The company had been developing equipment to this end and trials were under way, notably in Stratford-allocated Class 37 No D6818. The last Class 20s from No D8217 had an electronic closed-loop control system, which might be considered to have been a precursor of the new locomotives. DP2 offered an ideal test bed for the control scheme to be fitted to the Class 50s, and it went to Vulcan Foundry on 31 January 1966 for modifications, emerging in June. During November EE engineers fitted further equipment at Finsbury Park depot. EE technicians always rode on DP2 when it was in service and this allowed the new systems to be assessed in the field.

were in full flight. Mr Ratter recommended an order for a small fleet of DP2s, in part to evaluate the design, and in part because there was only one supplier, whereas three companies were involved with the Class 47. Six days later the BRB accepted Mr Ratter's report, instructing him to negotiate with EE for the hiring of 50 locomotives on a mileage and availability basis. The Board also impressed on Mr Harrison, the CME, the importance of his department to the running of the railway – perhaps coded language for sorting out poor locomotive availability.

Certainly EE came up with two novel (for Britain) features. Based on DP2's performance, the company offered an availability guarantee of 84% for the new design. This meant 42 locomotives available for traffic at 9am Monday to Saturday, with an assumed two in works for overhaul, five on depot for maintenance and one 'spare'. The other benefit was an offer to lease, rather than sell, the locomotives to BR. EE was already leasing large computers to industry and had a company set up for this purpose. Leasing benefited BR because the lease payments were treated as revenue expenditure in its accounts and not a capital item, a key difference in accounting terms. Fuller details of the leasing arrangement can be found in *Class 50s In Operation*.

On 12 November 1965 BR signed a letter of intent with EE for 50 100mph locomotives. However, the contract was not signed until

Why opt for electronics for locomotive control? The main reason was more precise control of power, coupled to the facility to build in additional features, such as slow-speed control. Control of the main and ETH generators was by way of two KV10 electronic field supply units (one per generator), and these were part of a closed-loop scheme that included several sub-systems for slow-speed operation, dynamic braking, wheelslip detection/correction and tractive effort control.

This latter facility offered drivers a more precise way to control power than the power handle, and was intended for use under poor rail conditions, when slipping was likely. There is a correlation between main generator current and tractive effort, as well as sustainable adhesion and tractive effort. On a dry rail the EE driver's manual instructed the application of full power once the train was well on the move at about 5mph. However, if rail conditions were poor, this technique would induce wheelslip. Leaving the power handle open fully, the driver could reduce power by using the tractive effort control until slipping stopped. Having found the highest sustainable tractive effort (basically, pulling effort) for the conditions, the train would accelerate at the fastest possible speed. Fine control of the main generator was only possible by the use of electronics, and this was also true of the slow-speed system facility for maintaining speed at 2mph.

English Electric used the 16CSVT diesel engine, rated at 2,700hp at 850rpm, which had worked so well in DP2. The main generator was the EE840/4B, rated continuously at 1,746kW, 1,800A, 970V at 850rpm, driven directly from the coupling flange on the diesel engine flywheel and very similar, apart from the drive arrangements, to that also used in DP2. An EE915/1B ETH generator was driven off the outboard end of the main generator by a cardan shaft with rubberised flexible couplings and was rated at 320kW at 800V. The auxiliary generator was overhung from the ETH machine, an assembly arrangement that was unique in British diesel locomotive practice. Unfortunately, BR later settled on 850V for its coaching stock, which caused some problems for the ETH generator when working at full rating. In this respect, the rating also proved low and locomotives of other types that were converted during the 1970s to supply ETH at a higher output.

Six EE538/5A traction motors were fitted and had three stages of field weakening. They were interchangeable with those installed in both the Class 37 and the Class 55, with the same gear ratio. Arranged in three series pairs, connected in parallel, the power train (from engine to motors) provided a versatile mixed-traffic traction characteristic. Maximum tractive effort was 48,500lb (limited by maximum permitted main generator current), continuous tractive effort was 33,000lb at 23.5mph, and full engine output was usable between 15 and 87mph; above 87mph main generator unloading began to reduce power.

From new, only No D400 had a full set of multiple jumper cables and ports. No D401 had a single connecting port, whereas the remainder had blanking plates fitted over the wiring on the cab front. In this snowy January 1968 scene, No D401 heads a Birmingham to Glasgow working north of Wreay on the descent to Carlisle. *R. H. Leslie*

This view of Docker Viaduct in the Cumberland fells is considerably more overgrown today than on 8 September 1969 when an unidentified Class 50 coasted down Grayrigg bank at the head of a Glasgow to Euston service.
David N. Clough

Although the design top speed was 105mph, in service the limit was 100.

During the first few months of 1966 various external styling options were proposed. EE put forward an attractive cab front proposal that featured wrap-around windscreens and a train headcode box below the cab windows, similar to the Class 47. BR rejected this and opted for the less attractive siting of the route indicator box above the cab windows, which were straight, following the precepts of a full-size cab mock-up built at Derby. BR also stipulated a sleek bodyside, without opening windows, and a sealed roof, dispensing with the bodyside air filter grilles found on earlier designs.

Naturally, there had to be an arrangement to supply combustion air to the engine and to cool the generators, and some intakes were fitted at roof height. These enabled air to be drawn into the locomotive by means of a pressurising fan, which kept the engine room at a higher pressure than the remainder of the locomotive. Air flowed first through a large inertial filter, which was mounted behind and above the generator group; a second inertial filter was sited at the other end of the engine. Although inertial filtration was EE's idea, the company was concerned from the start that there would be insufficient air flow for adequate air supply and to cool the engine room; DP2's bodyside windows were generally left open for that purpose.

Whereas Class 37 and 40 locomotives used a shaft from the 'free' end of the engine to rotate the radiator fan, and the Class 47 employed a pressurised hydrostatic drive, the Class 50s mirrored the BR-built 'Peaks' in employing an electric motor to drive the shaft. Electronics were even used in its control circuitry; this linked into a pneumatic system, which opened and closed the radiator shutters in line with the cooling demands being placed on the radiator panels.

EE had an eye to bigger locomotives up to 4,000hp and it is possible that this inspired the inclusion of wiring for bogie weight transfer compensation equipment. When a locomotive is pulling hard at low speed, there is a tendency for it to 'sit back' on the rear axle of each individual bogie and thus reduce adhesion weight on the leading axle; consequently wheelslip can affect the leading axles. EE devised a bellows arrangement, fitted to the bogies, to prevent this tilting, but in the event only No D417 received a full set of the apparatus.

Being a big 'sweaty' engine, the 16CSVT used quite a lot of coolant, and inadequate coolant could cause engine shutdown. A semi-rotary pump was therefore fitted, in combination with a bucket, so that drivers could refill the radiators from a shore supply – instances known about involve the use of river water and assistance from a farm!

If the above technical description is insufficient to emphasise how different the emerging design was from EE's tender, an internal memo of 28 March 1966 from Vulcan Foundry's CMEE confirmed that what was being produced bore little resemblance to what EE had intended. The changes were, however, to be viewed as to everyone's satisfaction. Perhaps some at least within EE saw the Class 50 contract as an opportunity to move forward.

Production slipped because the Bradford works of EE could not produce main generators fast enough, while Vulcan suffered persistent labour problems, and by March 1967 only two complete power units had been supplied to Vulcan Foundry. The delays had almost been predicted, because on 22 February 1966 the BR CME wrote to the Chief Operating Officer to comment specifically about delays in 1965 new builds from Vulcan due to persistent labour disputes at the works. Two revised dates for hand-over of the first of the class came and went, and it was not until 19 August that D400 moved under its own power for the first time. The livery was BR Corporate Blue, with yellow cab fronts and black for the buffers, undergear and bogies. All received the 'D' prefix to their numbers, which ran from D400 to D449, though BR officially dispensed with this prefix after the end of steam, and the 38th class member was thus merely No 437.

Trials and tribulations

During September 1967 No D400 went to Crewe for trials, which included a maximum load trip over Shap and Beattock with a Stanlow to Dalmarnock oil-tank train. There were also trials with passenger stock at up to 100mph. After a return to Vulcan Foundry for modifications, final trials based on Crewe saw an acceptance certificate being issued by BR on 3 October. Driver training between Crewe and Rhyl commenced thereafter, with two daily return trips.

During the remainder of 1967 there was a trickle of locomotives from Vulcan Foundry, the slow pace due to the need to incorporate certain modifications within the electronic systems. Once Nos D401/2/4 were in traffic, crew training at Carlisle, Glasgow Polmadie and Perth could begin; No D403 proved difficult during commissioning and was not issued with an acceptance certificate until 1968.

Surprisingly, the first service use was on the overnight Euston to Inverness 'Royal Highlander' between Crewe and Perth. During a journey on which No D401 was allocated, one of EE's engineers noted from instrumentation fitted for measurement that the locomotive was producing around 2,900hp during acceleration. Crewe Diesel Depot, where the class was based, did not have a load bank facility at the time, so No D401 was returned to Vulcan Foundry, but

On 4 September 1969 No D447 approaches Oxenholme with a Glasgow to Euston train. Note that the radiator shutters are fully open, signifying that the locomotive has been working hard.
David N. Clough

Exhaust haze confirms that No D434 is pounding away as it passes the long-closed Shap station on 8 September 1969 while working the 07.50 Glasgow to Euston train. *David N. Clough*

its test house showed engine power at the correct setting. Eventually, it was ascertained that the electronic control system was causing the engine to 'over-power' under certain conditions and revised instructions were issued for the setting-up of engine output. The upshot was that full rated output was only available to the driver during acceleration of the train, irrespective of whether he was demanding maximum effort.

Production rates across EE meant that four or five locomotives each month began to be delivered to BR during 1968. Newly commissioned machines were sensibly used for crew training to permit any shakedown issues to be dealt with before deployment on service trains. Notable instances of the sphere of operation planned for the class can be seen by No 443 going to Manchester's Newton Heath depot, while No 444 went to Glasgow Eastfield for training purposes directly after being commissioned.

In early February 1968 No D406 was appropriated by the Railway Technical Centre and prepared for a full set of road trials, using the WR's dynamometer car. Before the trials began, however, they were cancelled on cost grounds, a great shame because the opportunity to compare the design to the results obtained from similar trials involving Class 47s and 52s some years earlier was lost. In the event, the only tests carried out were to assess wheelslip protection in comparison with a Class 47. These were staged on the recently closed Butterley branch, but, embarrassingly, the specialised coupling between locomotive and dynamometer car was broken, causing red faces all round, and even these tests were abandoned in consequence.

There was already concern about the internal air management arrangements, due to oil contamination of the pressurising fan motor. No D406 was therefore retained at Derby for examination before returning to Vulcan Foundry on 26 February 1968. Eventually baffles were fitted to separate off the engine room from the generator set and the remainder of the locomotive interior at the No 2 end.

By all accounts drivers did not take to the class, preferring the Class 47. One can sympathise to a degree because the new arrivals were more difficult to fault-find when on the road and also more likely to fail as shakedown issues were resolved in service use. Proving the point, one driver failed No D400 at Carlisle with 'persistent wheelslip' but no fault was found. When No D405 proved incapable of building pressure in the train brake system at Crewe, the driver declared his machine a failure; too late the cause was found to have been the malicious unhooking of the brake pipe on the end Freightliner wagon, something that could only have happened after arrival from the south behind an AC electric locomotive. Back on depot, No D405 could not be faulted.

No D401 was the centre of an incident at Motherwell on 21 February 1968 while heading the 09.20 Crewe to Perth train. The driver was unable to clear an overload fault, even after isolating all six traction motors. Help was summoned and it transpired that the driver had used the wrong procedure to clear the overload trip; the locomotive now refused to take power and was declared a failure. Of course, the reason it would not take power was that all its traction motors were isolated! Many drivers and depot staff blamed malfunctioning electronics for virtually every problem. EE wisely stationed a site engineer at Crewe, Carlisle and Glasgow depots, where the class was most likely to be found, to deal with issues, and they quickly learned to look for the obvious when fault-finding, rather than exchanging electronic components. A simple example was a report by a driver of 'low power', which was actually traced to a seized turbocharger and not the control system. Drivers also inadvertently set the current limit potentiometer below maximum.

On 7 April 1968 No D405 was borrowed for trials on a push-pull rake between Edinburgh and Glasgow. The Scottish Region wished to improve its service on the route beyond the 1958-built 70mph DMUs, and a push-pull train set, using the control system already built into the Class 50, would have been ideal. On the day, 100mph running was achieved for the first time over the route, but the Region's aspirations were thwarted because insufficient 50s were available to be diagrammed on these services. It was to be 1979 before Type 4 power could be spared for the route, in the shape of Class 47s, and several further years before the Class 47/7 sub-class was cleared for 100mph running.

Service experience

English Electric had given an availability guarantee in its contract with BR covering Class 50 and this had been based on the performance of the company's prototype, DP2. Of course, the new Type 4 was different in many ways, but it was far from true to say that it was the new features that caused all the trouble during the first couple of years. True, the electronics were not trouble-free. The train heat generator provided power for the radiator fan motor and was therefore in use constantly when the locomotive was working. A protection circuit, the train heat over-voltage relay (HOVR), tended to trip and cause the engine to shut down purely due to a 'spike' occurring in the circuitry, rather than the voltage really being too high. Electronic 'spikes' were common in other control sub-systems and represented a pitfall of first-generation railway electronics. In an effort to reduce their occurrence, the HOVR was made less sensitive, while the push-pull train operation control system was isolated. The KV10 generator field supply units had a

tendency to 'lock on' in the 'full' state; this meant that even the smallest opening of the driver's power handle would bring full generator excitation, so a change of the offending component was then needed. Both the HOVR and KV10 issues still affect Class 50s.

Fitting baffles on the engine room to improve air management proved unsuccessful and a bulkhead was substituted. Even so, siting the inlet ducts for the air filters at roof level behind the engine exhaust ports was not ideal because greasy exhaust gas tended to be sucked into the filter system and locomotive interior. As a consequence filter surfaces became sticky and detritus stuck to them, reducing their effectiveness. It did not take long for the locomotive interior to become filthy, leading to the inertial filters being dubbed the 'filthy filters'.

Components that had been 'through the mill' with DP2 also caused problems. Main generator failures due to flashover were far too common and often in sympathy with one or more traction motor flashovers. Even the battle-hardened 16CSVT diesel proved not to be immune from problems. The piston scraper rings were too severe, causing piston seizures due to a lack of oil. Worst of all, the cylinder heads began to develop cracks, which allowed coolant into the cylinders when the engine was shut down. Coolant does not compress and combust and the result was inevitably a bent connecting rod or worse. The cylinder head issue was due to defective casting of the components, which arose when production was switched between EE

Mail bags are much in evidence at Carlisle at around 19.00 on 30 November 1968 as the 14.05 Euston to Glasgow makes its booked stop. No D436's footplate crew are not in evidence – the lights are on but no one's at home! *Geoffrey J. Jackson*

Class 50s performed most of the mail, parcels and Freightliner work on the WCML north of Weaver Junction. No D431 arrives at Crewe with the 08.32 Kendal to Euston parcels. *David Wharton*

group factories. Eventually a revised design was substituted.

The foregoing gives an overview of the issues faced by not only BR staff, both footplate and maintenance, but also by EE, which suffered financially because of poor availability. Despite the rate of production at Vulcan Foundry slipping towards the end, due to staff realising that EE was not winning new orders at home or overseas, No 449 brought the order to completion when it entered traffic on 11 December 1968. By then the class had taken over all the main Anglo-Scottish passenger and most of the freight turns north of Crewe, as well as some services in North West England and Central Scotland. By August displaced diesels of other types allowed steam traction to be eliminated in the North West and thus across the entire BR main-line network.

North of Weaver Junction, the northern limit of West Coast electrification, the railway had not been modernised in any way and speeds reflected this fact. Indeed, there was a blanket 75mph upper limit across the whole of Scotland, due to signal spacing. The West Coast line was no racetrack in consequence and there was little opportunity for Class 50s to show their high-speed capabilities. Nevertheless, there were some rousing exploits climbing to Shap from Carlisle and in hauling upwards of 500 tons at 90mph between Preston and Lancaster. Route

modernisation began in 1969 with track relaying for higher speed, which gave the opportunity for accelerated schedules from May 1970, but that is taking the story beyond the scope of this book. There is no doubt that the initial experience with the Class 50 proved most inauspicious, but by the end of the decade most of the issues had been resolved, to a greater or lesser degree.

Length	68ft 6in
Width	9ft 1½ in
Height	12ft 9¹/₁₆ in
Weight	117 tons
Sanding gear	Not Fitted
Fuel tank capacity (gallons)	1,055
Minimum curve radius (chains)	4
Maximum speed (mph)	100

Engine
EE 16CSVT Mark 2

Engine output (bhp)	2,700

Tractive effort (lb)

Maximum	48,000
Continuous	33,000 at 23.5mph

Gear ratio
53:18

EE contract No CCT 1421
EE progressive Nos 3770-3819; Vulcan Foundry Nos D1141-90

At a meeting of the BTC on 23 May 1957, K. W. C. Grand, the WR's General Manager, referred to his interest in acquiring a 3,000hp locomotive to work heavy coal trains. On 16 July 1959 the BTC authorised the construction of 74 Type 4 diesel-hydraulics at a cost of £9,990,000, which were to complete the requirements for Area 1, west of Bristol. Perhaps understandably, the BTC expressed the hope that the actual cost would be markedly less. In the event, the cost per locomotive was around £120,000, which excluded spare power trains.

The locomotives were ordered on 27 August 1959 as part of the 1961 building programme; the first 35 were to be built at Swindon, and the remaining 39 at Crewe, the latter's solitary foray into main-line diesel-hydraulic construction. Deliveries were to commence from Swindon during August 1961 and from Crewe in December 1961. Plans changed, however, during December 1961, when, on the 21st, the BTC endorsed a recommendation from the Works & Supply Committee to transfer the building of 10 examples from Swindon to Crewe so that Swindon could start on the production of a new design of diesel-hydraulic Type 1. In the event, only five of Swindon's original allocation, Nos D1030-4, were built at Crewe.

The addition of charge cooling, or intercooling, had begun by the date of the order, and Maybach Motorenbau GmbH had modified its Maybach MD650 unit, used in Class 42. The intercooled MD655 12-cylinder power plant was set at 1,380hp at 1,500rpm, a relatively modest increase from the 1,135hp of the earlier model and well below the 1,500 metric horsepower UIC rating. The two MD655s fitted gave a combined power of 2,760hp, though the combined output of both engines has generally been quoted as 2,700hp. Rather than use a Maybach-Mekydro hydro-mechanical transmission combination, Swindon – the lead drawing office – chose a Voith transmission, model L630rV, which could take an input of 1,270hp from each MD655 engine, 2,540hp for the two. Swindon assigned Lot No 450 to the order.

To a large degree, the new Type 4 followed the mechanical design of the Class 42, including the use of stressed-skin bodywork construction and KM-pattern bogies. Of course, the intercoolers increased the engine size, while the extra power developed raised the cooling demand and so called for larger radiators.

On entering traffic, the Class 52 was first used on the Paddington to Wolverhampton Low Level route. No D1000, the first of the design, was given a livery of Desert Sand, which had been considered for the West Coast AC electrics. On 11 June 1962, possibly still being used for driver training, the locomotive eases out of Wolverhampton Low Level, after arriving with the 11.50am from Stourbridge Junction via Dudley, a service that was withdrawn six weeks later. *Michael Mensing*

Several experimental liveries were tried, with all-over green applied on several examples, one of which was No D1003, photographed on 15 June 1962. Note how the side cab windows are cut in from the rest of the body profile. *H. Wheeler*

These and other scaling-up issues increased locomotive weight beyond what was acceptable for a BB wheel arrangement, so a three-axle bogie was designed. A Spanner Swirlyflo train heat steam generator was fitted and the resultant locomotive weighed 108 tons.

External styling went through a long but fascinating evolutionary process. As with all the new designs that were commissioned after the Pilot Scheme, BR's recently established Design Panel held a watching and co-ordinating brief. The following information has been extracted from one of the Design Panel files now in the National Archive.

On 31 October 1958 Professor Misha Black (an external design consultant, engaged by the Design Panel to advise the WR on the 'Warships') reported to Christian Barman (head of public relations at the BTC, but also an architect and industrial designer of many years' standing) about a meeting earlier in the month, which dealt with progress on the Class 42. In his letter, Black refers to the WR mentioning during the meeting that it was in the preliminary planning stage of a scheme for a new, larger, Type 4 design. Mr Scholes of the Swindon drawing office expressed the view that he hoped Black would be commissioned to assist with the new project.

Some delicate, carefully crafted, political manoeuvres then took place. First, there had been some dissatisfaction in certain quarters about No D800's front-end styling. On 28 November 1958 Mr Barman wrote to Mr Grand. He first refers to the No D800 styling replicating that of the German Class V200 on Mr Grand's insistence, then says that he had hoped that the locomotives would be distinctive from the other Pilot Scheme products, but that they were just another series of BR diesel locos with a 'nose', the only material difference being the shape of the nose. Barman picks out the styling of the front-end windows as praiseworthy and says that development of this feature in the new Type 4 would result in a really distinctive locomotive. Cunningly, he says that this would publicise the WR, rather than Krauss-Maffei (KM) or German Federal Railways. In concluding, Barman suggests that, if Grand is in agreement, he should tell the WR CME (R. A. Smeddle) that, as General Manager, he would like to explore a fresh approach, but without this representing a commitment.

What could Mr Grand do but agree? This letter from a BTC board member to a Regional General Manager clearly shows how much power the latter post-holder retained at the time as regards locomotives for his Region. January

1959 saw the start of design work on what was to become the No D1000s. A meeting on the 5th reported that Mr Sly (the Swindon draughtsman) was working on stress calculations, which would dictate the position of the main structural framing members; this was crucial because the position of the framing members could be varied slightly to accommodate styling requirements. The position of the side vents was more or less fixed by the needs of the power units, but Swindon was willing to consider slight modifications. A curved windscreen glass was debated, and Swindon had already decided to suggest the curved sides for the bodywork to improve panel finishing.

Misha Black proposed high but narrow windscreens to generate an impressive appearance; this would involve a lowering of the cantrail, but Mr Scholes was opposed to this because of the risk of weakening the body structure. By May a model had been produced at Swindon, but the body profile prompted adverse comment on safety grounds by BTC member Sir Steuart Mitchell. He considered that the gap between lineside structures and the cab windows would be too small and put footplate crew at risk when reversing a locomotive. Sir Steuart added that he thought the styling replicated a French Railways diesel class, used on the route to La Rochelle.

By July 1959 a rethink of the styling was in progress; a fresh model had been produced and had won acceptance, even though Chris Bond, the BTC Chief Officer (Traction & Rolling Stock) preferred high nose ends. The issue of 'sleeper flutter' affecting the driver of a flat-fronted locomotive during high-speed running was raised, and setting back the driver's seat was put forward as a means to combat this.

Professor Black did, however, ask whether AC electric locomotive-style cast stainless steel numbers and crest could be used, as well as a break-away from sombre dark green. By April 1960 Mr Grand had left Paddington for the BTC and had been replaced by R. Hammond, who was also an ex-GWR man. Mr Hammond's departure in January 1962 brought this lineage to an end, and Stanley Raymond was appointed to the top job at Paddington. For whatever reason, Swindon thinking had now reverted to a D800 form of styling. Despite the first delivery being due in the summer of 1961, a number of details remained unresolved. Professor Black was unhappy at siting the warning horns on the cab roof and felt that the radius of the plating round the cab was greatly 'discouraging'. A lack of communication between Swindon's drawing office and the works was blamed, but Mr Smeddle promised that the radius would be increased to 1 inch from about the sixth locomotive.

No D1005 calls at Solihull with the 4.50pm Pullman from Paddington in 1963. *David Adams*

Mr Scholes wanted to move to a more striking livery, though his seniors did not. He also felt that bodyside stencils should remain because the design was tight within the loading gauge. George Williams of the Design Panel suggested that two livery options be prepared, one based on green and the other possibly beige/grey, which he had suggested for the 'Deltics'. Blue was out because this had been selected for the AC electrics. By November there was talk of four livery options, including turquoise and light brown (WR coaching stock continued the GWR chocolate and cream scheme), while Smeddle now wanted the choice to be 'as distinctive as possible'. The Design Panel ruled out 'lining out' in favour of a broad band along the bottom of the bodyside in a contrasting colour.

As late as 21 April 1961 a fifth livery option of maroon was added. Five days later Mr Williams sent four options to Mr Smeddle – desert sand, turquoise, standard green and red – and said that the Design Panel would prefer either of the first two. Scholes came under pressure to paint No D1000 in desert sand, but he felt that the WR management would object. The rest, of course, is history.

Unusually, the public was asked to comment on the three trial liveries actually used – desert sand, green and maroon. As if this was not enough, in July 1962 Brian Haresnape (who provided input to the Design Panel) suggested something similar to Stroudley yellow (William Stroudley had been CME on the London, Brighton & South Coast Railway, where the colour was actually – bizarrely – called 'improved locomotive green'). Interestingly, the WR was keen to explore this option, otherwise the Region threatened to adopt maroon to match the new livery chosen by the BTC for coaching stock. This was no idle threat, because on 16 August Smeddle wrote to Williams to say that the WR General Manager had decreed maroon, except for Stroudley yellow, aka golden ochre, which had been produced by Haresnape from a mix of diesel-pipework orange and WR chocolate brown.

Professor Black was disappointed, considering that maroon was 'distressing' and acted as a camouflage. When No D1015 was viewed in its trial scheme, his verdict was that 'it looks very brown to me'. Mr Williams was also unconvinced, noting that it 'seems to live' under certain light conditions, but is rather dull in others. Golden ochre was not replicated.

The foregoing provides a wonderful vignette of design evolution, showing how competing ideas struggled for pre-eminence. While Misha

A busy scene outside Birmingham Snow Hill, now much changed, finds No D1011 bringing the 3.35pm Wolverhampton Low Level to Paddington service past a 4-6-0 steam locomotive during the autumn of 1962. *David Adams*

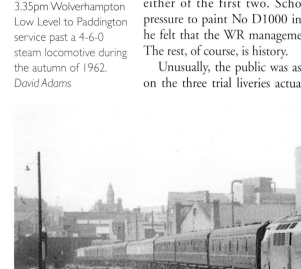

Black is generally attributed with the external styling, it is clear how his ideas had to be modified to take into account practicalities and personalities.

Into service

No D1000's construction at Swindon was reported on several times by visitors to the Works, and on 5 November 1961 it was noted to be complete but unpainted. A month later painting was complete and the date of acceptance was 20 December 1961, with allocation to Laira. As with all the class, cast numberplates and fabricated nameplates were fitted prior to leaving the Works, the name carried being *Western Enterprise*. Only this machine received a cast BR emblem, the remainder having a transfer in the form of the BR Coaching Stock cypher, of the type used on coaching stock. No D1001 did not enter traffic until 12 February 1962. Meanwhile no doubt Crewe was following behind, drawing on Swindon's experience, because its first 'Western', No D1035, was not commissioned until 27 July 1962 and also became a Laira locomotive.

As the story goes, it was a secretary at Swindon who came up with the idea of prefixing with the word 'Western' a list of names that had been drawn up for the class. It is also said that Swindon envisaged a production run of a further 226 machines, such was the lack of understanding of how few diesels were needed compared to steam traction.

With the transfer of Nos D1030-4 to Crewe, No D1034 completed the Crewe order; it was noted at Crewe shed on 25 March 1964 and was commissioned on 15 April. Swindon's last true main-line locomotive, No D1029, was complete by 20 April 1964 when it left the Works for evaluation of modifications to the bogie. Entry to service did not come until 14 July.

No D1000 was painted in desert sand, with black roof hatches (but only from behind the cab) and black cab window surrounds, and red buffer-beam and front skirt. The nameplate and numberplate backgrounds were black. No D1001 received maroon, with mid grey for the roof hatches behind the cab and white window surrounds, but a yellow buffer-beam and front skirt. Nos D1002-4 (from Swindon) and Nos D1035-8 (from Crewe) emerged in standard

By 3 June 1965 No D1000 had been repainted in maroon, the standard livery for the class. It awaits departure from Paddington with the 17.00 service to Fishguard.
Anthony A. Vickers

locomotive green, mid grey roof hatches, small yellow warning panels on the front ends and, apparently, red backgrounds to the nameplates. No D1015 duly received the golden ochre scheme, with black roof hatches. Following the national consultation, maroon was adopted as the standard livery, with black roof hatches, together with (eventually) small yellow warning panels. By the end of 1962 Nos D1001/7 were reported to have lost their yellow buffer-beams but had received yellow warning panels instead. In 1967 No D1030 became the first of the class to receive BR Rail Blue (including the roof) with small yellow ends. Landore had a small allocation of 'Westerns' and chose to repaint their roofs black, which included the hatches over the cabs.

No D1000's service debut seems to have been on 20 December 1961 at the head of the 6.55am Cheltenham to Paddington train forward from Swindon, piloting No D0280 *Falcon*. This was the working customarily used by Swindon for trial running, with the 1.34pm Paddington-Plymouth vans as far as Swindon forming the return leg. Initial feedback from drivers was that the Brush prototype, which also had two MD655 engines but electric transmission, was more powerful than the 'Western', yet No D0280 had its engines set to produce a combined 2,800hp, against 2,760hp for D1000.

By 28 January 1962 No D1000 was at Laira for driver training, being attached as pilot on

eastbound service trains as far as Newton Abbot. *Trains Illustrated* for July 1962 noted that No D1004 was at Oxley for training purposes, in advance of the type taking over Class 1 duties along the Paddington to Wolverhampton and (later) Shrewsbury corridor, which eventually saw the class penetrate as far as Chester while hauling London-Birkenhead through services. The first diagram on the route for a 'Western' commenced on 25 June and was quickly followed by deliveries to date being concentrated there. The Winter 1962 timetable called for 13 class members for an accelerated service. Such utilisation no doubt helps to explain the transfer of the early deliveries to Old Oak Common during October 1962, because those concerned moved away in March 1964 after displacement by Class 47s.

By now there had been a change in the top personnel on the WR at Paddington and hydraulic transmission was no longer in favour. Technical problems with the Class 52s allegedly prompted a request for the first batch of Class 47s (Nos D1500-19) to be reallocated to the Region, once the ER had received deliveries from No D1520 onwards. These first 20 Brush/Sulzer machines had ETH equipment and the WR was rather frustrated by the poor performance of the steam train heat generators installed in the 'Westerns'.

With the WR main line to Birmingham established as the first sector for utilisation of the new Type 4, the focus now moved to South Wales. On 4 October 1962 No D1009 worked a parcels train ex-works from Swindon to Cardiff. From mid-October No D1041 was on a turn into South Wales on the 1.08pm from Leeds and the 3.15pm return. This working, which was between Gloucester and Cardiff, continued into November, but with No D1012.

Further penetration into South Wales came with No D1045's appearance at the partly completed diesel depot at Landore during February 1963. Interestingly, most of the early activity in the Principality seems not to have been on passenger diagrams. By June Landore-based units were reaching Whitland and Margam yard, while on 28 April one had taken a hand on coal traffic in the western valley near Aberbeeg. From 15 July 'Westerns' took over the sheet steel workings from Birmingham that originated at Scunthorpe and ran to Margam via Bromsgrove.

On the passenger front, from the Summer 1963 timetable the class resumed work between Cardiff and Shrewsbury on Liverpool services and Swansea to Manchester. Another interesting Summer 1963 turn was diagramming on the 'Pines Express' between Oxford and Crewe. From 3 June the class began regular passenger work to Neyland, using No D1064 based at Carmarthen. On 15 August 1963 D1040 was in collision with a freight at Knowle & Dorridge, near Solihull, while hauling a spare Pullman rake. Accelerations between Paddington and South Wales commenced from the winter timetable and were based on the new arrivals.

Boundary changes in 1962 transferred the section of the Paddington to Birmingham line north of Banbury from WR to LMR control, and the latter decided that it did not want Class 52s on the expresses that travelled this way. As soon as sufficient newly built Class 47s were to hand, the 'Westerns' were displaced; the changeover was due to take place on 23 December 1963, but was postponed until 13 January 1964 because the usurpers did not have WR-pattern AWS. A similar switch took place with the 'Pines Express' on 22 February. Cascaded Class 52s migrated to the Paddington to Bristol route in place of the 'Warships'.

With all 74 examples in traffic and confined virtually exclusively to WR metals, a revised, faster timetable between London and the West Country was mapped out for Summer 1964, including a new businessmen's train, up in the morning and back in the late afternoon. Cecil J. Allen made a return footplate journey as far as Plymouth on the 'Cornish Riviera Express' in the summer of 1965. Although the 4-hour schedule was retained, the load limit was raised from 10 to 12 coaches and calls were made at both Taunton and Exeter. Comparison should be made to a journey on the same train described in the Class 42 section.

Picking out the key points from the trip, No D1058 had a 13-car load of 475 tons gross out of Paddington. Mr Allen commented that full power was used extensively. A signal check before Slough to 52mph was followed by a maximum of 80 on level track to Maidenhead. Climbing the Kennet Valley, speed was in the low 70s, while Brewham summit was topped at 69mph. Top speed was 88mph at Curry Rivel Junction and net time was just about kept to Taunton. Restarting, there was an easing for a pws before Norton Fitzwarren, with 60 attained on the climb to Whiteball, where the rate had fallen back to 46 against the grade. On the final section to Plymouth, Dainton and Rattery were both surmounted at a minimum of 26.

In the up direction the following day, Mr Allen rode No D1045, which had to contend with 14 coaches, grossing 525 tons full. A pws before Plympton prevented Hemerdon bank being charged and speed fell away to 17½ mph. It is likely that the locomotive was driven hard throughout between Exeter and Whiteball, not least because the train was more than 10

minutes behind time due to various delays. Speed peaked at 71mph past Tiverton Junction before falling off to 56½ past Whiteball, but three-quarters of a minute had been lost on the section. A similar situation appertained during the running from Taunton to passing Castle Cary, with a loss of half a minute and no higher speed than 82mph. Brewham was cleared at 50 and, with the train still well behind schedule at Heywood Road Junction, there followed an acceleration from 77½ to 80½ on level track to Lavington; this was superior to the 80mph on level track of No D1058 the day before with a coach less. Top speed for the run was 87½ at Slough before signals intervened.

An assessment of these performances produces disappointing rail horsepower figures. Between West Drayton and Maidenhead the value was a mere 1,600, slightly higher at 1,650 between West Drayton and Slough. Climbing to Whiteball a somewhat higher 1,825 was being produced, but in a speed range where this was to be expected. At around 75-80mph predicted values are roughly 2,000 rhp, and in the speed range climbing to Whiteball 2,150. It is reasonable to conclude that No D1058's engines were turning out 2,350hp, well below the nominal setting. Mr Allen's presence on the

No 1040 looks in very good external condition at the head of a Paddington-bound working, rounding the sea wall at Teignmouth on 14 June 1969. *David N. Clough*

footplate confirmed that the sections used for these assessments were taken at full power. No D1045 was clearly a superior traction unit, though around 1,880rhp on the climb to Whiteball was still below the predicted performance.

Lest it be thought that these runs were unrepresentative, Mr R. I. Nelson also footplated the down 'Riviera' in the summer of 1965 aboard No D1048, hauling 15 vehicles grossing 545 tons. Continuous full power between Acton and Maidenhead failed to quite achieve 80mph before Reading, with 1,880rhp developed. Climbing the Kennet Valley, progress was around the 70 mark and a calculation of rail horsepower over 17 miles at full power gives nothing better than 1,725. Restarting from Taunton, nearly 1½ minutes was lost ascending to Whiteball, despite full controller, and the minimum at the summit was 36mph in a time of 13min 56sec.

David Adams made a number of journeys with the class and possibly his best was a 1967 effort by No D1042 trailing 14 cars for 530 tons gross. A creditable 86mph was reached by Maidenhead and, over the same section as No

D1048 just described, the power was 1,925rhp. By contrast, No D1042 was also typically 5mph quicker throughout the ascent of the Kennet Valley. However, even this standard might be regarded as unremarkable when set against similarly powered diesel-electric traction and also when ranked alongside the Class 42 'Warships'. Mr Adams's records on the Birmingham route amplify this conclusion, with the 2,750hp Class 47 typically 5mph faster climbing Hatton Bank than a Class 52.

During the 1960s the 'Westerns' were rarely free of trouble. The steam generator failures have already been referred to, and following swiftly on their heels the whole class was taken out of service on 6 November 1963 due to severe wear, close to collapse, of a transmission roller bearing. Detection came during a routine strip-down of a transmission on No D1000 after 100,000 miles, and 20% of the fleet were found to exhibit this trouble. Resolution was achieved by taking six out of traffic at a time and fitting replacement bearings; using four spare transmissions on a component exchange basis kept down-time to two days. Even before this, availability had been as low as 50% or less, caused notably by

The Class 52s had a long association with the West of England main line. By June 1969 No 1029 had been repainted into Corporate Blue guise. The train, the 07.37 Ealing Broadway to Penzance, is skirting Horse Cove between Dawlish and Teignmouth. *David N. Clough*

attention to bogie suspension and bogie final drive units. Sixty design modifications had already been authorised.

Having a similar KM-pattern bogie to the Class 42 and 43, it was hardly surprising that similar problems over ride quality developed. In view of this issue emerging with the older design during construction of the later Type 4, no explanation has ever been offered as to why Swindon did not appreciate that modifications to the 'Westerns' would be required prior to construction being concluded. In any event, by mid-1963 all the 'Westerns' were limited to 80mph pending rectification, which was carried out in priority to Class 42 and 43. Ride quality was good at low speed, less so at high speed; a peculiar 'corkscrew' roll occurred at around 60mph, causing drivers of the milk trains to run at either 55 or 65mph.

As with the 'Hymeks', a shortage of engine components during 1964/5 caused locomotives to be out of traffic. The design of the horizontal torque reaction members on the axle drive casings were the source of transmission troubles, and were resolved with the substitution of vertical-pattern arms, among other modifications. The short life of the riveted-type cages of the output shaft bearings of the Voith transmission was diagnosed as due to torsional oscillation in the system. Materials substandard to Maybach's specification within engines of Bristol Siddeley manufacture have been cited for a range of failures. The supporting frames were also susceptible to bending following even low-speed collisions. Unlike the Class 35, the 'Westerns' took up power quite slowly, which was useful during shunting.

The above description of technical issues is by no means exhaustive but does help to explain the poor availability. Eventually Swindon worked through these matters, but failures were also allegedly due to indifferent maintenance by depot staff, whereas the complicated engineering of the Maybach required careful attention. The converse, of course, was proved with, say, EE's Class 20, which used uncomplicated engineering and rugged construction.

It was therefore doubly unfortunate for the Class 52 that the trials conducted by Swindon in 1962 found its road performance to be inferior to the Class 47. Although the maximum tractive effort is usually quoted as 72,000lb, the best achieved under test was 65,900, inferior to its diesel-electric counterpart. The Brush/Sulzer locomotive was also able to deliver a consistently higher rail horsepower and the conclusion drawn was that there was a mismatch between the Maybach engine and Voith transmission. The trial results established no performance advantage for diesel-hydraulic locomotives, once their weight advantage over diesel-electric equivalents had effectively gone. The average mileage per locomotive during 1964 was only 65,400, compared to 95,100 for the Class 42 or even 80,000 for the less-reliable Class 43, and this shortfall cannot be explained away by the 'Western's spending more time on freight diagrams. One must therefore conclude that the Class 52 was something of a disappointment, and expensive, during the 1960s.

Length	68ft
Width	9ft
Height	13ft 1in
Weight	108 tons
Sanding gear	Fitted
Fuel tank capacity (gallons)	850
Minimum curve radius (chains)	4½
Maximum speed (mph)	90

Engines (two per locomotive)
Maybach MD 655

Engine output (bhp)	2 x 1,380 at 1,500rpm

Tractive effort (lb)

Maximum	66,770
Continuous	45,200 at 14½ mph

Gear ratio
N/a

Class 55

Deltic – the prototype

EE had been a key partner with both the pre-nationalisation London, Midland & Scottish Railway and the Southern Railway in their production of large main-line diesel-electric locomotives. These prototypes offered the highest installed power available at the time from an EE engine, which, despite technical development over several years during the gestation of the locomotives in question, still offered nothing more than 2,000hp in a 135-ton machine; this meant that sustained road performance was no better than could be achieved by a Class 7 'Pacific' steam locomotive. Being aware of this, and having D. Napier & Sons Ltd as a subsidiary, EE embarked on a speculative venture that was to have a profound impact on Britain's rail scene.

In response to a request from the Royal Navy in 1946 for a lightweight/high-power diesel for patrol boats, Napier had produced an opposed-piston engine that was based on a German military design. The naval engine, the D18-11B, had 18 cylinders and a 1-hour rating of 2,500bhp at 1,500rpm. Napier recognised that this would not be suitable for rail applications and pursued additional development. The resultant engine was the D18-12A, which had a rating of 1,650bhp at 1,500rpm continuously for rail traction application. Importantly, the interval between overhauls was pushed up from 1,000 to at least 4,000 hours. Being a quick-running engine, the D18-12A was small and lightweight relative to the medium-speed diesels fitted in the pre-nationalisation prototypes; consequently, two could be fitted in a single locomotive, thereby offering 3,300hp.

On 20 November 1951 an internal order was generated within EE for the production of a locomotive of entirely new design that was aimed at both home and overseas markets. The shape of the opposed-piston layout of the engine was roughly 'D'-shaped, and since in Greek the letter D is 'delta', the engine was dubbed the 'Deltic', which also proved to be the name given to the resultant prototype locomotive. After the erection work was completed by EE's Preston Works in October 1955, static testing was undertaken before handover to BR for service running on the LMR, which commenced on 28 November. During August and September 1956 Deltic was rigged up and put through a full series of dynamometer car trials over the Settle & Carlisle line.

The road trials pretty much confirmed the theoretical road performance of the design, which was considerably in advance of any other British diesel locomotive either extant or planned. Return to service with the LMR brought a range of duties, none of which taxed Deltic's capabilities because no train was scheduled or loaded for a 3,300hp traction unit. By this time the ER was taking an interest, and the prototype moved there in January 1959 for trials, followed by service running.

The production-series 'Deltics'

There is arguably no better person to explain why BR ordered a fleet of locomotives based on the prototype Deltic than Gerard Fiennes, who held a senior post within the ER's Operating Department, and who was instrumental in the

The 'Deltic' production line inside Vulcan Foundry is in full production during this 1961 view of No D9005 being lowered onto its bogies. *GEC*

Class doyen No D9000 makes its debut on BR metals outside Vulcan Foundry on 22 February 1961. *E. N. Bellass*

procurement of the locomotives. Mr Fiennes's contribution to *The Deltics – A Symposium* (Ian Allan Ltd, 1978) provides a fascinating insight.

In planning for the long-term survival of inter-city passenger services, Fiennes concluded in the mid-1950s that end-to-end journeys must be at an average of 75mph in order to compete with road and air journeys up to 300 miles. At that time the BTC had embarked on its Pilot Scheme, with the most powerful diesels being of the order of 2,000hp. The decision to order motive power under the Scheme was essentially driven by the Mechanical Engineering Department and no provision was made to call for traction of greater power. Fiennes was scathing about this because he appreciated that nothing ordered to date would be capable of delivering the 75mph target. He saw the Pilot Scheme as continuing the long-standing railway practice of the engineers deciding what the operators might want, instead of the operators telling the engineers what they actually wanted.

Fiennes was right. He had been instrumental in getting the initial tranche of the first BR Standard steam locomotive design, the 'Britannias', for the ER's Great Eastern Section, in order to speed up services between Liverpool Street and Norwich. He then negotiated for the first batch of Type 4 diesels, the EE Type 4, later

Class 40, to be allocated to these services, yet the design's installed 2,000hp offered no advantage over what a 'Britannia' in good condition could achieve between London and Norwich.

By 1957 Fiennes had moved to the Great Northern Section and was planning electrification of the East Coast route to Scotland. Following a meeting with the BTC, it was evident that modernisation was highly likely to be sanctioned, but electrification was not. Coincidentally, Fiennes says that he had heard about *Deltic*'s dynamometer trials and he was immediately attracted to its installed 3,300hp and 105mph top speed. Opposing forces, notably from the CME's Department, countered that such a top speed was unusable, the high-speed engines were too complicated and the locomotive was out of gauge for use north of York.

The contract

The ER prepared a case for a fleet of *Deltic*-type locomotives as a ten-year stopgap before electrification and to replace 55 'Pacific' steam locomotives. A BTC board meeting on 23 May 1957 discussed the ER's recommendation for the early purchase of about 20 locomotives and agreed 'favourable consideration' of it, subject to concurrence by the North Eastern and Scottish

This official view captures a Class 55 in the landscape, speeding towards King's Cross. *EE*

Regional boards. Two caveats were put on the recommendation: first, the price needed to be 'acceptable', and second, there would have to be some arrangement with the manufacturers to ensure that the Commission was relieved of 'a proportion of the risk inherent in the purchase of these expensive locomotives, whose sustained serviceability had yet to be proved'.

While the ER was lobbying the BTC for a fleet of 'Deltics', it is hardly surprising that EE was also working to achieve a sale. The EE Chairman and the BTC met on 30 September 1957 to discuss the possibility of the use of a fleet of production locomotives on the East Coast line.

The BTC first discussed the ER's plans at its meeting on 11 September 1957, noting that EE had been asked for assurances concerning maintenance and performance. Correspondence with the EE Chairman about these assurances was reported to the meeting on 19 September, this correspondence having elicited some proposals from the manufacturer. The matter progressed to the 13 November meeting, where a cost for 23 locomotives was estimated at £3,450,000. On the 21st Commission approval was given to the purchase, subject to satisfactory arrangements with EE concerning the financial and technical matters and parts maintenance.

But had Fiennes and the ER General Manager been pushing at an open door with the BTC? It has always been assumed that the BTC did not want anything more powerful than the largest Pilot Scheme diesels, but this was far from true. The board minutes for 26 July 1956, pre-dating *Deltic*'s trials, and therefore ahead of Mr Fiennes's interest in the concept, had emphasised the need for diesels of 3,000-3,500hp, ahead of electrification of routes. Thus the BTC needed no convincing of the benefit, nay need, for a locomotive of *Deltic*'s power, merely whether it was conceptually sound. In building up his part as a trail-blazer of high-powered, single-unit diesels, Mr Fiennes had merely drawn the same conclusion as the BTC itself.

Even now, the Commission minutes expressed concern at the value of the outlay for an unproven design, somewhat ironic when set against the many other orders for unproven designs! Nevertheless, the view was expressed that the new fleet needed to be delivered as soon as possible, but the Commission asked that the ER Operating Department reconsider whether a reduction below 23 locomotives was possible. The BTC meeting of 28 February 1958 recorded an order for 22 'Deltics' at a total cost, including spares, of £3,410,000, subject to the agreement of the North Eastern and Scottish Regional boards. A CME Department schedule records the order date as 1 May 1958.

English Electric recognised the need to modify its prototype design for squadron service application, perhaps the principal change being the need to comply with the space envelope of the L1 loading gauge (*Deltic* had been built to the L2 gauge). Certain BR standard equipment also had to be fitted, including a steam generator, AWS, fire protection, and external restyling. EE also recognised that other modifications were needed; for example, greater radiator capacity would be essential to dissipate the heat from the engines, which would be working much harder than had been necessary for *Deltic*.

During late 1957 and into 1958 it became obvious to EE that, because of additional requirements from BR, replication of *Deltic* was not going to happen. Just one of these requirements, the minimum curve radius to be negotiated by the design being reduced to 4 chains, involved revision of the underframes. Additionally, a bogie with a shorter wheelbase was to be substituted to assist in this respect; this bogie was to become an EE 'standard' design and would also be used for the Class 37, DP2 and Class 50.

One of the adverse factors in the design, as perceived by elements within BR, was the complication of the opposed-piston 'Deltic' engine. Perhaps to address this, EE not only sought to achieve a sale, but also proffered a five-year maintenance contract for the fleet. Under this, EE would supervise the maintenance while Napier would carry out work on the engines. A guarantee was given to BR covering annual utilisation, with a penalty against EE for any shortfall.

A different main generator from that fitted in *Deltic* was used. The 10-pole EE829/1A, one per engine and rated at 1,090kW, 1,650A, 660V continuously, was driven at a maximum speed of 1,125rpm through reduction gears rather than being bolted onto the engine driveshaft. This change from the model fitted to the prototype was to reduce the risk of flashover and to improve commutation.

The auxiliary generator was a 4-pole EE913/A, rated at 38kW, 345A, 110V at 1,000-2,480rpm. As explained in relation to the Class 37, in early 1958 EE developed a new traction motor, the EE538, as a replacement for the EE526 used in *Deltic* and the Class 20 and 40. Not only was the EE538 used also for the Class 37 and 50, but its 53:18 gear ratio was also standardised, which

The 'Deltics' had bodyside windows that could be opened in order to provide extra ventilation to the engine room. On 2 June 1963 the driver has taken advantage of this with No D9004, which is heading the 10.00am Sundays King's Cross to Edinburgh service out of Potters Bar Tunnel. *Brian Stephenson*

This official view was taken to mark the 100th anniversary of the 'Flying Scotsman' and depicts the train on Welwyn Viaduct on 13 April 1962. Note that the 'Deltic' warning horns were in their original position at buffer-beam height. *BR*

was different from the two gear ratios used on the prototype.

Six were fitted to the Class 55 (the TOPS classification for the production 'Deltics'), one per axle, each rated at 320kW, 533A, 600V. Tests at Vulcan Foundry with *Deltic* determined that traction motor blower capacity was inadequate to cool the motors, if the full capacity of the locomotive was used, so larger-capacity blowers were substituted. A Spanner Mk III steam generator for train heating was installed, with Class 40 No D248 being provided with an example as a test bed.

Deliveries were to commence on 30 March 1960 and conclude on 15 March 1961. Nevertheless, the essential aspects of the design were not finalised until November 1958, and Vulcan Foundry was contracted to carry out construction.

Styling a leading lady

The new fleet was to be the top-flight traction between London and Edinburgh. Public reaction towards the styling and livery of *Deltic* had been mixed, and in 1955 the industrial design sector had lobbied for thought to be given to the appearance of the Pilot Scheme designs in general. In response BR set up a Design Panel in 1956, and E. G. M. Wilkes was

awarded the contract for the styling of the new fleet. He is said to have been unimpressed by *Deltic*'s appearance, but several factors constrained change. First, *Deltic* was out of gauge for running in Scotland, so addressing this was an issue. Second, while Wilkes considered that the nose end impeded forward visibility, others countered that it reduced the risk of 'sleeper flutter' (the rapid passage of track sleepers) for the footplate crews on flat-fronted locomotives. Third, the body shape was typical EE, which viewed the 'Deltic' order as important, but small, bringing a disinclination towards change.

Responding to these parameters, Wilkes improved the shape of the nose end, including raking back the front plate. Three, rather than two, cab windows were used, with the outer two wrapping round slightly. Neither BR nor EE was sold on the restyling and, ultimately, the changes were largely confined to cleaning up the nose end.

Concerning the livery, a BR Design Panel minute dated 8 December 1960 reports as follows. A drawing was submitted illustrating the proposed livery, and after many experiments with lining design on different types of locos, the conclusion was reached that better results could be achieved by the use of a two-colour livery, with part of the body in a lighter colour. A drawing was submitted that showed the lower part in a light green, and this was approved. That was not, however, the end of the matter.

On 23 March 1961 E. S. Cox, who was head of the BR Design Office, wrote to J. F. Harrison, the CME. He had recently seen a locomotive and considered that the light-green lower band was 'far too light and sickly looking'. An alternative colour was provided for consideration, which Mr Harrison approved and gave instructions for its use on the 'Hymeks' and later builds of 'Deltics', instructing Beyer Peacock and EE accordingly. There was also a change in window livery. On 20 January 1962 Mr Wilkes wrote to Mr Williams at the BR Design Panel to notify him that, as he had requested, there had been a change to aluminium from light grey.

Now the East Coast had a squadron of 3,300hp traction units, weighing around 100 tons, in the making. Concurrently, BR's workshops were beginning to turn out the latest version of its design of Type 4, with the Sulzer engine uprated to 2,500hp, but weighing almost 140 tons. Although the ER was to receive an allocation of the latter for East Coast duties alongside the 'Deltics', one can understand why it rejected them, as well as EE's No D200 series Type 4s of only 2,000hp. This stance reflects exactly the WR's reaction towards NBL's 117-ton Type 4 offering, and Swindon's counter-proposal for an 80-ton product of the same power.

Naming principal passenger classes had been a long railway tradition, and this continued with the 'Deltics'. The ER opted for racehorse names, recalling Nigel Gresley's use of such names for his 'A3' 'Pacifics'. In contrast, both the NER and ScR chose regimental names for their allocations.

Into service

Initial allocations were to be eight each at Finsbury Park and Haymarket, with six at Gateshead. Originally, deliveries were to start in April 1960, with ten locomotives in traffic by September and 16 by Christmas. Naturally, the new arrivals would revolutionise East Coast train operation, and accordingly a fully recast

In 1965 the railway at Retford was remodelled, with the Worksop to Gainsborough route provided with an underbridge rather than a flat crossing of the ECML. On 14 June a Class 55 brings the up 'Flying Scotsman', with its distinctive headboard, over the new dive-under line. *BR*

This beautiful picture is so redolent on the 1960s railway scene. Inverwick, a wayside station between Edinburgh and Berwick, has a rake of coal wagons and its North British Railway-pattern box to represent a timeless aspect, while the modern railway is represented by No D9020 and new maroon Mark 1 train set on the up 'Heart of Midlothian'. *W. A. C. Smith*

timetable was prepared during 1959. Implementation was to be by way of phasing in the class on an increasing number of selected trains.

In late 1959 a visitor to Vulcan Foundry saw no sign of construction and was told that priority was being given to an export order for Sudan. 1960 came and went without the appearance of a locomotive, and in January 1961 EE promised three examples by the end of February. Further slippage arose, caused by the need to modify the bogies fitted to Class 37s, which were identical to those for the 'Deltics'. A decision at BR board level gave priority to Class 37 delivery over the Class 55 in order not to disturb the GE Section's recast Summer 1961 timetable.

No D9001 was the first to depart Vulcan Foundry when it moved to Doncaster on 16 January 1961; the following day it went to Stratford (London) and was placed on display at Liverpool Street on the 18th. Back at Doncaster, the next few weeks passed without record, presumably due to examination by BR. Allocated to Finsbury Park on 23 February 1961, trial running continued with a run

between King's Cross and Edinburgh on 15 March. Meanwhile No D9000 arrived at Doncaster on 28 February 1961, and it too worked a trial on 15 March between Doncaster and New Southgate before arriving at its home shed of Haymarket on the 22nd. No D9002 followed in early March, but it was not seen at Gateshead Depot until the 22nd. Sufficient machines had now arrived to permit a few diagrams to commence in September 1961.

The business case for the 'Deltics' anticipated an annual mileage per locomotive of 220,000, but in practice during the 1960s there was insufficient work for this parameter to be achieved. Only during the 12-week period of the Summer timetable did the mileage equate to an annual equivalent of that amount. Generally, locomotives put in between 150,000 and 180,000 miles annually, though the 1963 Summer timetable saw more than a million miles accumulated across the fleet. In fact, 1963/4 proved to be the mileage high point, with 3.96 million miles. BTC minutes accord the East Coast operators a plaudit for this performance. Thereafter, 3.6-3.7 million miles became the norm, due to changes to the timetable and locomotives being out of traffic for the fitting of train air brake equipment during 1967/8.

Class 55 deliveries were at a rate of two or three per month during 1961, but the last three were accepted in December, February and May 1962. The first full 'Deltic' timetable did not therefore begin until Summer 1962, with all the fleet pooled for any ECML diagrams, irrespective of Regional allocation. Faster journey times and shorter intervals between arriving at the destination and taking up the next departure facilitated the oft-quoted statistic that 22 diesels could displace 55 'Pacific' steamers. Even so, in 1962 the ECML had not benefited from any of the realignments, track upgrading or resignalling that permitted major improvements in later years, notably during the 1970s.

Thus the timings were based around superiority in acceleration and hill-climbing over the potential of a Class 8 'Pacific'. The headline service was the 'Flying Scotsman', where the London to Edinburgh booking was cut by an hour to 6 hours. Between 1961 and 1970 the London to Doncaster schedule for an 11-coach consist was pared by 9½ minutes to 2 hours, net of recovery time, while the recovery allowance was also slimmed from 14 to 9 minutes.

During No D9001's trial run in March 1961 referred to above, the 11-coach load of 380 tons gross was accelerated from 65mph at Wood Green to 75 at Potters Bar up the 1 in 200. Stoke bank was cleared at 83. Mr D. S. M. Barrie recorded No D9020 on a nine-coach formation, which passed Doncaster in 109¾ minutes, inclusive of several delays, an average of 85¼ mph. Of note was an acceleration from 96 to 99mph up the 1 in 200 at Leys. Demonstrating accelerative potential, Gordon Pettit's journey on No D9004 with an 11-coach train is illuminating. Departing northbound from Doncaster on generally level track, 70mph was attained in 2 miles, 85 in 4¼ miles and 100 by Heck, 11 miles. Finally, putting No D9001's run in March 1961 in the shade, No 9007 hauled a 13-coach service grossing 490 tons out of King's Cross and, despite the two extra coaches, passed Wood Green at the same

Enthusiasts crowd round No D9018 at Waverley station, Edinburgh, as it waits to depart with the up 'Heart of Midlothian' on 18 April 1966. Note that the BR emblem is now located under the locomotive number in order to make way for the nameplate.
The late Derek Cross

speed as No D9001 and Potters Bar at only a slightly lower 72. Restarting from Peterborough, the train was worked up to 92mph through Little Bytham on the climb to Stoke, with a minimum of 87 before easing to 75mph for a restriction at the summit. This last run, in particular, illustrates not only Class 55 potential but also the not infrequent occurrence of performance levels above what might be predicted. Mr Fiennes must have been pleased!

Service problems

The first of a number of issues to emerge was fracturing of the fabricated bogies, which arose on Nos D9000 and D9001 within weeks of delivery. The bogie was a new design and the same issue had arisen with the first batch of the Class 37s on the Great Eastern Section. Locomotives were returned to the works for attention, but as mentioned above priority was given to remedying the Class 37 so that the Summer 1961 timetable diagrams for that class could be implemented.

Deltic had accumulated 400,000 miles, but not at the levels of power unit loading demanded from the production series, because she was hauling trains on schedules compiled for motive power of much lower capability. The higher engine load factors demanded from Class 55s brought to light shortcomings not found previously. Wear was found on spline shafts as well as cavitation cracking of the cylinder liners during pre-delivery testing undertaken by Napier. Unburned lubricating oil tended to collect in the engine exhaust drum, but faulty welds in the drum caused cracks to appear and the oil to leak out. A drain was added to remove the oil, but this frequently became blocked and the oil could then be ignited by the hot exhaust gases. Severe cylinder liner corrosion emerged, while the engine underspeed switch proved too sensitive and caused unnecessary shut-down.

Napier continued to develop the 'Deltic' engine, pushing up the rating of the 18-cylinder version to nearly 4,000hp, and these improvements found their way into the units installed in the BR locomotives, albeit still set to deliver 1,650hp. While engine overhauls were originally scheduled after 4,000 hours, by 1968 the interval had risen to 5,000. A side effect, however, was that major attention to the engines, mechanical and electrical parts and running gear got out of phase, so that locomotives were being shopped for different reasons rather than all components being dealt with in one hit.

Engine noise had been identified as an issue during *Deltic*'s trials and, unsurprisingly, this carried across into the production series. Eventually, full-height acoustic damping panels were fitted behind the two cab seats, with a padded curtain that could be drawn across to close the gap between the two; however, this curtain made the cab very cramped.

The load regulator, which matched engine output to the power being taken from the main generator, only had a small number of notches at the beginning of its travel. Heavy-handed operation of the driver's power controller during starting could therefore cause a surge in power. Under poor rail conditions, wheelslip could occur very easily and, during the early days, it was not uncommon for trains to slip to a stand in the tunnel at the exit from King's Cross. Subsequently a load regulator with more contacts at the start of its travel was fitted.

Across the whole diesel fleet, machines fitted with steam generators always suffered reduced availability during winter months because these generators proved unreliable for various reasons. Unsurprisingly, Class 55s were not immune from this problem and modification work involved taking locomotives out of traffic, which impacted on availability.

It is claimed that the maintenance contract concentrated EE's mind towards keeping availability and reliability high and therefore addressing problems with impetus. This contract was renewed with some revisions in 1966. EE stationed a team of technicians at King's Cross to deal with problems, accompanied by a representative from Napier. Locomotives arriving at the London terminus with a fault were assessed, then agreement had to be reached between BR and EE as to responsibility for rectification. The work was undertaken locally, apart from major engine defects, which involved a trip to Doncaster Works.

When the contract came up for renewal again in 1969, BR decided against it. Sensibly, Doncaster Works had undertaken a successful pilot by overhauling the 'Deltic' engines fitted to the Class 23 'Baby Deltics'. It was always accepted that the 'Deltics' would cost more than a conventional medium-speed diesel-fitted locomotive such as a Class 47, but examination of costs on comparable work by the ER suggested, surprisingly, that the overall cost per mile favoured the Class 55. Mr Fiennes's judgement had been vindicated, notably once East Coast modernisation permitted quicker journey times of an order not possible by the West Coast operators on the non-electrified section north of Crewe. Equally, the BTC's concern at an unproven design had been overcautious, because the 'Deltics' were no more troublesome than most of BR's diesel fleet during the 1960s. Finally, Freddy Harrison, the BR CME, who was heavily committed to Sulzer engines, was proved wrong in his belief that the 'Deltic' engine was too complicated for rail use.

Length	69ft 6in
Width	8ft 9½ in
Height	12ft 10in
Weight	99 tons
Sanding gear	Fitted
Fuel tank capacity (gallons)	900 (later 826)
Minimum curve radius (chains)	4
Maximum speed (mph)	100

Engines (two per locomotive)

Napier D18-25B	
Engine output (bhp)	2 x 1,650 at 1,500rpm

Tractive effort (lb)

Maximum	50,000
Continuous	30,500 at 32½ mph

Gear ratio

53:18

Bibliography

AEI/Sulzer *Operating Manual British Railways Locomotives D5176-299 D7500-7677*
BR Operating Manuals for Classes 45 and 46
National Archive records of the BTC and BR

Allen, Cecil J. *The Deltics – A Symposium* (Ian Allan)
Beasant, E. H. Paper on Class 47 in the *Journal of the Institution of Locomotive Engineers,*
    20 November 1967
Clough, David N. *Diesel Pioneers* (Ian Allan)
Class 50s In Operation (Ian Allan)
Ell, S. O. *Design Problems Of Diesel Locomotives* (Institution of Locomotive Engineers)
Endacott, Geoff *'Westerns', 'Warships' & 'Hymeks' At Work* (Ian Allan)
Haresnape, Brian *British Rail Fleet Survey, Part 3* (Ian Allan)
Harris, Roger *The Allocation History Of BR Diesels & Electrics, Parts 1, 2, 3 & 5* (Roger Harris)
Nelson, R. I. *Locomotive Performance: A Footplate Survey* (Ian Allan)
Nock, O. S. *The GWR Stars, Castles and Kings* (David & Charles)
Oakley, M. J. *BR Class 26/27 Diesels* (Bradford Barton)
BR Class 31 Diesels (Bradford Barton)
Oakley, M. J. and Perkins, Chris *BR Class 24/25 Diesels* (Bradford Barton)
Oakley, M. J. and Tiller, Robert *BR Class 33 Diesels* (Bradford Barton)
Reed, Brian *Diesel-Hydraulic Locomotives of the Western Region* (David & Charles)
Tayler A. T. H. *Sulzer Types 2 and 3* (Ian Allan)
Tayler A. T. H., Thorley, W. G. F. and Hill, T. J. *Class 47 Diesels* (Ian Allan)
Webb, Brian *The Deltic Locomotives of British Rail* (David & Charles)
English Electric Main Line Diesel Locomotives of British Rail (David & Charles)
Sulzer Diesel Locomotives of British Rail (David & Charles)
Wood, Roger B. *1983 Locomotive Stock Book* (RCTS)

Issues of *Diesel Railway Traction, Modern Railways, Merseyside Railway Society Journal* and *Trains*
    Illustrated